In the name of Allah, the Compassionate, the Merciful

Who are the Believers?

An Islamic Perspective

Dr. Muhammad A. Hafeez

ISBN: 1507832370
ISBN 13: 9781507832370

Library of Congress Control Number: 2015901780

.Who Are The Believers?: An Islamic Perspective / Muhammad A. Hafeez
(docmhafeez@hotmail.com)
1. Islamic practices, 2. Human ethics, 3. Islam and justice,
4. Qur'an teachings, 5. Theological anthropology

CreateSpace Independent Publishing Platform
North Charleston, South Carolina

VERSE ON THE FRONT COVER - QUR'AN 11:88
" ... : O my people! ... . I only desire (your) betterment to the best of my power (ability); and the
success (in my task and efforts) can only come from Allah. In Him I trust, and unto Him I look."

Dedicated to the Believers—

(People Who Live as God Commands)

"Say: the things that my Lord has indeed forbidden are:
shameful deeds, whether open or secret; sins and trespasses against truth or reason;
assigning of partners to Allah, for which He has given no authority;
and saying things about Allah of which you have no knowledge."

The Qur'an 7:33

Acknowledgement

The importance of learning what God commands in the Qur'an is such that people should exert all their efforts to accomplish this task, and no one is exempt from this duty. Although the Messenger[PBUH] was *Ummi* (unlettered), God commanded him, "Read in the name of your Lord Who created—created man from a clot. Read, and your Lord is Most Honorable..." (Qur'an 96:1-3).

In understanding the Qur'an, I have benefited from both Urdu and English translations and *Tafsir* (commentary) by Syed Abul Ala Maududi, as well as from English translations by 'Abdullah Yusuf Ali, Zafar Ishaq Ansari, Muhammad Marmaduke Pickthall, M. H. Shakir, and Dr. M. M. Khan and Dr. M. T. Al-Hilali. I am indebted to the scholarly writings of Dr. Malik Ghulam Murtaza, Adil Salahi, Sheikh Ali Tantavi, Sheikh 'Abdullah Bin Muhammad Al-Muhtaj, M. Al-Ghazali, and Hamza Yusuf. I acknowledge that their contributions have greatly helped me in my pursuit of knowledge. I am grateful to Mirza Iqbal Ashraf, author of Introduction to World Philosophies, Islamic Philosophy of War and Peace, and Rumi's Holistic Humanism, for his invaluable review and comments.

The Qur'an was revealed for the benefit of all humanity, and God thusly enjoined Adam in Paradise: "We said: 'Get you down all from here; and if, as is sure, there comes to you guidance from Me, whosoever follows My guidance, on them shall be no fear, nor shall they grieve" (Qur'an 2:38). God also promised that, "As for those who were led to the guidance, Allah increases them in their guidance and causes them to grow in their piety" (Qur'an 47:17). Every human being is divinely blessed with a capacity to comprehend God's guidance.

This has indeed encouraged me and will encourage whoever wants to learn about his/her obligations as God's trustee on Earth. God has reminded us in that, "We have indeed made the Qur'an easy to understand and remember; then is there any who will receive admonition?" (Qur'an 54:17). As members of humanity, for our own good, both in this life and in the Hereafter, we should say, "Yes," to God's invitation to His guidance.

Dr. Muhammad A. Hafeez
January 3, 2015

Contents

Preface

Who are the Believers? God created mankind blessed with a conscience, free will and gave guidance. He conceived each one of us male or female, rich or poor, to be His Trustee on earth, to serve Him by implementing His commands in managing our affairs and building a just human society in the world. God desires people to be His trustees on earth. It is up to us to accept or reject God's offer of trusteeship. Those who accept the assignment become the believers. They take this assignment as a challenge and a trial from Him. The believers have the desire and intention to succeed as God's trustee on earth. Since it is through knowledge and understanding that people attain closeness to God, believers strive to gain knowledge. They strive to read and understand the Qur'an and follow His Messenger[PBUH] (peace be upon him) as their role model.

Those who do not know Arabic and find it difficult to understand the Qur'an in its original form should benefit from translations of the Qur'an in the language they know. Since God does not expect individuals to perform beyond their abilities, they should honestly follow to the best of their abilities what they understand from the Qur'an through its translations, *Tafsirs* (commentaries) and *Ahadith* (sayings of the Messenger[PBUH]). Reading and reflecting on the essence of the Qur'an is like having God Himself tell the reader how to live his/her life as an individual and as a member of society. While studying the Qur'an it is one's duty, to the best of one's ability, to listen to God attentively and to follow what He is commanding.

The purpose of this book is to introduce the divinely ordained path in a systematic way to the believers as individuals and as members of humanity. My effort in this subject was prompted by a sincere desire to explain what God commands and forbids the believers in the fulfillment of their obligations. The Qur'an covers every sphere of our life that needs to be understood and followed. Since it is each believer's obligation to know what God commands in the Qur'an and then to live accordingly, this book is an easy-made explanation of most, but not all, of the Qur'anic injunctions.

Nonexistence of a true Islamic model society anywhere in the world confirms that we as a society and as parents have miserably failed to inculcate Islamic values among ourselves and continue to neglect learning them and then teaching our children those values and character traits which form the backbone of Humanity. All we have is the past of which we should always be proud. Contrary to the teachings of the Qur'an, we have divided ourselves into various sects, and we no longer treat our fellow Muslim brothers with respect. Perhaps we have stopped learning the basic teachings of Islam from the Qur'an.

The teachings of the Qur'an are very simple and are meant to be understood by both the most simple and the most sophisticated human beings. Humans, because of the divinely gifted power of free will, are prone to obedience and disobedience. Their obedience to God alone makes them powerful and strong. Their worship of the Ultimate Power makes them feel powerful, and feeling free and strong they become responsible members of humanity. By virtue of obedience to God's commands, humanity feels safe and protected. Their own conscience of obedience watches over them, and in such a state they cannot err or commit sin. Disobedience leaves one alone, and thus by saying no to power it becomes easy to err and to sin. We therefore need to keep God in our hearts and minds all the time, know His commands, and make their practice a part of our life.

The current book demonstrates how inculcating Qur'anic invocations and teachings into one's life transforms a person by focusing on God's commandments, His rewards, and His warnings. As such, this book serves as a quick reference for self-evaluation and development. The translation of the Qur'an by Abdullah Yusuf Ali, with minor modifications as required for clarity, has been used in this study.

Dr. Muhammad A. Hafeez

A Prelude to

What God Commands

As believers, our efforts in obeying certain rules in this world do not mean that we will be saved from suffering only in the Hereafter. Who benefits here on Earth? Does the benefit of our compliance accrue to someone else or to God? God does not benefit by our obedience to or compliance with His rules; we do. The Messenger^PBUH quotes God in a sacred *Hadith* saying: "My servants, it is but your deeds that I reckon up for you and then recompense you for (in this world). Therefore, let him who finds good praise God, and let him who finds other than good blame no one but himself" (Sahih Muslim 32.6246).

Faith can be defined as something that is well established in people's minds and hearts and to which credence is given by practice. Therefore, faith is not an academic theory or an abstract idea. Its practical effect has to be seen so that the claim of being a believer is seen to be true. Hence, Islam is an embodiment of statements and practices. According to the Messenger, "Islam is built on five pillars: the declaration that there is no deity save Allah and that Muhammad is His Messenger, regular attendance to prayer, the payment of *Zakat*, fasting during *Ramadan*, and pilgrimage to the Sacred House when a person is able to do so" (Sahih Bukhari 1.2.7).

1
Islam is Built on Five Pillars and Righteous Deeds

Although Islam is built on five pillars, it needs a lot of good deeds to complete its structure. None can be expected to perform beyond one's capacity. God tells people in *Surah Al-Baqarah* that, "On no soul does Allah place a burden greater than it can bear. It gets every good that it earns, and it suffers every ill that it earns. ..." (Qur'an 2:286). Since people's abilities vary, the following *Hadith* illustrates the minimum that is required from a person of the least ability. People are accountable according to their abilities and the blessings that God has bestowed on them.

It is narrated by Talha bin 'Ubaidullah that, "A man from Najd with unkempt hair came to Allah's Apostle and we heard his loud voice but could not understand what he was saying, till he came near and then we came to know that he was asking about Islam. Allah's Apostle said, 'You have to offer prayers perfectly five times in a day and night.' The man asked, 'Is there any more (praying)?' Allah's Apostle replied, 'No, but if you want to offer the *Nawafil* prayers (you can).' Allah's Apostle further said to him: 'You have to observe fasts during the month of *Ramad'an*.' The man asked, 'Is there any more fasting?' Allah's Apostle replied, 'No, but if you want to observe the *Nawafil* fasts (you can.)' Then Allah's Apostle further said to him, 'You have to pay the *Zakat* (obligatory charity).' The man asked, 'Is there any thing other than the *Zakat* for me to pay?' Allah's Apostle replied, 'No, unless you want to give alms of your own.' And then that man retreated saying, 'By Allah! I will neither do less nor more than this.' Allah's Apostle said, 'If what he said is true, then he will be successful (i.e. he will be granted Paradise)'" (Sahih Bukhari 1.2.44).

2
Unlawful Earnings Spoils All Worship and Good Deeds

Abu Hurairah reported God's Messenger saying: "O people, Allah is pure, and He therefore accepts only that which is pure." God commanded the believers as He commanded the Messengers by saying: "O Messengers, enjoy (all) things good and pure, and do good deeds; verily, I am aware of what you do" (Qur'an 23:51). And He said: "O those who believe! Eat of the good things that We have provided for you" (Qur'an 2:172). "The Messenger then made mention of a person who travels widely, his hair disheveled and covered with dust. He lifts his hand towards the sky (and thus makes the supplication): 'O Lord, O Lord,' whereas his diet is unlawful, his drink is unlawful, and his clothes are unlawful and his nourishment is unlawful. How can then his supplication be accepted?" (Sahih Muslim 5.2214).

3
Injustice and bad behavior lands even believers in Hell

Abu Hurairah reported God's Messenger saying, "Do you know who is poor? They (the companions) said: 'A poor man among us is one who has neither *Dirham* with him nor wealth.' He (the Messenger) said: 'The poor of my *Umma* (Muslim community) will be he who will come on the Day of Resurrection with prayers, fasts, and *Zakat* (obligatory charity). (However, he will find himself bankrupt on that day because he has exhausted his fund of virtues). Since he hurled abuses upon others, brought calumny against others, unlawfully consumed the wealth of others, shed the blood of others, and beaten others, his virtues will be credited to the account of one (who suffered at his hand). If his good deeds fall short in clearing the account, then his victim's sins will be entered into (his own account), and he would be thrown in the Hellfire" (Sahih Muslim 32.6251).

COMMANDS

Items given below do not represent a complete list of all commands given to the believers in the Quran. The believers are to read, understand and implement in their lives what God commands people in the Quran to become good Muslims or the believers.

I. BELIEFS AND THE LAW OF NATURE

1. Believe in God and in Prophet Mohammad (peace be upon him).
2. Believe in all Prophets, and make no distinction among them.
3. Believe in God's books and their original messages.
4. Believe in Angels who carry out God's commands and who worship Him.
5. Believe in the Day of Judgment and in the accountability for one's deeds done in this world.
6. Believe in *Qadar* or the laws of nature that God has put in place.

II. WORSHIP AND PROPAGATION OF VIRTUE

1. Establish regular prayer, which will help you accept God's commands and will help prevent you from doing prohibited things.
2. Earn your living honestly with hard work. Use part of it to help fellow Muslims in their needs and to promote and uplift communities around you.
3. Fast to achieve self restraint and piety.
4. Perform Hajj as prescribed if you are physically and financially able.
5. Join others in doing what is good, and forbid what is evil.

III. INDIVIDUAL CHARACTER

1. Eat what God has allowed you, and stay away from what He has prohibited.
2. Don't say things about God about which you have no knowledge.
3. Refrain from anger, and forgive others (both believers and unbelievers) even when you are angry.
4. Exercise patience when in pain and when suffering difficulties.
5. Don't be arrogant and extremist; be humble and moderate.

IV. INDIVIDUAL BEHAVIOR

1. Be kind to your parents, and pray for their salvation.
2. Refrain from shameful deeds in open and in secret.
3. Never intentionally kill another person.
4. Do not kill your children or commit adultery
5. Fulfill all promises and contracts you make with others.
6. Don't lie, be not dishonest, and do not use your resources to spread corruption.
7. Don't steal or defraud others.
8. Respect fellow Muslims; remain united; don't spy and backbite.

V. FINANCIAL DEALINGS AND JUSTICE

1. Don't eat up your property among yourselves in vanities, but let there be traffic and trade among you in mutual good will.

2. Stand for justice, and speak the truth on a witness stand even if it goes against your relatives, and regardless of whether the one for whom or against whom you are testifying is rich or poor.

3. Be kind and just in all of your dealings with people. Whether you are dealing with family, relatives, friends, colleagues, employees, or servants, do so without discrimination or favor.

4. Give measure and weight with (full) justice. Don't defraud and be dishonest with others; honor your promises and contracts

VI. SELF-DEFENSE AND FIGHTING OPPRESSION

1. Defend yourself against those unbelievers who attack you and expel you from your houses.

2. Fight oppression until truth and justice prevails in your community. Yet, have no animosity towards unbelievers unless they harm you.

REWARDS

1. God gives guidance when you believe in His message and seek His guidance.

2. God cancels your bad deeds that result from human weakness with the good deeds you perform.

3. If you fear God for your inability to fulfill His commands, He will remove ills from you and enlarge His reward for your efforts.

4. God is sufficient in giving you resources to succeed in this life while following His commands and to achieve ultimate success in the Hereafter.

5. God does not place the burden of one upon the shoulders of another, and no burden is placed upon a soul greater than it can bear.

6. God creates ease after difficulty for His believers.

7. God is Oft-Forgiving and Most Merciful. There is no type of sin and no limit to the number of sins He will forgive if forgiveness is requested with sincere repentance.

8. The believers shall be rewarded many times for their good deeds and will reside in Paradise in their eternal lives.

WARNINGS

1. Everybody will be accountable for his own deeds on the Day of Judgment. Even the relatives of prophets will answer for and suffer the consequence of their misdeeds.
2. God does not guide those who do not believe in His message; in fact, they go astray.
3. The disbelievers and wrongdoers will reside in Hell forever.

Chapter 1

Introduction
(Believers are God's Trustee on Earth)

God created humankind with a conscience, intellect, and free will to be His *Khalifah* (Trustee) on earth. It is up to each individual to choose whether to be or not to be God's trustee on earth. Although God created both humans and jinn to serve Him, He specifically appointed humans to be His trustee on earth, if they so choose, and manage their affairs on earth as God commands them.

The Qur'an and *Sunnah* (religious examples) of the Messenger[PBUH] (peace be upon him) are a guidance for all people, the descendants of Adam and Eve. Islam is not a blind faith. People need to be convinced that it is the truth before freely accepting it. Since one's religion is a great responsibility, people should learn, reflect, and then believe.

Whatever God commands in the Qur'an is obligatory for those men and women who believe and have accepted God's offer to be His trustee on earth. Their general duties can be summarized as follows:

KNOW THE CREATOR OF THE UNIVERSE—through worshiping and remembering Him. God's remembrance is to learn, know, remember, and follow His commands in one's daily activities.

KNOW WHAT GOD COMMANDS—Learn from His books (the Qur'an) and learn from His Messengers[PBUT] (peace be upon them) of what He desires from the believers and what He commands.

GOD'S WILL AND HIS WAYS—Like all physical laws, God's Will and His Ways are eternal and well-established. God does not change His Will or His Ways for benefit or punishment in an unscientific or unsystematic way. Each act, good or bad, has its own built in consequence according to nature. For example, injustice will be followed by anarchy in all unjust communities, irrespective of the fact that injustice is being done in Muslim or non-Muslim societies.

KNOW ISLAM AND FOLLOW IT—Life of this world (*Dunya*) is a part of Islam. Islam does not distinguish between *Deen* (religion) and *Dunya* (life on earth), but *Deen* consists of two parts: *Dunya* and the Hereafter. Any worldly activity of a believer in which God's commands are not violated is a part of his/her religion or *Deen* and the worship of God.

1
MOBILIZATION OF PEOPLE AS GOD'S TRUSTEE

The believers strive to know themselves and their weaknesses and to develop such character and behavior so as to be God's trustees which are hardworking, honest, just, and helpful in their own individual area of dealings and influence. The believers cannot discriminate, exploit, or oppress others.

1.1 SELF-PRESERVATION AND DEVELOPMENT—Learning and honestly earning one's subsistence are of utmost importance, as all of our other activities depend on them. For our preservation, we have to work and not steal or beg; we have to be honest and not fraudulent; we have to be true and just and not cruel or oppressive. In short, we have to treat others like we want others to treat us.

1.2 REPENTANCE AND REFORMATION—Since people have free will, perfection of their character and behavior without divine guidance is not possible. What Islam teaches is an attitude that leads to continual improvement in individual character and the society. Everyone is prone to err, and everyone makes mistakes. However, when the believers err, they seek God's forgiveness, which is forthcoming when the request is genuine. Human character is improved each time one acknowledges, regrets, and makes a genuine effort not to repeat a mistake. A person may be committing errors throughout the life, but whenever one realizes his/her mistakes and repents, seeking God's forgiveness, God forgives if he/she turns to Him in genuine repentance.

1.3 SEEKING GOD'S PLEASURE AND MERCY—A believer's purpose in life is to please God, and He is pleased when people follow His commandments. Therefore, people who believe must believe by their actions—, by worshiping God and doing good deeds. It is true that none will achieve salvation or success without God's Mercy, but the believers have to believe, worship God, and do good deeds to become a candidate for His Mercy.

1.4 WORSHIPING GOD AND HONEST LIVING—All human activities in which God's commands are not violated are acts of servitude and worship to God. Obligatory worship is designed to motivate people to reform and nurture human values: For example, "Recite what is sent of the Book by inspiration to you, and establish regular prayer: for prayer restrains from shameful and unjust deeds; and remembrance of Allah (God) is the greatest (thing in life) without doubt. And Allah knows the (deeds) that you do" (Qur'an 29:45). God tells the believers that, "O you who believe! Fasting is prescribed to you as it was prescribed to those before you, that you may (learn) self-restraint" (Qur'an 2:183).

Learning to develop a capability to earn an honest living is obligatory, and working hard in one's selected professional area for earning an honest living is an act of God's Worship. Misappropriating property or using it to bribe judges is forbidden in Islam. God commands, "And do not eat up your property among yourselves for vanities, nor use it as bait for the judges, with intent that you may eat up wrongfully and knowingly a little of (other) people's property" (Qur'an 2:188).

1.5 UNDERSTANDING WHAT GOD COMMANDS —Hearing, listening, and learning what God commands in the Qur'an is another obligation. God asks, "Do they not then earnestly seek to understand the Qur'an ...?" (Qur'an 47:24). Since God does not demand of people what is beyond their capability, each individual is equipped to learn what one needs to learn from the Qur'an. God assures the believers, "And Allah does advance in guidance those who seek guidance: and the things that endure, good deeds, are best in the sight of your Lord, as rewards, and best in respect of (their) eventual return" (Qur'an 19:76).

Religious teachers, or *Tafsirs* of the Qur'an written by them and *Ahadith* of the Messenger[PBUH] can help as needed. Those who do not know Arabic should read the meanings of the Qur'an in their own language asking, 'What does God command me to do in my environment?' One should take notes for remembering God's command and implement them as needed. God warns the believers, "Be not like those who say, we hear, but listen not: for the worst of beasts in the sight of Allah are the deaf and the dumb—those who understand not" (Qur'an 8:21-22). The believers should make sure that the Messenger will not say about them in front of God on the Day of Judgment, "Then the Messenger will say: 'O my Lord! Lo! Mine own folk made this Qur'an of no account'" (Qur'an 25:30). Whatsoever God commands in the Qur'an is an obligation. The believers have to know and follow them. All of His commands are important. God does not command without purpose—commands are given either for the betterment of individuals themselves or of the society in which they live.

2
GUIDANCE IS FOR THOSE WHO DESIRE GUIDANCE

God created humankind with a conscience, free will, and rational thinking based on truth and reason. Only those people who, without any compulsion, believe in God with all of His attributes, who have respect for Him, and who are sure about needing to account for their deeds, desire His guidance. With all this realization they say, "In the name of Allah, the compassionate, the merciful, praise be to Allah, the cherisher and sustainer of the worlds; Most Gracious, Most Merciful; master of the Day of Judgment" (Qur'an 1:1-4). It is not blind faith but rational thinking and understanding that motivate people to declare, "You do we serve, and Your aid we seek. Show us the straight Way" (Qur'an 1:5-6). Such people are genuine candidates for receiving guidance. This guidance, implemented individually and socially, will lead to, "The Way of those on whom You (Allah) have bestowed Your Grace, those whose (portion) is not wrath, and who go not astray" (Qur'an 1:7).

2.1 God's Will is— He guides those who seek guidance

The Qur'an confirms that, "Those who believe not in the Signs of Allah— Allah will not guide them, and theirs will be a grievous penalty" (Qur'an 16:104). "And Allah will not mislead a people after He has guided them, in order that He may make clear to them what to fear (and avoid) ..." (Qur'an 9:115). These verses confirm the need for divine laws and the messengers in order to justify punishment. The Qur'an also says, "... He (Allah) does not misguide, except those who transgress" (Qur'an 2:26), and "...Allah will leave, to stray, those who do wrong ..." (Qur'an 14:27). It is clear that the just and virtuous people are not led astray, but those who transgress His laws become lost. God says in the Qur'an, "Verily We have revealed the Book to you in truth, for (instructing) mankind. He then that receives guidance benefits his own soul, but he that strays injures his own soul..." (Qur'an 39:41). Hence God's guidance and humanity's misguidance constitute part of the workings of natural laws. These natural laws are uniform and not at all capricious. Had they been capricious, no scientific invention would have been possible. The Qur'an says that there is no changing in God's creation (laws), "... No change (let there be) in the work (wrought) by Allah: that is the standard Religion ..." (Qur'an 30:30).

2.2 The guidance is given to those who seek guidance

People have been assured in the Qur'an that, "And Allah does advance in guidance those who seek guidance: And the things that endure, good deeds, are best in the sight of your Lord, as rewards, and best in respect of (their) eventual return" (Qur'an 19:76). "And those who strive in Our (Cause), - We will certainly guide them to Our paths: for verily, Allah is with those who do right" (Qur'an 29:69). "... Allah chooses to Himself those whom He pleases, and guides to Himself those who turn (to Him)" (Qur'an 42:13).

3
Human Mission on the Earth

God created people with a conscience and free will, and He gave guidance. He offered each one of us, male or female, rich or poor, to be His *Khalifah* (trustee) on earth by serving Him, implementing His commands in managing their affairs, and building a just human society in the world: "Behold, your Lord said to the angels: 'I will create a vicegerent (trustee) on earth.' They said: 'Will You place therein one who will make mischief therein and shed blood? - while we do celebrate Your praises and glorify Your holy (name)?' He said: 'I know what you know not'" (Qur'an 2:30).

God desires people to be His trustee on earth. Those who wish to be God's trustee, they believe in and worship Him, learn to be human, reform themselves, and do good deeds. They take this assignment as a challenge and a trial from Him. It is up to us to accept or reject God's offer of trusteeship. Those who accept the assignment become the believers. As a token of acceptance to be God's trustee, the believers worship Him and remember Him during every moment of their lives, in order to develop a relationship and a trust with Him.

The believers have the desire and intention to succeed as God's trustee on earth. Since it is through knowledge and perception that people attain closeness to God, the believers strive to gain knowledge. They strive to read and understand the Qur'an and follow His Messenger as their role model. The importance of learning what God commands in the Qur'an is such that people should exert their efforts to the best of their ability to accomplish this task, and no one is exempt from this duty.

Why is it important to learn what God says in the Qur'an? God has shown us in numerous ways that He loves people. That is why He commands only those things that are good for us. God says that we should serve Him and our families, neglecting neither. It is by serving God that we learn the importance of serving our families. Who are the members of our family? They are our children, relatives, neighbors, countrymen, and people all over the world. Islam does not distinguish between living the life for this world and living the life for the Hereafter. It (Islam) expects its followers to live their lives following all moral and ethical principles. How we live in this world will very much determine our life in the Hereafter. People's welfare in this life, as well as in the Hereafter, depends on their efforts and good deeds. God reminds us that: "Every soul is (held) in pledge for its deeds" (Qur'an 74:38).

In human development, all aspects of life need to be addressed in order to nurture an honest, hardworking, and competent individual. God desires that a well-balanced human personality be developed for the progress of humanity. That is why He has given people an ability to endeavor in all areas of learning, "And He taught Adam the names of all things…" (Qur'an 2:31). Therefore, education that only addresses either religious or secular aspects of life is not helping the society. People need an integrated educational system for teaching students in various areas of learning and for developing all human faculties.

Currently, the most prevalent route to acquire knowledge that will help build human character and behavior is through self-study of the Qur'an and *Ahadith*, supplemented by the writings of religious scholars. In the past, Arabic was the only way to study the Qur'an, and thus many people recited the Qur'an without understanding its meanings. This was due to the non-availability or limited availability of translations of the Qur'an. Since translations and interpretations of the Qur'an are now available in almost every known language, one can also learn and understand the Qur'an in one's own language. Although learning and understanding the Qur'an in its original Arabic language is highly preferred, the importance of knowing what God commands is so important that nothing should discourage people. God tells the believers, "… Be not like those who say, we hear, but listen not: for the worst of beasts in the sight of Allah are the deaf and the dumb— those who understand not" (Qur'an 8:21-22). And then He asks— why "Do they not then earnestly seek to understand the Qur'an…" (Qur'an 47:24).

Chapter 2

Divine Law and Human Destiny

(*Qadar, Taufiq, Taqdir,* God's Mercy and Forgiveness)

What does belief in *Qadar* mean? Complete belief is a thing which may not be understood by everyone. When one believes in pre-destination or *Qadar*, it must be understood that for those without belief, arguments may not be sufficient or satisfactory to convince them of it. It implies a belief that among people, no one has absolute power, absolute knowledge, or absolute will, but one's power, knowledge and will are controlled by God not arbitrarily but according to certain laws or *Qadar* to determine ones destiny or a decree or *Taqdir*. God reaffirms, "Verily, all things have We created in proportion and measure (*Qadar*)" and, "... Verily, for all things has Allah appointed a due proportion (*Qadar*)" (Qur'an 54:49; 65:3).

It is a belief in *Qadar* that no one has control over such things as birth, death, looks, talents, etc., but that people have a limited control over their doings: either to follow a right way that brings reward or to follow a wrong way so as to bring punishment. It is a belief that all our deeds or efforts are subject to *Qadar* or divine law, defined as the law of nature that God has put in place. In another way, all our deeds, good or bad have built in consequences (or a decree or *Taqdir*), according to their *Qadar*. It is a belief that we must go on working to the best of our abilities, thereby shaping our own destinies or *Taqdir* (Modified from Al-Hadith Vol., 3, Chapter 32).

Again, God grants *Taufiq* only to those who honestly try their best in the area of their choice. This is another law of nature which God has put in place.

Similarly, there are certain requirements which have to be met before the believers can expect to receive God's Mercy and His Forgiveness.

1
GOD CREATED THINGS ON THEIR NATURE

"Glorify the name of your Guardian-Lord Most High, Who has created, and further, given order and proportion; Who has ordained laws (*Qadar*). And granted guidance" (Qur'an 87:1-3). Ali reported that the Messenger[PBUH] of God said: "No servant believes till he believes in four things—he bears witness that there is no deity but Allah; that I am the messenger of Allah Who sent me with truth; and he believes in death and resurrection after death; and he believes in pre-measurement (*Qadar* or predestination)" (At-Tirmizi, Ibn Majah, Al-Hadith, vol., 1, no. 36, page 112).

A miser does not give alms unless compelled by unforeseen calamities. At such a time, he takes a vow of charity provided a certain calamity is removed. Abu Hurairah and Ibn Omar reported that the Messenger[PBUH] of God said: "Don't take a vow, because a vow has no effect against pre-decree (*Qadar*)" (Agreed; Al-Hadith, vol., 2, no. 21, page 465). Jaber bin Samorah reported: "I heard the Messenger[PBUH] of God say: 'There are three things that I fear from my followers: (1) seeking rain with the position of the stars, (2) oppression of a ruler (3) and disbelief in predestination (*Qadar*)'" (Ahmad, Baihaqi; Al-Hadith, vol. 2, no. 363w, page 565).

1.1 DIVINE WILL OR THE WORKINGS OF THE LAWS OF NATURE
Divine will is not capricious and arbitrary. It follows the natural laws created by God. The limited will of people also follows the divine laws; those who follow these laws will be happy, and those who transgress them will suffer. Divine law instructs people to stay away from fire to save themselves from its harm. Similarly God instructs us to stay away from the fire of Hell by following His commands. If we obey them, we will be in bliss. If not, we will suffer Hellfire. This is the natural law both in the material and spiritual worlds. As for those who follow the laws, God leads them to guidance just as He grows crops for those who cultivate and sow. As far those who do not follow the laws, God misguides them just as He does not grow crops for those who do not cultivate and sow.

Belief in *Qadar* can best be explained by what God says in *Surah Al-Rahman*, "The sun and the moon follow courses (exactly) computed; and the herbs and the trees— both (alike) bow in adoration. And the sky has He raised high, and He has set up the balance (of justice), in order that you may not transgress (due) balance. So establish weight with justice and fall not short in the balance" (Qur'an 55:5-9). In these verses, God is telling people that like the physical laws that control the universe, He has set up moral laws that have adverse consequences if violated.

1.2 EVERYTHING GOES BY LAW, PROPORATION AND MEASURE

God's creation is not haphazard. Everything goes by law, proportion, and measure. Everything has its appointed time, place, and occasion, as also its definite limitations. *Qadar* is the Arabic word which is translated in English as—in due proportion or in proportion and measure. In other words, nothing happens but according to God's plan, and every deed, word, and thought of a person has its fullest consequences, except insofar as the Grace and Mercy of God intervenes, and that is also according to a law and a plan. About God and His creation, people are told that, "To Him is due the primal origin of the heavens and the earth: When He decrees a matter, He says to it: 'Be' and it is" (Qur'an 2:117). Again people are told that God is, "He to Whom belongs the dominion of the heavens and the earth: no son has He begotten, nor has He a partner in His dominion: it is He Who created all things, and ordered them in due proportions (*Qadar*)" (Qur'an 25:2).

While in the life of created things there is 'proportion and measure', and a lag of time or distance or circumstance. In God's command, the design, the word, the execution and the consequence are but a single act like the twinkling of an eye. In *Surah Al-Qamar*, people are told that, "Verily, all things have We created in proportion and measure. And Our Command is but a single (Act), - like the twinkling of an eye" (Qur'an 54:49-50). Again in *Surah Al-Talaq*, God tells those who trust Him that, " ... Sufficient is (Allah) for him. For Allah will surely accomplish His purpose: Verily, for all things has Allah appointed a due proportion (*Qadar*)" (Qur'an 65:3).

1.3 GOOD OR BAD DEEDS HAVE THEIR BUILT-IN CONSEQUENCES

Taqdir is the end result of *Qadar* or natural law, ordinance or a divine procedure, and as such it is not inconsistent with freedom of will; on the contrary, it helps it. It is a *Taqdir* that out of a male and female's union an issue will be born under certain circumstances and that seed of one kind cannot produce another kind.

God asks people, "Have We not created you from a fluid despicable? - Which We placed in a place of rest, firmly fixed, For a period (of gestation), determined (according to need)? For We do determine; for We are the best to determine (things)" (Qur'an 77:20-23). God's direct interference is not at all necessary. The natural law (*Qadar*) must operate. If it is pre-written that an animal can move then that animal will move around. Hence, the movements of men have been pre-written. Thus, the whole universe is being governed according to certain immutable laws of *Qadar*.

1.4 PEOPLE WILL FIND NO CHANGE IN GOD'S WAY OF DEALING
God does not discriminate among people. His law is for all people irrespective of their religion. Those who fail in their trust today, will be dealt exactly like the previous nations who failed in their trust. Arrogance and the spread of evil will have the same consequences for people as it has in the past.

God tells people that, "On account of their arrogance in the land and their plotting of Evil, but the plotting of Evil will hem in only the authors thereof. Now are they but looking for the way the ancients were dealt with? But no change will you find in Allah's Way (of dealing): no turning off will you find in Allah's Way (of dealing)" (Qur'an 35:43).

1.5 *TAQDIR* MAY BE CHANGED BY REPENTANCE AND PRAYERS
However, it is a part of the Divine Law or *Qadar* that a decree or *Taqdir* can be averted by God if He so Wills. Salman Al-Farsi reported that the Messenger[PBUH] said: "Nothing but invocation averts a decree, and nothing but righteousness increases life" (At-Tirmizi; Al-Hadith, vol. 3, no. 11, page 711). But the repentance and prayers fail when the results of people's misdeeds become evident. After they see God's punishment, they can neither profess Faith nor repent. At that moment their fate is sealed.

God tells people, "But when they saw Our Punishment, they said: We believe in Allah,- the One God - and we reject the partners we used to join with

Him. But their professing the Faith when they saw Our Punishment was not
going to profit them. (Such has been), Allah's way of dealing with His Servants
(from the most ancient times). And even thus did the Rejecters of Allah perish!" (Qur'an 40:84-85).

2
TAUFIQ IS FOR THOSE WHO STRIVE

It is practice that makes people perfect in the area of their endeavors. God
grants people *Taufiq* (ability) to do good or bad according to their individual
efforts. He grants *Taufiq* to those who honestly try their best in the area of their
choice. The Islamic concept of life demonstrates the perfect balance between
asserting that God's Will is absolute in shaping all events and that it comes
into operation through man's own actions. The divine laws of nature establish
a cause and effect relationship in all matters, but causes do not initiate effects
alone— without God's Will or *Qadar*.

The operative force is that of God, Who determines effects on the basis
of causes according to His Will. He then requires man to work hard, fulfill
his duties, and meet his obligations. It is in relation to how far man discharges
his responsibility that God determines the results. This means that results will
always depend on God's Will, for it is He alone Who brings them into being
whenever and however He Wills. Equilibrium is thus established between the
basic concept of a believer and his actions. A believer works as hard as he can
and knows that the results of his actions depend on God's Will.

2.1 GOD GUIDES THOSE WHO BELIEVE TO A STRAIGHT PATH
God reaffirms that He Guides all those, "… Whoever holds firmly to Allah,
will be shown a Way that is straight" (Qur'an 3:101). Contrarily, God neither
forgives nor guides, "Those who believe, then reject Faith, then believe (again)
and (again) reject Faith, and go on increasing in unbelief—Allah will not forgive them nor guide them on the Way" (Qur'an 4:137).

God also confirms that He guides all those who seek His guidance,
"Wherewith Allah guides all who seek His good pleasure to ways of peace

and safety, and leads them out of darkness, by His Will, unto the light—guides them to a Path that is Straight" (Qur'an 5:16).

2.2 GOD GIVES ABILITY TO ENJOY GOOD— TO GOOD PEOPLE

People's ability (*Taufiq*) to enjoy the good things God has provided them does not change unless their own behavior deteriorates. Contrarily, people's condition will not improve before they improve their own collective behavior.

People are to keep a strict watch over their conduct and deeds, "Because Allah will never change the Grace which He has bestowed on a people until they change what is in their souls: and verily Allah is He Who hears and knows (all things)" (Qur'an 8:53). And again people are assured, "… Verily never will Allah change the condition of a people unless they change what is within themselves …" (Qur'an 13:11).

2.3 ABILITY TO DO GOOD INCREASES BY DOING GOOD DEEDS

People's ability (*Taufiq*) to do good increases with every good deed they do. Similarly, people's ability to do evil will increase with every bad deed they do.

God tells the believers, "And establish regular prayers at the two ends of the day and at the approaches of the night: for those things that are good remove those that are evil: In that is remembrance to those who remember (their Lord)" (Qur'an 11:114).

2.4 GOD'S FEAR AND SUPPLICATION HELPS REMOVE ONE'S ILLS

Communication is the only way to develop any relationship in this world. It is our discourse and dealings by which we know each other. In the same way, the believers develop their relationship with God and know Him. The believers develop their relationship with God by talking to Him during their prayers and by listening to Him while reading the Qur'an in the language they understand and then— by living as He commands, they know Him and take His advice. People who fear and trust God, He will remove their weaknesses and difficulties and will enlarge their reward.

It is God's promise that, " ... And for those who fear Allah, He prepares a way out, and He provides for him from (sources) he never could imagine. And if any one puts his trust in Allah, sufficient is (Allah) for him. For Allah will surely accomplish his purpose. Verily, for all things has Allah appointed a due proportion (*Qadar*).", "That is the command of Allah that He has sent down to you, and if any one fears Allah (and supplicates), He will remove his ills from him and will enlarge his reward" (Qur'an 65:2-3, 5).

3
Conscience, Intentions, Efforts and *Taqdir*

People are reminded: "That man can have nothing but what he strives for" (Qur'an 53:39). The Messenger[PBUH] quotes God in a sacred *hadith* saying: "My servants, it is but your deeds that I reckon up for you and then recompense you for, so let him who finds good praise Allah and let him who finds other than that blame no one but himself" (Sahih Muslim: 32.6246). In other way— One's deeds, according to their *Qadar*— results in their *Taqdir* or the consequence *(Taqdir)* of one's deeds as a reward or the punishment is according to their *(Qadar)*. Therefore, people must go on working to the best of their abilities, thereby shaping their own destinies or *Taqdir.*

3.1 People will have nothing but what they strive for
All deeds have their consequences, good or evil. But there is always room for repentance and amendment in this life. With repentance, God's mercy comes into action. It can blot out the consequence of one's evil deed. and the 'reward' for a good deed is nearly always greater than its merit. The working of the law of efforts and rewards has many manifestations: The first is that one's spiritual burden—the responsibility of one's sin—must be borne by the sinner himself and not by someone else. The second is that one must strive or there will be no gain. The third is that if one does strive, its results must soon appear in sight and the reward will be there in full measure. The fourth one is that all things return to God and all our hopes should be in Him and we should fear no one but Him; and that He alone can give life and death.

God tells people how His reward system works, "Namely, that no bearer of burdens can bear the burden of another; That man can have nothing but what he strives for; That (the fruit of) his striving will soon come in sight: Then will he be rewarded with a reward complete; That to your Lord is the final Goal; That it is He Who grants Laughter and Tears; That it is He Who grants Death and Life" (Qur'an 53:38-44) God has promised people that He will raise them after death into a new life in the hereafter and reward them according to their deeds. "That He has promised a Second Creation (Raising of the Dead)" (Qur'an 53:47).

3.2 GOOD INTENTIONS LEAD PEOPLE— TO RIGHTEOUS DEEDS

Human conscience and divine guidance tells people what is right or wrong for them to do in their daily lives. People select for themselves with their free will about what they intend to do, and then go after their goal. If their selection and intention are good, then they will do righteous deeds. Their deeds according to their *Qadar* or the pre-destined law of nature which God has put in place will result into their fate, destiny or *Taqdir*. In other words, *Taqdir,* the destiny or fate of a person depends on his/her efforts or deeds, according to the *Qadar* or the law of nature which God has put in place.

About human conscience, people are told in *Surah Al-Shams* that, "By the Soul, and the proportion and order given to it; And its enlightenment as to its wrong and its right;-

1. Truly he succeeds that purifies it,
2. And he fails that corrupts it" (Qur'an 91:7-10).

3.3 DIVINE LAW AND DECREE HELP PEOPLE TO ACHIEVE GOAL

God has ordained His law and decrees (or *Qadar and Taqdir*) by which people can develop themselves and fit into His scheme of evolution for all His creation. He has measured exactly the needs of all, and given them instincts and physical and psychic predispositions which fit into His Decree. He has given them guidance so that they are not at the mercy of some mechanical laws but they exercise their reason and their will during their struggle to achieve their goal and destiny in life.

About *Qadar* and guidance, people are told in *Surah Al-A'la* that, "Glorify the name of your Guardian-Lord Most High, Who has created, and further, given order and proportion; Who has ordained laws (*Qadar*). And granted guidance" (Qur'an 87:1-3).

3.4 *TAQDIR* IS THE OUTCOME OF PEOPLES DEEDS AND *QADAR*

Human origin as an animal is lowly indeed. But what additional faculties and capacities has not God granted to people? Besides their animal bodies, in which they also share in all the blessings which God has bestowed on the rest of His creation, people have been granted numerous divine gifts which entitle them to be called 'His Vicegerent on earth' (Qur'an 2:30). People have a will, they have spiritual perception: they are capable of divine love; they can control nature within certain limits, and subject nature's forces to their own use. They have been given power of judgment, so that they can avoid excess and defeat, and follow the middle path. And that path, as well as all that is necessary for their life in its manifold aspects has been made easy for them.

Though all these blessings and stages have been provided by God's Grace for the good of people yet the unrighteous people fail to carry out the purpose of their creation and life. God tells people that He created and molded them according to their *Qadar*, "From a sperm-drop: He has created him, and then molded him in due proportions (*Qadar*);

1. Then does He make His path smooth for him (With One's Efforts, Deeds and *Qadar*);
2. Then He causes him to die, and putts him in his grave; (Causes and *Qadar to Taqdir*)
3. Then, when it is His Will, He will raise him up (again)" (Qur'an 80:19-22)

4

GOD IS MERCIFUL TO THE BELIEVERS

God's Mercy is there for those believers who really believe and follow what He commands to the best of their abilities. It is true that none will achieve salvation or success without God's Mercy, but the believers have to believe, worship Him, and do good deeds to become a candidate for His Mercy, "The believers, men and women, are protectors of one another. They enjoin what is just and forbid what is evil. They observe regular prayers, practice regular charity, and obey Allah and His Messenger. On them will Allah pour His Mercy, for Allah is Exalted in Power, Wise." And, "Those who believed and those who suffered exile and fought (and strove and struggled) in the path of Allah, they have the hope of the Mercy of Allah, and Allah is Oft-Forgiving, Most Merciful" (Qur'an 9:71, 2:218).

However, along with God's Mercy, good deeds are needed for salvation in the Hereafter. Since people will be judged with justice, the believers earn their salvation with their good deeds. It will be assured to people in the Hereafter that they inherited Paradise due to their good deeds which they used to do in their life on earth.

4.1 GOD IS MERCIFUL TO THOSE WHO REPENT AND REFORM
There are many people among Muslims in society who believe that they will eventually be forgiven because God is Oft-forgiving, Most Merciful. Perhaps they forget that people who die without repentance, God warns them, that on the Day of Judgment, no excuse of theirs will avail them, nor will they be invited at that time to seek grace by repentance.

How a person qualifies for God's Mercy, He tells the believers, "O you who believe!

1. Devour not usury, doubled and multiplied, but fear Allah that you may (really) prosper. Fear the Fire that is prepared for those who reject Faith, and obey Allah and the Messenger that you may obtain mercy" (Qur'an 3:130-132).
2. "Allah accepts the repentance of those who do evil in ignorance and repent soon afterwards; to them will Allah turn in mercy, for Allah is full of knowledge and wisdom" (Qur'an 4:17).

Among people who die without repentance, God warns them, "So, on that Day no excuse of theirs will avail the transgressors, nor will they be invited (then) to seek grace (by repentance)" (Qur'an 30:57).

4.2 FOLLOW THE REVEALED TO THE BEST OF YOUR ABILITY
An individual is responsible only to the extent of his or her ability. God does not demand from us what is beyond our abilities. That is why He commands people to follow what He has revealed, to the best of their abilities and understanding.

God tells the Messenger to, "Say: 'O my servants who have transgressed against their souls! Despair not of the Mercy of Allah, for Allah forgives all sins, for He is Oft-Forgiving, Most Merciful. Turn to your Lord (in repentance) and bow to His (Will) before the penalty comes on you. After that, you shall not be helped. And follow the best of (the courses) revealed to you from your Lord ..." (Qur'an 39:53-55).

4.3 ALONG WITH GOD'S MERCY GOOD DEEDS ARE NEEDED
God has promised His Mercy and salvation only to those who believe and do good deeds, "....Allah has promised those among them who believe and do righteous deeds forgiveness, and a great Reward" (Qur'an 48:29).

To enjoy a life of good pleasure in the Hereafter, people will need plenty of good deeds to qualify for God's Mercy. He tells people that, "Every man's fate We have fastened on his own neck: On the Day of Judgment We shall bring out for him a scroll, which he will see spread open. (It will be said to him:) Read your (own) record: Sufficient is your soul this day to make out an account against you" (Qur'an 17:13-14).

People are told about their destiny or fate on the Day of Judgment as, "Then, he whose balance (of good deeds), will be (found) heavy, will be in a life of good pleasure and satisfaction. But he whose balance (of good deeds), will be (found) light, - Will have his home in a (bottomless) Pit (of Hell)" (Qur'an 101:6-9).

4.4 BELIEVERS EARN THEIR SALVATION WITH THEIR DEEDS
God does not expect from the believers what is beyond their capacity, "But those who believe and work righteousness,- no burden do We place on any

soul, but that which it can bear,- they will be Companions of the Garden, therein to dwell (for ever)" (Qur'an 7:42).

The believers are also reminded that they can achieve their salvation and Paradise only by their belief and good deeds, "Such will be the Garden of which you are made heirs for your (good) deeds (in life). You shall have therein abundance of fruit, from which you shall have satisfaction" (Qur'an 43:72-73).

Entering Paradise the believers will be told that they have inherited Paradise because of their good deeds, ".... And they shall hear the cry: Behold! the Garden before you! You have been made its inheritors, for your deeds (of righteousness)" (Qur'an 7:43).

4.5 GOD WILL REWARD PEOPLE WITH JUSTICE IN HEREAFTER
God is Oft-Forgiving, Most Merciful. He forgives people after they repent and reform during their life on earth. But, after completing their life on earth, when people will return to God in the Hereafter, He will reward them with justice. He has also warned the believers that after the accountability process is completed, "Hypocrites (who do not repent and reform) will be in the lowest depths of the Fire: no helper will you find for them" (Qur'an 4:145).

God rewarding people with justice has been confirmed in *Surah Yunus* as, "... that He may reward with justice those who believe and work righteousness; but those who reject Him will have draughts of boiling fluids, and a penalty grievous, because they did reject Him" (Qur'an 10:4).

Historically, "To every people (was sent) a messenger: when their messenger comes (before them), the matter will be judged between them with justice, and they will not be wronged." and "At length, it will be said to the wrongdoers: 'You taste the enduring punishment! you get but the recompense of what you earned.'" Concluding the process of accountability, people will be told that, "Every soul that has sinned, if it possessed all that is on earth, would fain give it in ransom: They would declare (their) repentance when they see the penalty: but the judgment between them will be with justice, and no wrong will be done unto them" (Qur'an 10:47, 52, 54).

5

God Forgives Those Who Forgive Others

God tells the believers, if they desire to be forgiven by Him, they should forgive people. They should forgive people even if they are angry. The believers forgive people, are charitable, and they restrain their anger. The believers are to forgive all people whether those they are forgiving are believers or unbelievers. With the Doctrine of Forgiveness, Islam tries to eliminate violence from society.

God commands the believers to forgive the unbelievers. Even those people, He Himself has cursed are to be forgiven by the believers. It is God Who guides people so the believers freely forgive the unguided people. They are commanded to forgive and overlook the People of the Book (e.g., Jews and Christians). Although there is a stipulation that allows demanding eye for an eye, and although the heirs of the slain person can demand *Qisas* (blood money), God tells the believers that to forgive the guilty is better. While the believers should know their enemies among their relatives, they are commanded to forgive them. Further they should overlook and cover up their faults.

5.1 God guides people, so freely forgive the unguided

God has created the universe for a purpose and it is operating as He planned. People should not be impatient, if there appears to be, to their limited vision, apparent injustice. They must bear and forebear, and as far as their feelings are concerned, they must not judge but overlook other people's faults and forgive them freely. Their behavior will certainly be judged on the Day of Judgment.

Therefore, God tells people that, "We created not the heavens, the earth, and all between them, but for just ends. And the Hour is surely coming, so overlook (any human faults) with gracious forgiveness" (Qur'an 15:85).

5.2 BELIEVERS FORGIVE THE UNBELIEVERS AS COMMANDED

One of the laws of nature that God has put in place, is that 'people are rewarded for what they do.' This will become manifest on the Day of Judgment, when God will recompense people for what they have earned. Since, the unbelievers do not believe in the accountability of their deeds, their conduct is not based on human values as commanded in the Qur'an, but they follow only selfish desires.

Since it is for God to take people into account, the Messenger has been asked to, "Tell those who believe to forgive those who do not look forward to the Days of Allah. It is for Him to recompense (for good or ill) each people according to what they have earned" (Qur'an 45:14).

5.3 BELIEVERS ARE TO FORGIVE THE PEOPLE OF THE BOOK

The believers' belief is God's blessing and a sign of His mercy for them. The People of the Book know this, and therefore out of jealousy wish the believers back to unbelief. Even so, the believers forgive them and overlook their behavior, for they know that God will eventually punish them.

God tells the believers that "Quite a number of the People of the Book wish they could turn you (the believers) back to infidelity after you have believed, from selfish envy, after the truth has become manifest unto them: but forgive and overlook till Allah accomplishes His purpose, for Allah has power over all things" (Qur'an 2:109).

5.4 BELIEVERS FORGIVE EVEN THOSE WHOM GOD HAS CURSED

God cursed the People of the Book because they broke their contract with Him by withdrawing His overflowing grace from them. This made their hearts grow hard and they were no longer protected from the assaults of evil and even His message of forgiveness and mercy was withdrawn from them.

But the believers forgive even those people whom God Himself has cursed because they are commanded to do so, "Allah did aforetime take a Covenant from the Children of Israel, and We appointed twelve captains among them. And Allah said: 'I am with you: If you...' But because of their breach of their

Covenant, We cursed them and made their hearts grow hard. They change the words from their (right) places and forget a good part of the message that was sent them. Nor will you cease to find them, barring a few, ever bent on (new) deceits, but forgive them, and overlook (their misdeeds), for Allah loves those who are kind" (Qur'an 5:12-13).

5.5 FORGIVE UNBELIEVERS AND OVERLOOK THEIR BEHAVIOR

Citing the example from the behavior of the People of the Book who, due to their selfish envy, were trying to turn back the believers to infidelity. The believers were commanded to forgive them, even when angry, and overlook their actions. Forgiving people has been commanded along with being steadfast in prayer and regular in charity. This indicates that forgiving people should be practiced by the believers with the same zeal as prayer and charity. They cannot be excused from this duty even if they are angry.

God commands the believers to forgive, and overlook the behavior of the unbelievers "Quite a number of the People of the Book wish they could turn you (the believers) back to infidelity after you have believed, from selfish envy, after the truth has become manifest unto them:

1. But forgive and overlook (the behavior of the unbelievers), till Allah accomplish His purpose; ...
2. And be steadfast in prayer and regular in charity:

And whatever good you send forth for your souls before you, you shall find it with Allah: for Allah sees well all that you do" (Qur'an 2:109-110).

God tells in *Surah Al-Shura* that the believers forgive people even if they are angry.

3. "…And when they are angry even then forgive" (Qur'an 42:37).

5.6 AN EYE IS FOR AN EYE BUT TO FORGIVE PEOPLE IS BETTER

God does not love those who do wrong. If wrong is tolerated or encouraged by allowing it to run rampant, instead of preventing it, people fail in their duty to God. On the other hand, It is harder to be patient and forgiving yet it gets wrong— corrected. It may look futile but in realty, it is the highest and noblest form of courage and resolution. It may reform the guilty and help eradicate evil even better than punishment.

God tells the believers to show patience and forgive the guilty, for a better reward from Him,

1. "The recompense for an injury is an injury equal thereto (in degree), but if a person forgives and makes reconciliation, his reward is due from Allah, for (Allah) loves not those who do wrong—

But indeed if any do help and defend themselves after a wrong (done) to them, against such there is no cause of blame. The blame is only against those who oppress men with wrongdoing and insolently transgress beyond bounds through the land, defying right and justice: for such there will be a penalty grievous.

2. But indeed if any show patience and forgive, that would truly be an exercise of courageous will and resolution in the conduct of affairs" (Qur'an 42:40-43).

5.7 HEIRS OF THE SLAIN EITHER DEMAND *QISAS* OR FORGIVE

The believers kill no one wrongly, but if it happens by mistake then compensation is required. It could be that, either a life should be taken for a life destroyed or reasonably compensated, if the heirs of the person slain accept it. God tells the believers that, "Never should a believer kill a believer; but (if it so happens) by mistake, (compensation is due): ... If a man kills a believer intentionally, his recompense is Hell, to abide therein (for ever): And the wrath and the curse of Allah are upon him, and a dreadful penalty is prepared for him" (Qur'an 4:92-93).

Life is absolutely sacred in the Islamic society but mistakes sometime happen like in a car accident with no guilty intentions of the accused. Under such cases, the family of the deceased could demand either a compensation or forgive the accused. God commands the believers, "Nor take life, which Allah has made sacred, except for just cause. And if anyone is slain wrongfully, We have given his heir authority (to demand *Qisas* or to forgive), but let him not exceed bounds in the matter of taking life; for he is helped (by the law)" (Qur'an 17:33).

5.8 KNOW ENEMIES AMONG YOUR KIN BUT FORGIVE THEM

Sometimes, the family (i.e., wife and children) demands may conflict with a person's moral and spiritual convictions and duties. Under such circumstances, he must not abandon his duties to their requests and desires, and must not treat them harshly. He must make reasonable provision for them, and if they persist in opposing his clear duties and convictions, he must forgive them and not expose them to shame or ridicule, while at the same time holding on to his clear duties.

Hence, God tells the believers, "O you who believe! Truly, among your wives and your children are (some that are) enemies to yourselves, so beware of them! But if you forgive and overlook and cover up (their faults), verily, Allah is Oft-Forgiving, Most Merciful" (Qur'an 64:14).

5.9 RESOLVE NOT AGAINST HELPING YOUR KIN BUT FORGIVE

Referring to the incident of slandering the Messenger's wife 'Aisha, her father, 'Abu Bakr, wanted to withdraw his support from his relative who took part in the incident, God tells the believers that they should forgive people even if they are guilty of a serious misconduct. A generous person should not, in personal anger, withdraw his support even for serious faults, if the guilty repents and mends his ways. If God forgives people, then who are we to refuse forgiveness to our fellows.

God commands the believers to forgive others if they want to be forgiven by Him, "Let not those among you who are endued with grace and amplitude of means resolve by oath against helping their kinsmen, those in want, and those who have left their homes in Allah's Cause. Let them forgive and overlook; do you not wish that Allah should forgive you? For Allah is Oft-Forgiving, Most Merciful" (Qur'an 24:22).

5.10 BELIEVERS ALSO FORGIVE EVEN WHEN THEY ARE ANGRY

As one can see 'forgiving people even when angry' is one of seven major characteristics of the believers—The believers, 1) believe, and trust God, 2) avoid greater crimes and shameful deeds and 3) forgive people even when they are angry. They 4) fear their Lord, establish prayers and 5) consult each other in their daily affairs. They, 6) are charitable, and 7) fight with the oppressors to defend themselves.

God assures such believers that, "Whatever you are given (here) is (only) a convenience of this life, but that which is with Allah is better and more lasting. (It is) for those who believe and put their trust in their Lord; Those who avoid the greater crimes and shameful deeds and when they are angry even then forgive; Those who hearken to their Lord and establish regular prayer, who (conduct) their affairs by mutual consultation, who spend out of what We bestow on them for sustenance. And those who, when an oppressive wrong is inflicted on them, help and defend themselves" (Qur'an 42:36-39).

Chapter 3

Divine Guidance for Humanity

(Human Conscience, Divine Guidance, and Humanity)

After describing the salient features of the worst and the best of humanity, various ways of distinguishing each have been highlighted. Listening honestly to one's conscience and following what God commands in the Qur'an are the best tools available to people if they desire to progress in humanity. God desires people to excel, which is why He has been sending His Guidance and His Messengers as human role models. By His guidance and the divine requirement of good deeds for salvation in the Hereafter, God motivates people and provides direction as well as means to excel in Humanity.

1
THE WORST AND THE BEST OF HUMANITY

Life on earth is like a steep road that helps people to ascend to new heights of humanity. Those who tread the steep road, believe in God, follow His law, and join others in the establishment of a just human society which strives to fulfill the demands of virtue and righteousness, are the best of humanity. Their virtue is reflected in their honest earnings and by spending their wealth to help the orphans and the needy.

1.1 LIFE IS HARD WORK AND INDIVIDUAL ACCOUNTABILITY

Life is hard work, and all human activities have good or bad consequence. In *Surah Al-Balad*, after citing the city of Makkah, the hardships being faced by the Messenger and the general condition of people, as a witness to the truth,

God tells people that this world is not a place of rest and ease for them, where they are born to enjoy life; rather, they are created to toil and struggle, "Verily We have created man into toil and struggle" (Qur'an 90:4). This makes it clear that people's ultimate future depends on their efforts and struggles. In addition, some people's mistaken belief that they are in charge of this world without any accountability of their behavior and deeds has been refuted in this *Surah*.

In contrast, people are told: "That man can have nothing but what he strives for" (Qur'an 53:39). And that: "Every soul is (held) in pledge for its own deeds" (Qur'an 74:38). About accountability, the Messenger[PBUH] quotes God in a sacred *hadith* saying: "My servants, it is but your deeds that I reckon up for you and then recompense you for, so let him who finds good praise Allah and let him who finds other than that blame no one but himself" (Sahih Muslim: 32.6246).

1.2 ROAD TO SUCCESS IS IN AN HONEST AND MODEST LIVING

Surah Al-Balad also points out the wrong criterion of merit and greatness that many people have adopted. Such people squander heaps of wealth for ostentation and display, take pride in their extravagances, and enthusiastically admire themselves for it. Whereas God, Who is watching over their deeds, sees by what methods and ways they obtained their wealth and with what motives and intention they spend it. The road to success is in living on honest earnings, in avoiding extravagance and not wasting resources and wealth.

Although God has created man into toil and struggle but:

1. "He (the misguided man) thinks that none has power over him?
2. He may say (boastfully); wealth have I squandered in abundance!
3. He thinks that none beholds him?" (Qur'an 90:5-7).

1.3 HUMANITY LACKS CONSCIENCE AND NEGLECTS GUIDANCE

People are endowed with knowledge and the faculties of thinking and understanding. They need a conscience and divine guidance to succeed. God has allowed people free will to chose between the ways of virtue or of vice. The easy way leads to moral depravity, while the right way leads to moral heights, although it is a steep uphill road. People have to exercise self-restraint in scaling this uphill road.

Unfortunately, human weakness is such that it prefers slipping down into the abyss rather than scaling up a cliff. A person representing the worst of humanity 'thinks that none has power over him. He may say (boastfully), 'Wealth have I squandered in abundance!' Does he think that no one beholds him?'

God asks such person, "Have We not made for him a pair of eyes, and a tongue, and a pair of lips, and shown him the two highways (of good and evil)?" (Qur'an 90:8-10). But such person makes no haste on the path that is steep and leads to the best of humanity. This path can only be tread by following one's conscience and the divine guidance as described in the Qur'an.

1.4 REFORMING AWAY WHICH IS THE WORST FOR HUMANITY
Greed and other such human weaknesses can be overcome by listening and following one's conscience and divine guidance. When people use reasoning to control and manage their selfish desires successfully then they are— the best of creatures. People who cannot control or manage their selfish desires are— the worst of creatures. Such people use reasoning to justify their selfish desires.

God tells people that, "Those who reject (truth), among the People of the Book and among the polytheists ... they are the worst of creatures. Those who have Faith and do righteous deeds—they are the best of creatures. Their reward is with Allah: Gardens of Eternity, beneath which rivers flow; they will dwell therein forever, Allah well pleased with them, and they with Him. All this for such as fear their Lord and Cherisher" (Qur'an 98:6-8).

1.5 DEVELOPING VALUES THAT ARE THE BEST FOR HUMANITY
Although humanity has made tremendous progress in harnessing God's bounties that are scattered around the globe, it has weakened itself by an increased greed in some segments of the society, depriving part of the population from the benefits of progress in science and technology.

God tells people, "But he (humanity) has made no haste on the path that is steep. And what will explain to you the path that is steep?

1. (It is) freeing the bondman, or
2. (It is) the giving of food in a day of privation to the orphan with claims of relationship or to the indigent (down) in the dust.
3. Then will he be of those who believe,
4. And enjoin patience (constancy and self-restraint),
5. And enjoin deeds of kindness and compassion.

Such are the companions of the right hand. But those who reject Our Signs, they are the (unhappy) companions of the left hand. On them will be fire vaulted over (all round)" (Qur'an 90:11-20).

2
LISTENING TO THE HUMAN CONSCIENCE

People's fate depends on how they use their sense of discrimination, free will, and judgment to develop their goodness and suppress their evil tendencies. Progress in developing one's inner goodness and in getting rid of one's evil inclinations will attain ultimate success. However, if one suppresses the good and promotes evil tendencies of the human self, that will lead to disappointment and failure.

2.1 BELIEVERS WHO DO GOOD AND EVILDOERS ARE NOT ALIKE
Goodness and Evil are not alike in results. Like the sun and the moon, the day and the night, and the earth and the sky, which are different from each other and contradictory in their affects and results, so are good and evil deeds different from each other and contradictory in their affects and results. Neither are alike in their outward appearance, nor can they be alike in their results.

God tells people: "Assuredly the creation of the heavens and the earth is a greater (matter) than the creation of men. Yet, most men understand not. Not equal are the blind and those who (clearly) see, nor are (equal) those who believe and work deeds of righteousness and those who do evil. Little do you learn by admonition! The Hour (of Judgment) will certainly come. Therein is no doubt. Yet, most men believe not" (Qur'an 40:57-59).

God has also promised, His help in this world, as well as in the Hereafter, to anyone who calls upon Him. "Your Lord says: 'Call on Me. I will answer your (prayer), but those who are too arrogant to serve Me will surely find themselves in Hell—in humiliation'" (Qur'an 40:60). Since God's promise is true, people should be patient and ask for His help while trying their best to do good deeds. They are commanded, "Patiently then persevere, for the promise of Allah is true. And ask forgiveness for your fault, and celebrate the praises of your Lord in the evening and in the morning" (Qur'an 40:55).

2.2 HUMAN CONSCIENCE HELPS TO SEPERATE GOOD FROM EVIL
After giving people their bodies, intellect, and wisdom, God has not left them uninformed in the world. He blessed each person with a spontaneous inspiration that distinguishes between good and evil, right and wrong. As such, there is some basic understanding that what is good is beneficial and what is evil is harmful to human survival and success. The successful people follow their conscience.

God, swearing by His creation and human conscience, commands people that human conscience is to be kept pure and uncorrupted, "By the sun and his (glorious) splendor, by the moon as she follows (the sun), by the day as it shows up (the sun's) glory, by the night as it conceals it, by the sky and its (wonderful) structure, by the earth and its (width), by the soul and the proportion and order given to it and its enlightenment as to its wrong and its right—truly, he succeeds that purifies it, and he fails that corrupts it!" (Qur'an 91:1-10).

2.3 MESSENGERS AS ROLE MODELS TO INTERPRET CONSCIENCE
The inspirational knowledge of good and evil that God has placed in human nature is by itself not enough for the guidance of humanity. People sometimes assume wrong criteria and theories of good and evil, and they are thus misled. That is why God sent down clear and definite revelation to His Messengers, in order to augment people's natural inspiration or conscience, so that the messengers might explain to people what is good and what is evil. History confirms that all prophets were human role model for their people, who guided them by living as God

commanded. About the Messenger of Islam, God has Himself testified this in the Qur'an, "And you (stand) on an exalted standard of character" (Qur'an 68:4).

A Messenger recites divine revelations, sanctifies people, and guides them to Humanity. God tells people that, "Whatever is in the heavens and on earth, does declare the Praises and Glory of Allah, - the Sovereign, the Holy One, the Exalted in Might, the Wise. It is He Who has sent among the Unlettered a messenger from among themselves, to rehearse to them His Signs, to sanctify them, and to instruct them in Scripture and Wisdom,- although they had been, before, in manifest error" (Qur'an 62:1-2).

2.4 PEOPLE'S INTENTIONS HELP THEM LEARN FROM THE QUR'AN

The Qur'an is a book of guidance for those who strive to live as God desires, in righteousness, piety and good conduct. This is possible only for those who believe in their Creator and restrain one's tongue, hand, and heart from evil. Righteousness comes from a secure faith, from a sincere devotion to God, from an unselfish service to humanity and from the accountability of their deeds in the Hereafter.

The Qur'an provides guidance to those who desire guidance, "This (the Qur'an) is a Book; in it is guidance sure, without doubt, to those

1. Who fear Allah;
2. Who believe in the unseen,
3. (Who) are steadfast in prayer, and
4. (Who) spend out of what We have provided for them; and
5. Who believe in the revelation sent to you and sent before your time, and
6. (In their hearts they) have the assurance of the Hereafter" (Qur'an 2:2-4).

2.5 REFUSING TO SERVE GOD AND DENY HIS ACCOUNTABILITY

God's servitude is to live as He commands. The believers are those who have faith and serve Him. But there are people who like to live only to satisfy their own selfish desires—there is nothing but pity for those who reject truth, run after false worship, have no sympathy or charity for the needy and they even deny any future life. Such people try to mislead humanity by their idle tales and ignorance.

God commands the Messenger to tell people, "You (O Messenger) Say: 'I am but a man like you. It is revealed to me by inspiration that your Allah is one Allah: so stand true to Him, and ask for His forgiveness. And

1. Woe to those who join gods with Allah, -
2. Those who practice not regular Charity,
3. And who even deny the Hereafter" (Qur'an 41:6-7).

"But there are, among men, those

1. Who purchase idle tales, without knowledge (or meaning), to mislead (men) from the path of Allah
2. and throw ridicule (on the path).

For such, there will be a humiliating penalty" (Qur'an 31:6).

3
SEEKING GUIDANCE FROM THE QUR'AN

The Messenger and the believers cannot force people to believe or change their religion under compulsion. They are to seek advice and guidance on their own initiative. No one can be forced into believing, that is below the dignity of humanity, which is endowed with reasoning and free will. Humanity has a choice, "Allah is the protector of those who have faith. From the depths of darkness He will lead them forth into light. Of those who reject faith, the patrons are the evil ones. From light they will lead them forth into the depths of darkness; they will be companions of the fire, to dwell therein (for ever)" (Qur'an 2:257).

People are to know, learn and then believe in the truth themselves without compulsion. The believers are forbidden to overawe or force people to believe. The unbelievers could easily learn from the Qur'an if they desired so themselves. What the believers can do is to keep guiding people to manage their own affairs. They should also guide their kinsfolk, be kind with them, and trust God.

3.1 COMPEL NOT PEOPLE IN RELIGION: LET THE TRUTH PREVAIL

Truth stands out clear from the falsehood to the human mind. For this reason, people will refuse to believe by force. Therefore, God commands people, "Let there be no compulsion in religion. Truth stands out clear from error. Whoever rejects evil and believes in Allah has grasped the most trustworthy hand-hold that never breaks. And Allah hears and knows all things" (Qur'an 2:256).

Contrarily, "If it had been your Lord's Will, they would all have believed, all who are on earth! Will you then compel mankind, against their will, to believe! No soul can believe, except by the Will of Allah, and He will place doubt (or obscurity) on those who will not understand" (Qur'an 10:99-100).

3.2 DON'T OVERAWE PEOPLE: LET THE QUR'AN BE THEIR GUIDE

Human accountability on the Day of Judgment is not to overawe people or force them to behave in this world but it is a reality to motivate them to excel in humanity for which they will be rewarded. People may throw all sorts of doubt about the divine judgment of human behavior and deeds in the Hereafter. Therefore, the Messengers (or the believers) task is not to force them to accept anything but their task is only to deliver the message of the Qur'an, and to guide those who are ready to receive guidance, and to equip themselves to reach new heights of humanity.

God tells the Messengers and the believers that, "We know best what they (unbelievers, hypocrites) say, and you are not one to overawe them by force. So admonish with the Qur'an such as fear My warning" (Qur'an 50:45).

3.3 SO KEEP GUIDING PEOPLE: TO MANAGE THEIR OWN AFFAIRS

The Messenger or the believers are to teach and direct people to God's Way. They are not here to force their will on anyone or punish them for their misdeeds. Punishment belongs to God alone and it may present itself in this world or come in the Hereafter as He desires.

Since the Messenger's duty is only to guide people, he is commanded, "Therefore, you do give admonition, for you are one to admonish. You are not one to manage (people's) affairs. But if any turns away and reject Allah, Allah will punish him with a mighty punishment, for to Us will be their return. Then it will be for Us to call them to account" (Qur'an 88:21-26).

3.4 Trust God: guide your kinsfolk and be kind to them

A person can only try to guide one's kinsfolk. He is to command what is right and forbid what is wrong. At the same time, one should be kind, gentle and considerate with them. But if, then, any of one's flock do wrong, the responsibility lies with the wrongdoer. However, one should not leave hope, but continue teaching and trust that God will eventually guide them.

God commands the Messenger to, "Admonish your nearest kinsmen, and lower your wing to the believers who follow you. Then if they disobey you, say: 'I am free (of responsibility) for what you do!' And put your trust on the Exalted in Might, the Merciful" (Qur'an 26:214-217).

4

God Motivates People to Humanity

With the institution of repentance and forgiveness, God has provided people an opportunity for the continual improvement of their character and behavior. Although it is not possible for people to be perfect in dealing with others, the effort to improve their dealings with others produces positive results in their communities. Societies built on positive moral values are surely prosperous and peaceful. Happiness in the life to come also depends on one's efforts to improve the life in this world. This is very important, as individuals, irrespective of their situation or status in life, should improve their behavior and try to help others in their struggle in life. What makes us suffer or makes us happy are our intentions, attitudes, and deeds. As God administers absolute justice to all, our actions and intentions determine our present and our future. Corrupt people, who worship their own selfish desires and like to benefit from the injustice done to others, cannot build prosperous societies. Even the so-called rich countries, where most of the wealth belongs to a few individuals or corporations, cannot be really prosperous.

4.1 The continual improvement of—human society

Perfection of character and actions is not humanly possible. What Islam teaches is an attitude that leads to continual improvement in individual character and the society. Everyone is liable to make errors and mistakes, but when the believers do, they seek God's forgiveness, which is forthcoming when the request is genuine. Human character is improved with every incident of acknowledgment, regret, and effort made not to repeat the mistakes again.

In order to maintain good conditions in a society, people who commit sins are strongly urged to reform themselves through repentance, which God out of His grace has bound Himself to accept. Repentance that is deeply felt by an individual indicates that he has undergone a total transformation that is associated with sincerely regretting past mistakes. In such a case: "Allah accept the repentance of those who do evil in ignorance and repent soon afterwards; to them will Allah turn in mercy. For Allah is full of knowledge and wisdom" (Qur'an 4:17).

4.2 God accepts the repentance and forgives people

The opportunity for repentance after committing a sin, i.e., an action not compatible with God's commandments, even the most serious one, is there all the time. God doesn't close the door of forgiveness to anyone who turns to Him with sincerity and true repentance. Therefore, one should not lose hope. God may forgive all sins, as He has promised. The only requirement for the acceptance of repentance is that it should be made seriously and sincerely, and it should be coupled with a resolve not to repeat the sin again. God describes Himself in *Surah Al-Ghafir* as the One: "Who forgives sin, accepts repentance, is strict in punishment, and has a long reach (in all things). There is no god but He; to Him is the final goal" (Qur'an 40:3).

In contrast, the unbelievers who refuse to reform and do not improve their character and behavior are destroyed: "None can dispute about the revelations of Allah but the unbelievers. Let not then their (the unbelievers') strutting about through the land deceives you! But (there were people) before them who denied—the people of Noah and the confederates (of evil) after them, and every people plotted against their prophet to seize him and disputed by means of vanities, therewith to condemn the truth. But it was I that seized them, and how (terrible) was My requital! Thus was the decree of your Lord proved true against the unbelievers that truly they are the companions of the Fire" (Qur'an 40:4-6).

4.3 BELIEVERS TURN TO GOD IN REPENTANCE AND REFORM

There is a rule for repentance and a condition for its acceptance. Repentance begins with a genuine regret and desisting from bad deeds and is completed through doing good deeds to prove that repentance is serious and genuine. Good deeds produce a positive effect that favorably compensates for abandoning sin. A sin is an action that, when withdrawn, leaves a vacuum that must be filled with an action in the opposite direction. Otherwise, the feeling of emptiness makes one miss one's old sinful ways. This is a remarkable feature of the divine method of cultivating goodness within the believers. It is based on profound knowledge of human nature.

The believers acknowledge about God as: "He it is Who shows you His Signs and sends down sustenance for you from the sky, but only those receive admonition who turn (to Him). Call you (O believers) then upon Allah with sincere devotion to Him, even though the unbelievers may detest it" (Qur'an 40:13-14). God motivates people to repent and do good deeds by telling them that upon their resurrection, they will be rewarded according to what they did in the world. On that Day: "…every soul shall be requited for what it earned; no injustice will there be that Day, for Allah is swift in taking account" (Qur'an 40:17).

4.4 FOLLOW THE DIVINE LAW FOR PROSPERITY & PARADISE

God encourages people to strive to acquire good things of this life through lawful means, without exceeding limits. "O you who believe! Make not unlawful the good things that Allah has made lawful for you, but commit no excess, for Allah loves not those given to excess" (Qur'an 5:87).

God has provided sufficient means in the world for all people to live in prosperity. We have to exploit and properly manage these natural resources for the benefit of all humanity. God reminds people: "It is We Who have placed

you with authority on earth and provided you therein with means for the fulfillment of your life. Small are the thanks that you give" (Qur'an 7:10).

4.5 REPENT AND FOLLOW GOD'S COMMANDS TO PROSPERITY
Our individual and collective prosperity depends on how seriously and effec-
tively divine law is implemented. God tells people that if they fail to follow His
law, they should repent, correct the situation, and continue to strive to improve
their character and the society. This will, with God's help and His Mercy, make
them and their countries prosperous. God says (that Noah taught his people):
"Ask forgiveness from your Lord, for He is Oft-Forgiving. He will send rain
to you in abundance, give you increase in wealth and sons, and bestow on you
gardens, and bestow on you rivers (of flowing water)" (Qur'an 71:10-12).

People's repentance improves their character and transforms them into
hardworking, honest, and trustworthy individuals. When living together, such
people will develop into a safe and prosperous community. God commands
the Messenger to: "Say: 'O people! I am (sent) to you only to give a clear warning. Then (as for) those who believe and do good, they shall have forgiveness
and a sustenance most generous'" (Qur'an 22:49-50). God's forgiveness and a
generous sustenance from Him translate into a peaceful and prosperous society.
.

4.6 REPENT AND FOLLOW GOD'S COMMANDS TO PARADISE
The door of repentance is always open to admit anyone whose conscience is
reawakened and who desires improvement in his character and behavior. No
one is ever turned away from it, no matter who he might be or what sins he
might have committed. The only condition is to repent sincerely.

Anas reported that the Messenger[PBUH] said: "Allah the Almighty said: 'O
son of Adam, so long as you call upon Me and ask of Me, I shall forgive you for
what you have done, and I shall not mind. O son of Adam, were your sins so
numerous as to reach the clouds of the sky and thereafter you ask forgiveness
from Me, I would forgive you and I don't care. O son of Adam, if you were to
come to Me with sins nearly as great as the earth and then you were to face Me,
ascribing no partner to Me, I would certainly come to you with an earth full of
forgiveness'" (Al-Hadith: vol. 3, no. 96, page 756).

5

SALVATION NEEDS BELIEF AND GOOD DEEDS

Only belief in God and good deeds can assure individual salvation. God warns people that no one can save even the nearest kin from His punishment. It is narrated on the authority of 'Aisha that when the verse "And admonish your nearest kinsmen" (Qur'an 26:214). was revealed, the Messenger[PBUH] of Allah stood up on Safa' and said: "O Fatimah, daughter of Muhammad, O Safiya, daughter of Abd al-Muttalib, O sons of Abd al-Muttalib, I have nothing that can avail you against (the punishment of) Allah; you may ask me what you want of my worldly belongings" (Sahih Muslim: 1.401). Even God's Messenger Noah[PBUH] could not save his son because his son's conduct was unrighteous, and God's Messenger Lot could not save his wife. The angels who were sent to destroy Lot's people told Lot[PBUH] to leave the city behind and not turn back, but Lot's wife failed to follow this angelic advice and paid the consequences.

5.1 PEOPLE SEEK AND FOLLOW THE GUIDANCE TO SUCCEED

Divine guidance is there to remind people of their weaknesses which they have to overcome, to nurture their human character, and to adapt to all human values. The drowning of Noah's son and the destiny of Lot's wife prove that only belief in God and good deeds can assure individual salvation. Noah's people were destroyed because of their unbelief, and his son was drowned due to his unrighteous behavior.

Only belief and good deeds assure salvation. Noah's people's refusal of the guidance destroyed them, "They (Noah's people) said: 'O Noah! You have disputed with us, and you have prolonged the dispute with us. Now bring upon us with what you threaten us if you speak the truth.' He said: 'Truly, Allah will bring it on you if He Wills— and then, you will not be able to frustrate it'" ... And, "It was revealed to Noah: 'None of your people will believe except those who have believed already! So grieve no longer over their deeds. But, construct an ark under Our eyes and Our inspiration, and address Me no (further) on behalf of those who are in sin, for they are about to be overwhelmed'" (Qur'an 11:32-33, 36-37).

About the Noah's people's punishment, we are told that, "At length, behold! There came Our command, and the fountains of the earth gushed forth! We said: 'Embark therein, of each kind two, male and female, and your family—except those against whom the word has already gone forth—and the believers.' But only a few believed with him…Then the word went forth: "O earth! Swallow up your water. And O sky! Withhold (your rain)!' And the water abated, and the matter was ended. The ark rested on Mount Judi, and the word went forth: 'Away with those who do wrong!'" (Qur'an 11:40, 44).

5.2 EVEN MESSENGERS COULD NOT SAVE THEIR RELATIVES

God told Noah that those who did wrong would be drowned. "And Noah called upon his Lord and said: 'O my Lord! Surely my son is of my family! And Your promise is true, and You are the just of judges!' He (God) said: 'O Noah! He is not of your family, for his conduct is unrighteous. So ask not of Me that of which you have no knowledge! I give you counsel lest you act like the ignorant'" (Qur'an 11:45-46).

Noah's son lost his life for his unrighteous behavior, "So the ark floated with them on the waves (towering) like mountains, and Noah called out to his son, who had separated himself (from the rest): 'O my son! Embark with us, and be not with the unbelievers!' The son replied: 'I will betake myself to some mountain; it will save me from the water.' Noah said: 'This day nothing can save, from the command of Allah, any but those on whom He has Mercy!'— And the waves came between them, and the son was among those overwhelmed in the flood" (Qur'an 11:42-43).

Similarly, Lot was told, "O Lot! We are messengers from your Lord! By no means shall they reach you! Now travel with your family while yet a part of the night remains, and let not any of you look back. But your wife (will remain behind), to her will happen what happens to the people. Morning is their time appointed. Is not the morning around?" (Qur'an 11:81).

Chapter 4

Development of Human Society
(Believers, Unbelievers, and Human Conduct)

God has obligated people to follow His commands with dedication and sincerity for the development of a good relationship with Him and with other members of human family. The implementation of these commands individually and in the society, leads people to the best of humanity that can be developed on earth. In Islam, the spiritual, economic, social, and political systems are interconnected and interwoven in such a way that they cannot be isolated from one another. As such, the believers have to behave as God desires them to behave, in order to nurture the best of their humanity. God's commands cover all aspects of human activities without any distinction or division. This has been illustrated in the Qur'an, by all those group of verses in which two of the fundamental activities of the believers, i.e., that they pray and give charity, are repeated. These two activities, i.e., God's worship and charity, motivate people to fulfill all of their obligations towards God, and His people.

1
BASIC PRINCIPLES THAT DEVELOP HUMANITY

Throughout the Qur'an, God has explained and reminded people about the basic principles of Humanity. These principles, if followed, help reform and improve our character and behavior. Some of these principles are outlined below.

1. "... The guidance of Allah—that is the (only) guidance,..." (Qur'an 2:120). "...they (the past People) shall reap the fruit of what they did, and you of what you do, and you shall not be asked about what they did" (Qur'an 2:134, 141).

2. "To each is a goal to which Allah turns him; then strive together (as in a race) towards all that is good. ..." (Qur'an 2:148).

3. "Nor can goodness and evil be equal. Repel (evil) with what is better:..." (Qur'an 41:34). "Repel evil with that which is best: ..." (Qur'an 23:96).

4. "... Allah does not love mischief" (Qur'an 2:205). "... And had not Allah checked one set of people by means of another, the earth would indeed be full of mischief:..." (Qur'an 2:251).

5. "... Fulfill (all) obligations ..." (Qur'an 5:1). "Abandon all sin, open or secret: ..." (Qur'an 6:120). "... Do your duty to Allah, Seek means of approach unto Him, ..." (Qur'an 5:35);

6. "... Guard your own selves: ..." (Qur'an 5:105). "... Each person earns only on its own account; no bearer of burdens can bear the burden of another. ..." (Qur'an 6:164).

7. "... Help one another in righteousness and piety, but do not help one another in sin and transgression:..." (Qur'an 5:2).

8. "... Whoever believes in Allah and the Last Day and works righteousness— on them shall be no fear, nor shall they grieve" (Qur'an 5:69).

9. "... Not equal are things that are bad and things that are good, even though the abundance of the bad may dazzle you; ..." (Qur'an 5:100).

10. "He that does good shall have ten times as much to his credit. He that does evil shall only be recompensed according to his evil: ..." (Qur'an 6:160).

11. "To those against whom war is made, permission is given (to fight) because they are wronged— and verily Allah is most powerful for their aid—"(Qur'an 22:39).

12. "... Had not Allah checked one set of people by means of another, there should surely have been pulled down monasteries, churches, synagogues, and mosques in which the name of Allah is much-remembered. ..." (Qur'an 22:40).

2
BELIEVERS AND UNBELIEVERS IN THE SOCIETY

God is blissful to those people who are charitable, fear the accountability of their deeds, and do good. Contrarily, arrogance, greed and evil deeds make people miserable. This is because denial of truth destroys while devotion and charity saves. Therefore believers show their gratitude to God by being helpful to the orphans and the needy. They are humble, benevolent and content.

2.1 BELIEVERS' BLISS IS- GOD'S FEAR, CHARITY AND GOODNESS
There are wide contrasts in the nature and aims of people. These may be broadly divided into two classes, good and evil. Good people may be characterized by those that are large hearted, who strive in God's way and help humanity, the truthful who recognize and support all that is morally sound, and the righteous who fear their Creator and treat others with justice. Such people represent the best of Humanity.

God tells about such people, "By the night as it conceals (the light), by the day as it appears in glory, by (the mystery of) the creation of male and female, verily, (the ends) you strive for are diverse. So he who gives (in charity) and fears (Allah), and (in all sincerity) testifies to the best, We will indeed, make smooth for him the path to bliss" (Qur'an 92:1-7).

2.2 DENIERS' MISERY IS- ARROGANCE, GREED AND EVIL DEEDS
Evil people are characterized by their greed and denial of other people's rights, their arrogance and self-sufficiency, and their rejecting of the truth for material gains. The downward progression gathers speed throughout their lives resulting in nothing but misery. Such people represent the worst of Humanity.

God tells about such people, "But he who is a greedy miser and thinks himself self-sufficient, and gives the lie to the best, We will indeed make smooth for him the path to misery; nor will his wealth profit him when he falls headlong (into the pit)" (Qur'an 92:8-11).

2.3 DENYING TRUTH DESTROYS; DEVOTION AND CHARITY SAVE

God has taken the responsibility to guide people in order that they may achieve the best of humanity. Although, His unfailing laws are there to guide people along the right Path, He has also sent Messengers as role models for further teaching and guidance. The only thing people must realize is that denial of the truth will destroy humanity while their good intentions and striving for righteousness will save it.

God tells people that, "Verily, We take upon ourselves to guide, and verily unto Us (belong) the end and the beginning. Therefore, do I warn you of a fire blazing fiercely. None shall reach it but those most unfortunate ones who deny the truth and turn their backs. But those most devoted to Allah shall be removed far from it,

1. Those who spend their wealth for increase in self-purification,
2. And have in their minds no favor from anyone for which a reward is expected in return,
3. But only the desire to seek for the countenance of their Lord Most High;

And soon will they attain (complete) satisfaction" (Qur'an 92:12-21).

2.4 THANK GOD BY BEING KIND TO ORPHANS AND THE NEEDY

Citing from the life of the Messenger, God tells people that it is He Who gives loving care to the orphan, provides guidance to the unguided and helps the needy. One way or the other, all humanity is God's beneficiary and therefore people should remember His bounties and thank Him by being kind to orphans and by helping the needy.

God asks the Messenger, "Did He not find you an orphan and give you shelter (and care)? And He found you wandering, and He gave you guidance. And He found you in need, and made you independent.

1. Therefore, treat not the orphan with harshness,
2. Nor repulse the petitioner (unheard);
3. But the bounties of the Lord - rehearse and proclaim" (Qur'an 93:6-11).

3

Individual Attributes of Human Conduct

Life is not for play, but it is to believe and make efforts to eradicate what is evil. Therefore, the believers are benevolent, restrain anger and forgive people. They worship their Creator and practice righteousness. They remember and follow what God commands them and fear His accountability. They are not among those who are covetous but spend in charity.

3.1 Worship your Creator and practice righteousness

The believers pray and give charity, fulfill their contracts and promises. They are firm and patient, in pain and adversity, and throughout all periods of panic. Fulfilling contracts and promises, or being firm and patient has been commanded along with being steadfast in prayer and regular in charity. This indicates that fulfilling contracts and promises should be practiced by the believers with same zeal as prayer and charity. The believer is always hopeful and patient during difficulties.

Addressing people God commands as: "O you people!

1. Adore your Guardian-Lord Who created you and those who came before you that you may have the chance to learn (and practice) righteousness" (Qur'an 2:21).

"It is not righteousness that you turn your faces towards east or west; but it is righteousness—

2. To believe in Allah and the Last Day, and the angels, and the Books, and the messengers;
3. To spend of your substance, out of love for Him, for your kin, for orphans, for the needy, for the wayfarer, for those who ask, and for the ransom of slaves;
4. To be steadfast in prayer and practice regular charity;
5. To fulfill the contracts (promises) that you have made;
6. And to be firm and patient, in pain and adversity, and throughout all periods of panic.

Such are the people of truth, the God-fearing" (Qur'an 2:177).

Benevolence, restraining anger and forgiving people are three most important attributes which assures a believer God's forgiveness, and a place in Paradise.

God commands the believers to, "Be quick in the race for forgiveness from your Lord, and for a Garden whose width is that of the heavens and of the earth, prepared for the righteous—Those who spend, whether in prosperity or in adversity, who restrain anger and forgive (all) men—for Allah loves those who do good" (Qur'an 3:133-134).

3.3 LIFE IS NOT FOR PLAY, BUT TO BELIEVE AND SHUN EVIL
God created people for a purpose and appointed them His Trustee (*Khalifah*) to help flourish humanity on earth. Amusement and play have their specific value, but if we concentrate on them and neglect our duties to manage our lives as God has commanded, then we are failing in our duties. God commands us to believe, develop human values and guard against evil. This needs devotion and sacrifice in person and resources. The believers strive and spend in the Way of God for their own survival.

God tells people that,

1. "The life of this world is but play and amusement: and if you believe and guard against evil, He will grant you your recompense and will not ask you (to give up) your possessions. If He were to ask you for all of them, and press you, you would covetously withhold, and He would bring out all your ill feeling" (Qur'an 47:36-37).
2. "Behold, you are those invited to spend (of your substance) in the Way of Allah, but among you are some that are miserly. But any who are miserly are so at the expense of their own souls. But Allah is free of all wants, and it is you that are needy. If you turn back, (from the path), He will substitute in your stead another people; then they would not be like you" (Qur'an 47:38).

3.4 REMEMBER GOD AND SPEND IN CHARITY DURING YOUR LIFE

Riches and resources of all kind are but fleeting sources of enjoyment. They should not turn away the believer form his devotion to His Creator. The believers remember God by not violating His commands. Along with prayer and charity, God's remembrance includes every act of service and goodness, every kind thought and good deed, for this is the service and sacrifice which God requires from the believers to facilitate humanity on earth.

God reminds the believers that a way to remember Him is by spending in charity, "O you who believe!

1. "Let not your riches or your children divert you from the remembrance of Allah. If any act thus, the loss is their own.
2. And spend something (in charity) out of the substance that We have bestowed on you, before death should come to any of you …" (Qur'an 63:9-10).

3.5 FEAR GOD, SPEND IN CHARITY AND DON'T BE COVETOUS

Covetousness in people is caused by a lack of trust in God. The believers who trust God, fear Him, obey His commands are saved from the covetousness of their own souls. They spend in charity without any fear of poverty, and those who have no fear of poverty are prosperous.

God reminds people that, "Your riches and your children may be but a trial, but in the presence of Allah is the highest reward.

1. So fear Allah as much as you can,
2. listen and obey, and
3. spend in charity for the benefit of your own soul.

And those saved from the covetousness of their own souls—they are the ones that achieve prosperity" (Qur'an 64:15-16).

Chapter 5

Who are the Believers?
(Believers' Character and Behavior)

L ike bricks joined together in a house, human individuals have to be strong in character and beautiful in behavior in order to contribute in the accomplishment of the divine trust for eliminating corruption from human society. As raw bricks of ugly mold cannot increase the strength and look of a house, neither can an individual with a raw character full of ugly, selfish desires and undisciplined behavior strengthen society. The logical outcome of believing in God and of worshiping Him is the growth of people's moral character and the refinement of their behavior, without which they cannot fulfill their responsibility of being God's trustee on earth. Various attributes of the believers given at various places in the Qur'an are highlighted in this chapter. A believer is a paragon of most of these attributes and he/she considers all of them of equal value. The believers strive to adopt all of these attributes with an equal zeal.

1
BELIEVERS— LIVES ARE A TRUST FROM GOD

The believers' lives, abilities and assets belong to God. He has purchased their persons and their goods, for a place in Paradise. For this the believers fight in His Cause in this world to the best of their abilities. God's promise to the believers is: 'A promise binding on Him in truth, through the Law, the Gospel, and the Qur'an, and who is more faithful to his Covenant than Allah? The believers rejoice in the bargain that they will conclude in their lives with their good deeds. The believers are patient, firm and show self-control in their daily activities. They are true in their words and deeds, and start every day with a new resolve to do better under the watchful eyes of God.

Believers perform their duties diligently forsaking their selfish desires. Their adoration and zeal is shown not only in prayer and charity but also in all of their daily activities. This is because all activities of a believer, in which God's commands are not violated, are His worship and good deeds. The believers' character and behavior impacts on their grades and ranks in the presence of their Lord and their capacity and zeal to do good deeds elevates them.

1.1 BELIEVERS' LIVES, ABILITIES AND ASSETS BELONG TO GOD
Seven attributes of the believers that qualify them for a place in Paradise are: that they fight in His cause, they repent and reform, they serve and worship Him, they look out for opportunities to do good deeds to enhance humanity, they enjoin good and forbid evil, and they always respect the limit set by God—

God tells people about His bargain with the believers as, "Allah has purchased from the believers their persons and their goods, for theirs (in return) is the Garden (of Paradise).

1. They fight in His Cause, and slay and are slain:

A promise binding on Him in truth, through the Law, the Gospel, and the Qur'an, and who is more faithful to his Covenant than Allah? Then rejoice in the bargain that you have concluded; that is the achievement supreme.

2. Those that turn (to Allah) in repentance,
3. That serve Him and praise Him,
4. That wander in devotion to the Cause of Allah,
5. That bow down and prostrate themselves in prayer,
6. That enjoin good and forbid evil,
7. And observe the limit set by Allah—

(These do rejoice). So proclaim the glad tidings to the believers" (Qur'an 9:111-112).

1.2 BELIEVERS ARE PATIENT AND FOLLOW GOD'S COMMANDS

Along with establishing prayer and spending in charity, the believers are patient, firm and show self-control in their daily activities. They are true in their words and deeds, and start every day with a new resolve to do better under the watchful eyes of God.

This is due to the fact that, "... For in Allah's sight are (all) His servants, — (namely), those who say: 'Our Lord! We have indeed believed; forgive us, then, our sins, and save us from the agony of the Fire;'

1. Those who show patience, firmness, and self-control;
2. Who are true (in word and deed);
3. Who worship (follow all what God Commands to the best of one's ability) devoutly;
4. Who spend (in the Way of Allah); and
5. Who pray for forgiveness in the early hours of the morning (starting every day with a new resolve to do better)" (Qur'an 3:15-17).

1.3 BELIEVERS OF REVELATIONS ARE MODEST AND TRY HARD

The believers' attitude during their life on earth is characterized by that they accept and follow what God commands with dedication and humbleness. They perform their duties diligently forsaking their selfish desires. Their adoration and zeal is shown not only in prayer, and charity but also in all of their daily activities. This is because all activities of a believer, in which God's commands are not violated, are His worship and good deeds.

The believers are, "Only those believe in Our Signs, who, when they are recited to them, fall down in adoration, and celebrate the praises of their Lord, nor are they (ever) puffed up with pride. Their limbs do forsake their beds of sleep, the while they call on their Lord, in fear and hope, and they spend (in charity) out of the sustenance that We have bestowed on them. Now no person knows what delights of the eye are kept hidden (in reserve) for them— as a reward for their (good) deeds" (Qur'an 32:15-17).

1.4 BELIEVERS FEAR GOD AND THEY LIVE AS HE COMMANDS
There are various grades and ranks of the believers according to their character and behavior. Their capacity and zeal to do good deeds elevates them. The believers attributes which help them excel in life are given below:

1. "Verily, those who live in awe for fear of their Lord,
2. Those who believe in the Signs (revelations) of their Lord,
3. Those who join not (in worship) partners with their Lord,
4. And those who dispense their charity with their hearts full of fear because they will return to their Lord—

It is these who hasten in every good work, and these who are foremost in them" (Qur'an 23:57-61).

2
BELIEVERS— SERVE GOD AND HUMANITY

The believers know their Lord and love Him with all His Attributes. The divine knowledge strengthens their faith and trust in Him. They continue their friendship with God by His remembrance, prayer and charity. God's remembrance motivates them to reform by admitting their mistakes and mending their ways. The believers find strength and tranquility from their closeness to God in prayer and they strengthen their society by helping each other according to their needs and resources.

The believers never doubt their belief and they always strive in God's Way. A believer submits himself to God and follows His commands. This is a general statement describing Faith, which provides the believers and their community with absolute safety as long as they trust God. Their safety depends directly on their compliance and implementation of God's commands in society.

2.1 BELIEVERS FEAR GOD, WORSHIP HIM, AND SPEND FREELY

The believers know their Lord and love Him with all His Attributes. They strengthen their faith and trust in God by increasing their divine knowledge which makes them humble. They continue their friendship with God by His remembrance, prayer and charity. As a result, God takes care of them and overlooks their mistakes. Rather, God's remembrance motivates people to better themselves by admitting their mistakes and mending their lives as He commands. To such believers, God promises dignity, forgiveness and generous sustenance in this life and in the life hereafter.

Who are the true believers? People are told that, the "..., believers are those who,

1. when Allah is mentioned, feel a tremor in their hearts (love Him with all His attributes),
2. And when they hear His Signs rehearsed, find their faith strengthened,
3. And put (all) their trust in their Lord;
4. Who establish regular prayers
5. and spend (freely) out of the gifts We have given them for sustenance:

Such in truth are the believers: they have grades of dignity with their Lord, and forgiveness, and generous sustenance" (Qur'an 8:2-4).

2.2 BELIEVERS ESTABLISH PRAYERS AND SPEND IN CHARITY

If one looks around today, humanity seems to be in a similar situation as it was in *Makkah* during the early days of Islam, and perhaps it will remain the same, as long as the conflict between good and evil continues. During such times, believers find strength and tranquility from their closeness to God in prayer and they strengthen their society by helping each other according to their needs and resources.

God says, "Speak to my servants, who have believed, that they may establish regular prayers, and spend (in charity) out of the sustenance We have given them, secretly and openly, before the coming of a Day in which there will be neither mutual bargaining nor befriending" (Qur'an 14:31).

2.3 BELIEVERS DOUBT NOT AND STRIVE HARD IN GOD'S WAY

Who are the sincere believers? They never doubt their belief in God and His Messenger and they always strive in the Cause of God with all they have in person and in wealth.

Sincere believers are, "Only those are believers who have believed in Allah and His Messenger and have never since doubted, but have striven with their belongings and their persons in the Cause of Allah. Such are the sincere ones" (Qur'an 49:15).

2.4 BELIEVERS TRUST GOD, SUBMIT TO HIS WILL AND DO GOOD

A believer submits himself to God and follows His commands. This is a general statement describing Faith, which provides the believers with absolute safety as long as they trust Him. The believers' safety, then, depends on their own will and faith. God's help and protection will always be unfailing if they hold firmly to God and trust Him. Their safety depends directly on their compliance of what God commands.

God assures the believers that, "Whoever submits his whole self to Allah, and is a doer of good, has grasped indeed the most trustworthy handhold, and with Allah rests the end and decision of (all) affairs" (Qur'an 31:22).

3

BELIEVERS— ARE HONEST, TRUSTWORTHY AND PATIENT

It has been stressed to people that only those who listen and understand the Qur'an are guided by it. People should know what they are doing and for what purpose. Their purpose should be to reform themselves to be better people and to do good deeds. The believers honestly try to meet their obligations concerning God and His people. Believers are neither impatient nor miserly. They pray and share their fortunes with the poor and the needy. They are accountable for what they do and fear the displeasure of their Lord. They are chaste, honor their trusts and promises, and they honestly guard all their actions and deeds.

Islam—submitting one's will to God's Will, includes inculcating all attributes of believing men or women. These attributes include: Faith, hope, and trust in God; devotion and service in practical life; love and practice of truth in thought and intention, word and deed; patience and constancy in difficulties and right pursuits; humility, avoidance of an attitude of arrogance and superiority; charity to help the needy; fasting or self denial of food and other appetites; chastity, purity in sex life, purity in motive, thought, word and deed; and constant attention to the divine message and cultivating a desire to be near God.

3.1 BELIEVERS PATIENTLY PERSEVERE AND FULFILL PROMISES

It has been stressed to people that only those who listen and understand the Qur'an are guided by it. Following one's faith with full conviction and zeal is much better in results and affects than following it blindly. People should know what they are doing and for what purpose. Their purpose should be to reform themselves to be a better person as God desires and to do good deeds. The believers honestly try to meet all of their obligations concerning God and His people. The believers believe in God, follow His commands and honor their promises. Their behavior reflects that they are accountable for their actions. They worship their Lord and spend to help the needy. To please their Lord, they patiently persevere during all of their daily activities and they counteract evil with good.

God asks people, "Is then one who does know that which has been revealed unto you from your Lord is the Truth, like one who is blind? It is those who are endued with understanding that receive admonition—

1. Those who fulfill the Covenant of Allah and fail not in their plighted word;
2. Those who join together those things that Allah has commanded to be joined, Hold their Lord in awe, and fear the terrible reckoning;
3. Those who patiently persevere, seeking the countenance of their Lord; establish regular prayers, spend, out of (the gifts) We have bestowed for their sustenance, secretly and openly;
4. And turn off Evil with Good—

For such there is the final attainment of the (Eternal) Home" (Qur'an 13:19-22).

~~Human role models, believe in what~~ God commands, and patiently persevere during all of their daily activities— doing good deeds. God tells people that, "And We appointed, from among them, Leaders, giving guidance under Our command,

5. So long as they persevered with patience and
6. Continued to have faith in Our Signs" (Qur'an 32:24).

3.2 BELIEVERS ARE HUMBLE, AVOID VAIN TALK AND ADULTERY

The successful believers are humble in their prayers, avoid vain talk, participate in charitable deeds and abstain from adultery. They are trustworthy and honor their promises. Since all activities of a believer in which God's commands are not violated are His Worship, the believers strictly guard all of their daily activities like their prayers.

God tells people that, "The believers must (eventually) win through. Those (believers):

1. Who humble themselves in their prayers,
2. Who avoid vain talk,
3. Who are active in deeds of charity,
4. Who abstain from sex, except with those joined to them in the marriage bond, or (the captives) whom their right hands possess, for (in their case) they are free from blame, but those whose desires exceed those limits are transgressors—
5. Those who faithfully observe their trusts and their covenants;
6. And who (strictly) guard their prayers—

These will be the heirs who will inherit Paradise. They will dwell therein (forever)" (Qur'an 23:1-11).

3.3 BELIEVERS ARE HONEST, TRUSTWORTHY AND VIRTUOUS

The believers are neither impatient nor miserly. They pray and share their fortune with the poor and the needy. They are accountable for what they do and fear the displeasure of their Lord. They are chaste, honor their trusts and promises, and they honestly guard all their actions and deeds.

God tells people that, "Truly man was created very impatient—fretful when evil touches him and miserly when good reaches him—not so those devoted to prayer—

1) Those who remain steadfast to their prayer; 2) And those in whose wealth is a recognized right for the (needy) who asks and him who is prevented (for some reason from asking); 3) And those who hold to the truth of the Day of Judgment; 4) And those who fear the displeasure of their Lord—for their Lord's displeasure is the opposite of peace and tranquility— 5) And those who guard their chastity, except with their wives and the (captives) whom their right hands possess—for (then) they are not to be blamed, but those who trespass beyond this are transgressors— 6) And those who respect their trusts and covenants— 7) And those who stand firm in their testimonies—8) And those who guard (the sacredness) of their worship— Such will be the honored ones in the Gardens (of Bliss)" (Qur'an 70:19-35).

3.4 BELIEVERS ARE DEVOUT, TRUE, CONFIDENT AND PATIENT

Islam, or submitting one's will to God's Will, include inculcating all attributes of believing men or women. These attributes include: 1) Faith, hope, and trust in God; 2) devotion and service in practical life; 3) love and practice of truth, in thought and intention, word and deed; 4) patience and constancy in difficulties and right pursuits; 5) humility, the avoidance of an attitude of arrogance and superiority; 6) charity to help the needy; 7) Fasting or self denial in food and other appetites; 8) chastity, purity in sex life, purity in motive, thought, word and deed; and 9) constant attention to divine message and cultivating a desire to be near to God.

God has forgiveness and great reward, "For Muslim men and women—

1. For believing men and women,
2. For devout men and women,
3. For true men and women,
4. For men and women who are patient and constant,
5. For men and women who humble themselves,

6. For men and women who give in charity,
7. For men and women who fast (and restrain),
8. For men and women who guard their chastity, and
9. For men and women who engage much in Allah's praise,

For them has Allah prepared forgiveness and great reward" (Qur'an 33:35).

4
BELIEVERS— INCULCATE HUMAN VALUES

The believers obey God and His Messenger, protect each other, enjoin justice and forbid evil. They avoid all sins, help and forgive one another. Physical light is but a reflection of the True light in this world of reality, and the true Light is God. This light manifests itself in the form of divine attributes. Believers try to inculcate these attributes in themselves. They strive hard against evil and defend their beliefs. That is why they are strong against hostile unbelievers but to their brethren in faith— especially the weaker ones— they are mild and compassionate. They are humble before God and seek His pleasure. They are gentle, kind, forgiving, and helpful. Their reliance on God brings peace and calmness to them and their communities.

4.1 BELIEVERS PROTECT, ENJOIN JUSTICE AND FORBID EVIL
The believers; obey God and His Messenger, they protect each other, enjoin what is just and forbid what is evil, and they pray and give charity.

The believers' attributes who could expect to receive God's Mercy are,

1. "The believers, men and women, are protectors one of another.
2. They enjoin what is just and forbid what is evil.
3. They observe regular prayers,
4. Practice regular charity,
5. And obey Allah and His Messenger.

On them will Allah pour His Mercy, for Allah is Exalted in Power, Wise" (Qur'an 9:71).

4.2 BELIEVERS FORGIVE, HELP EACH OTHER AND AVOID SINS

Another set of attributes of the believers are that they, 1) believe, and trust God, 2) avoid greater crimes and shameful deeds and 3) forgive people even when they are angry. They 4) fear their Lord, and establish prayers and 5) consult each others in their daily affairs. They, 6) are charitable, 7) fight with the oppressors to defend themselves.

To such believers God assures a better and more lasting reward in the next life, "Whatever you are given (here) is (but) a convenience of this life, but that which is with Allah is better and more lasting.

1.   (It is) for those who believe and put their trust in their Lord—
2.   Those who avoid the greater crimes and shameful deeds,
3.   And when they are angry even then forgive,
4.   Those who hearken to their Lord and establish regular prayer,
5.   Who (conduct) their affairs by mutual consultation,
6.   Who spend out of what We bestow on them for sustenance,
7.   And those who, when an oppressive wrong is inflicted on them, (are not cowed but) help and defend themselves" (Qur'an 42:36-39).

4.3 BELIEVERS FOLLOW THE DIVINE LIGHT IN THEIR LIVES

The physical light is but a reflection of the True light in this world of Reality, and the true Light is God. But the perfect light of God is free from any defects or limitations of a physical light. The glorious parable of Light contains many layers of transcendental truth about spiritual mysteries. No notes can do adequate justice to its full meaning. Books have been written on this subject, the most notable being *Mishkat al Anwar* by al Ghazali.

The parable, 'God is the Light' as given in *Surah Al-Nur* is, "Allah is the light of the heavens and the earth. ... (Lit is such a light) in houses that Allah has permitted to be raised to honor; for the celebration in them of His name. In them is He glorified in the mornings and in the evenings (again and again), by men whom neither traffic nor merchandise can divert from the remembrance of Allah, nor from regular prayer, nor from the practice of regular charity.

Their (only) fear is for the Day when hearts and eyes will be transformed (in a world wholly new)—" (Qur'an 24:35-37).

4.4 BELIEVERS ARE STRONG AGAINST HOSTILE UNBELIEVERS

The believers strive hard against evil, but to their brethren in faith— especially the weaker ones— they are mild and compassionate. They are humble before God and seek His pleasure. They are gentle, kind, forgiving, and helpful. Their reliance on God brings peace and calmness to them.

To the believers, God has promised forgiveness and a great reward, "Muhammad is the messenger of Allah, and those who are with him are strong against unbelievers, (but) compassionate among each other. You will see them bow and prostrate themselves (in prayer), seeking grace from Allah and (His) good pleasure. On their faces are their marks, (being) the traces of their prostration. … Allah has promised, those among them who believe and do righteous deeds, forgiveness and a great reward" (Qur'an 48:29).

Chapter 6
What God Forbids People
(God Forbids All Shameful Deeds)

A ll shameful deeds against truth or reason, against one's own self, against fellow people and against public welfare are forbidden in Islam. God commands the Messenger to, "Say: 'The things that my Lord has indeed forbidden are: Shameful deeds, whether open or secret; Sins and trespasses against truth or reason; Assigning of partners to Allah, for which He has given no authority; And saying things about Allah of which you have no knowledge" (Qur'an 7:33).

1
DEEDS AGAINST TRUTH OR REASON ARE FORBIDDEN

God has forbidden all deeds that are done against truth or reason. It is reasonable that people should not eat such food which they have acquired by illegal means or which is not good for their health. Also, ascribing that which is false to God is unreasonable. If we have free will and can do whatever we desire, then it is reasonable that we should be responsible and accountable for what we decide and choose for ourselves. We belong to one human family; therefore, it is not reasonable to form groups within a family on any basis, especially in religion, when each one of us is responsible for one's own deeds and behavior in the final judgment before God.

God tells people in *Surah Al-Hujurat*, "O people! We created you from a single (pair) of a male and a female and made you into nations and tribes that you may know each other (not that you may despise each other). Verily, the most honored of you in the sight of Allah is (he who is) the most righteous of you..." (Qur'an 49:13). It is reasonable for people to treat others as they desire themselves to be treated.

1.1 Forbidden is to associate with God or defy parents

God has created the universe and people. Parents have to play a role in the life of their children. God's love for His creation and parental love for their children are both impartial. The seemingly inequality of provisions given to each one of us may indicate God's partiality due to our own imperfect knowledge and faith. Still there is no excuse for people to seek objects of worship other than God alone. If they do so, they will not only be disappointed, but will also lose respect for themselves for worshiping some one who is not worthy of worship.

Therefore, God commands His Messenger to, "Say: Come, I will rehearse what Allah has (really) prohibited you from: Join not anything as equal with Him; Be good to your parents; ... Take not with Allah another object of worship; or you will sit in disgrace and destitution" (Qur'an 6:151, 17:22).

1.2 Forbidden is to associate with God or split religion

God's purpose is to make humanity flourish and establish human brotherhood. Humanity is a single brotherhood under God, so people must unite to serve Him alone. People are reaffirmed that, "Verily, this brotherhood of yours is a single brotherhood, and I am your Lord and Cherisher: therefore serve Me (and no other). But (later generations) cut off their affair (of unity), one from another: (yet) will they all return to Us (for their accountability)" (Qur'an 21:92-93).

Again God reminds people that, "And verily this brotherhood of yours is a single brotherhood, and I am your Lord and Cherisher: therefore fear Me (and no other). But people have cut off their affair (of unity), between them, into sects: each party rejoices in that which is with itself. But leave them in their confused ignorance for a time" (Qur'an 23:52-54).

Therefore, the believers are commanded, "So set your face steadily and truly to the Faith. (Establish) Allah's handiwork according to the pattern on which He has made mankind; (let there be) no change in the work (wrought) by Allah. That is the standard religion, but most among mankind understand not.

1. You turn back in repentance to Him,
2. And fear Him:
3. Establish regular prayers,
4. And be not among those who join gods with Allah—
5. (And be not among) Those who split up their religion, and become (mere) sects— each party rejoicing in that which is with itself" (Qur'an 30:30-32).

1.3 Forbidden is to form sects as people did in the past

The believers are not to split their religion into various sects. Three eternal principles of past religions: 1) sincere devotion to God; 2) prayer and praise for drawing people nearer to God; and 3) the service of God's creatures by deeds of charity; were the same as in Islam but the followers of those religions split their religion into various sects.

About the People of the Book, God tells us, "Nor did the People of the Book make schisms until after there came to them clear evidence. And they have been commanded no more than this: to worship Allah, offering Him sincere devotion, being true (in faith); to establish regular prayer; and to practice regular charity. And that is the Religion Right and Straight" (Qur'an 98:4-5).

The believers are thus forbidden to form sects as people did in the past. People who form sects: 'their affair is with God: He will in the end tell them the truth of all that they did'. God tells the Messenger that, "As for those who divide their religion and break up into sects, you have no part in them in the least: their affair is with Allah: He will in the end tell them the truth of all that they did" (Qur'an 6:159).

1.4 Forbidden is to deny the reality of Judgment Day!

The believers firmly believe in the accountability of their deeds. Only sinners, who transgress all limits set by God, deny the reality of Judgment Day.

God warns people that, "Woe, that Day, to those that deny—those that deny the Day of Judgment. And none can deny it but the transgressor beyond bounds, the sinner! When Our Signs are rehearsed to him, he says, 'Tales of the ancients!'" (Qur'an 83:10-13).

1.5 FORBIDDEN IS INDULGENCE AND DENIAL OF THE HEREAFTER

The believers do not indulge too much in wealth and luxuries. People who persist obstinately in wickedness and do not believe in the accountability of their deeds—they will be, "The Companions of the Left Hand—What will be the Companions of the Left Hand? (They will be) in the midst of a fierce blast of fire and in boiling water, and in the shades of black smoke" (Qur'an 56:41-43).

God tells about such people that, "Nothing (will there be in the Hereafter) to refresh, nor to please (them):

1. For that they were wont to be indulged, before that, in wealth (and luxury).
2. And persisted obstinately in wickedness supreme!
3. And they used to say, 'What! When we die and become dust and bones, shall we then indeed be raised up again?'" (Qur'an 56:44-47).

1.6 FORBIDDEN IS TO EAT MEAT NOT PROPERLY SLAUGHTERED

The believers are forbidden to eat such meats which are not properly prepared. When a clear law has explained what is lawful and unlawful, it is wrong to raise fresh scruples to mislead people.

The believers are commanded to,

1. "So eat of (meats) on which Allah's name has been pronounced, if you have faith in His Signs. Why should you not eat of (meats) on which Allah's name has been pronounced, when He has explained to you in detail what is forbidden to you— except under compulsion of necessity?

But many do mislead (men) by their appetites unchecked by knowledge. Your Lord knows best those who transgress" (Qur'an 6:118-119).
2. "Eschew all sin, open or secret; those who earn sin will get due recompense for their earnings. Eat not of (meats) on which Allah's name has not been pronounced. That would be impiety. ..." (Qur'an 6:120-121).

1.7 FORBIDDEN IS TO EAT IMPURE MEAT OR UNLAWFUL FOOD

The believers offer gratitude to God by being modest and content in their sustenance by following as God commands them, " ... : Eat and drink: But waste not by excess, for Allah loves not the wasters" (Qur'an 7:31). Ingratitude for God's sustenance may be shown in various ways —By refusing to acknowledge the true source; by committing excesses in things lawful; by refusing to share them with others; or by ascribing false things to God.

Things forbidden by God to eat are:

1. "He has only forbidden you dead meat, and blood, and the flesh of swine, and any (food) over which the name of other than Allah has been invoked.

   But if one is forced by necessity, without willful disobedience, nor transgressing due limits,- then Allah is Oft-Forgiving, Most Merciful.

2. But say not - for any false thing that your tongues may put forth,- 'This is lawful, and this is forbidden,' so as to ascribe false things to Allah.

   For those, who ascribe false things to Allah, will never prosper" (Qur'an 16:115-116).

1.8 FORBIDDEN IS TO ASSOCIATE WITH WORKERS OF INIQUITY

As a general principle, one must not retaliate or return evil for evil. The hatred of the wicked does not justify hostility. Humanity is to help each other in righteousness and piety, not in perpetuating feuds of hatred and enmity. One must fight and put down evil; but never in a spirit of malice or hatred, but always in a spirit of justice and righteousness. God commands people to, "... You help one another in righteousness and piety, but you help not one another in sin and rancor:..." (Qur'an 5:2).

Since humanity is to propagate justice and righteousness, God commands people not to cooperate with those who do wrong, "And incline not to those who do wrong, or the Fire will seize you; and you have no protectors other than Allah, nor shall you be helped" (Qur'an 11:113)

1.9 Forbidden is to plead for the dishonest and guilty

The believers never advocate on behalf of the corrupt or those who betray their trust. In general, a believer is faced with all sorts of subtle temptations. The wicked will try to appeal to a believer's highest sympathies and most honorable motives to deceive and use him to defeat justice. Therefore, a believer should be careful and cautious and seek God's help and protection against deception and for courage in delivering justice without fear or favor. To do otherwise is to betray a sacred trust and the trustee must defeat all attempts made to mislead him.

God tells the believers that, "We have sent down to you the Book in truth, that you might judge between men, as guided by Allah:

1. So be not (used) as an advocate by those who betray their trust; But seek the forgiveness of Allah; for Allah is Oft-forgiving, Most Merciful.
2. Contend not on behalf of such as betray their own souls; for Allah loves not one given to perfidy and crime:

They may hide (their crimes) from men, but they cannot hide (them) from Allah, seeing that He is in their midst when they plot by night, in words that He cannot approve: And Allah does compass round all that they do. Ah! These are the sort of men on whose behalf you may contend in this world; but who will contend with Allah on their behalf on the Day of Judgment, or who will carry their affairs through?" (Qur'an 4:105-109).

1.10 Forbidden is to think those slain in *Jihad* as dead

People who die in God's Way are not dead - they live in a far higher and deeper sense than in the life they have left behind. In their case, through the gateway of death, they enter the true real life, as opposed to its shadow here on earth. Their carnal life is sustained with carnal food, and its joys and pleasure at their best are those which are projected on the screen of this material world. Their real life being sustained from the perpetual presence and nearness to God.

God consoles and reassures those left behind by saying to them as,

1. "Think not of those who are slain in Allah's way as dead. Nay, they live, finding their sustenance in the presence of their Lord;

2. They rejoice in the bounty provided by Allah: And with regard to those left behind, who have not yet joined them (in their bliss), the (Martyrs) glory in the fact that on them is no fear, nor have they (cause to) grieve.

They glory in the Grace and the bounty from Allah, and in the fact that Allah suffers not the reward of the Faithful to be lost (in the least)" (Qur'an 3:169-171).

2
DEEDS AGAINST ONE'S OWN SELF ARE FORBIDDEN

The believers are to fulfill all of their obligations. There are Divine obligations that arise out of our relationship with God. He created us and along with the intuition and reason; He implanted in us the faculty of knowledge and fore-sight. He made nature responsive to our needs and His Signs in nature are very instructive to us in life. He further sent Messengers, to inculcate human values in our conduct in individual, social, and public life. All these favors create corresponding obligations to fulfill. Besides, as a member of human society, we undertake many mutual obligations. We make promises, enter into commercial, social, or marriage contracts etc. All these relationships require that people must faithfully fulfill their obligations. There are obligations, as a citizen or of state official; as a host or of a guest; as a wayfarer or of a companion; as an employer or of an employee and all similar relationships among people. These obligations being interconnected, should conscientiously be discharged by each individual. Truth and fidelity are parts of religion in all these relationships.

2.1 FORBIDDEN IS TO BE UNJUST, FALSE AND UNTRUSTWORTHY
The believers fulfill all of their obligations. They take care of orphan's property, give measure with full justice, whenever they speak they speak for justice and fulfill their promises and covenants. They are not false, unjust or untrustworthy.

God reminds the believers to remember and follow His commands as,

1. "Come not near to the orphan's property, except to improve it, until he attains the age of full strength;
2. Give measure and weight with (full) justice—no burden do We place on any soul, but that which it can bear;
3. Whenever you speak, speak justly, even if a near relative is concerned;
4. And fulfill the Covenant of Allah.

Thus does He command you that you may remember (and follow His commands)" (Qur'an 6:152).

2.2 FORBIDDEN IS TO KILL OR COME EVEN NEAR TO ADULTERY

God has ordained human life to be equally sacred for all people at all times and places. Citing the story of two sons of Adam in which one of them regretfully killed the other, God ordained that, "... if any one slew a person— unless it be (the punishment) for a murder or for spreading mischief in the land— it would be as if he slew the whole people: and if any one saved a life, it would be as if he saved the life of the whole people. ..." (Qur'an 5:32).

This makes killing or taking life as one of the greatest sins, especially of children for any reason. Similarly, adultery is not only shameful in itself and inconsistent with self-respect or the respect for others, but it opens the road to many social evils. It destroy the basis of the family, it works against the interest of the children and it may cause feuds and murders, which are a deterrent to the welfare of society. Not only it should be avoided as a sin, but any approach or temptation to it should also be curbed.

The believers are therefore commanded,

1. "Kill not your children for fear of want:

We shall provide sustenance for them as well as for you. Verily the killing of them is a great sin.

2. Nor come near to adultery: for it is a shameful (deed) and an evil, opening the road (to other evils).

3. Nor take life— which Allah has made sacred— except for just cause.

And if anyone is slain wrongfully, we have given his heir authority (to demand *Qisas* or to forgive): but let him not exceed bounds in the matter of taking life; for he is helped (by the Law)" (Qur'an 17:31-33).

2.3 FORBIDDEN IS TO STEAL—A CRIME CARRING A PUNISHMENT

Stealing is to increase what one owns at the expense of someone else. The one who steals feels that his legitimate earnings are too little and, therefore, he wishes to add to it in an illegitimate way. He lacks contentment and his income does not satisfy his greed or his desire to be wealthy. He wants to assure a comfortable life without work. In short, the motive for stealing is to increase one's income or one's wealth. Islam counters this motive by prescribing the punishment of cutting of the thief's hand, since such a punishment will markedly decrease the thief's ability to work and reduce his income and wealth. When a thief is punished according to Islam, his ability to show off is greatly curtailed and his need to work hard is enhanced.

God prescribes a punishment for theft,

1. "As to the thief, male or female, cut off his or her hands: a punishment by way of example, from Allah, for their crime: and Allah is Exalted in power.
2. But if the thief repents after his crime, and amends his conduct, Allah turns to him in forgiveness; for Allah is Oft-forgiving, Most Merciful. ..." (Qur'an 5:38-40).

2.4 FORBIDDEN IS TO TAKE ANYTHING FROM ORPHAN'S PROPERTY

The believers give an orphans' property back to them when they are mature, honor their promises and fulfill their engagements. If an orphan's property is touched at all, it should be to improve it, or to give back something better than he had before— never to take advantage for the benefit of the guardian. The guardian should honor any promise or undertaking given for the welfare of his/her orphan ward.

God commands the guardians to take care of the orphans and,

1. "Come not near to the orphan's property except to improve it, until he attains the age of full strength;

2. and fulfill (every) engagement, for (every) engagement will be enquired into (on the Day of Reckoning)" (Qur'an 17. 34)

2.5 FORBIDDEN IS TO BE INDECENT, WICKED OR AN OPPRESSOR

The believers are just and do good even where perhaps they are not strictly demanded to by justice, such as returning good for evil, or obliging those who in worldly language 'have no claim' on them, and of course they fulfill the claim of those whose claims are recognized in life. Similarly the opposite is to be avoided: everything that is considered shameful, everything that is really unjust, and any inward rebellion against divine law or one's own conscience. Specifically, God forbids the believers: 1) All shameful deeds, 2) Injustice, 3) Rebellion, 4) Breaking Covenant of God and Oaths, and 5) Using oaths to deceive others for material gains.

To the believers, "God commands justice, the doing of good and liberality to kith and kin

1. but He (Allah) forbids all shameful deeds,
2. and injustice
3. and rebellion:

He instructs you, that you may receive admonition.

4. Fulfill the Covenant of Allah when you have entered into it, and break not your oaths after you have confirmed them; indeed you have made Allah your surety; for Allah knows all that you do.

And be not like a woman who breaks into untwisted strands, the yarn which she has spun, after it has become strong.

5. Nor take your oaths to practice deception between yourselves, lest one party should be more numerous (in gains) than another:

for Allah will test you by this; and on the Day of Judgment. He will certainly make clear to you (the truth of) that wherein you disagree" (Qur'an 16: 90-92)

2.6 Forbidden is to dishonor one's oaths and contracts

The believers know that dishonoring oaths and breaking contracts with people or God Himself for material gains is forbidden in Islam. Beside, any possible gain that one can make by breaking covenants of God or of divine law must necessary be miserable; while one's own benefit is far greater in obeying God's Will and doing what is right.

God commands the believers, "Nor sell the covenant of Allah for a miserable price: for with Allah is (a prize) far better for you, if you only knew. What is with you must vanish: what is with Allah will endure. And We will certainly bestow, on those who patiently persevere, their reward according to the best of their actions" (Qur'an 16:95-96).

2.7 Forbidden is drinking, gambling, shrines and oracles

Believers trust God and drive their strength and prosperity from Him. Since they have to follow what God commands, they neither follow superstitions, which are irrational nor do they seek undue stimulation in intoxicants nor search for some fake advantage in gambling. To some there may be temporary excitement or pleasure in these, but that is not the way to either prosperity or piety.

Therefore, God commands the believers to abstain from, "O you who believe!

1. Intoxicants and gambling, (dedication of) stones, and (divination by) arrows, are an abomination, - of Satan's handwork: eschew such (abomination), that you may prosper.

Satan's plan is (but) to excite enmity and hatred between you, with intoxicants and gambling, and hinder you from the remembrance of Allah, and from prayer: will you not then abstain?

2. Obey Allah, and obey the Messenger, and beware (of evil): if you do turn back, know you that it is Our Messenger's duty to proclaim (the message) in the clearest manner" (Qur'an 5:90-92).

2.8 FORBIDDEN IS TO WALK ON THE EARTH WITH INSOLENCE

Limited knowledge endowed to people does not qualify them to pursue any endeavor in life. Idle curiosity may lead people to venture into evil, without knowing that it is evil. People must guard against every such danger. They should only hear or see those things that are known to be good. People have to be careful because they will be called into account for the exercise of every faculty that has been given to them. The insolence, arrogance or undue elation at one's power or capacities is the first step to many evils. This has no justification, for all human capabilities are a God given trust and not individually acquired or owned.

Therefore, God commands the believers,

1. "And pursue not that of which you have no knowledge; for every act of hearing, or of seeing or of (feeling in) the heart will be enquired into (on the Day of Reckoning).
2. Nor walk on the earth with insolence: for you can not rend the earth asunder, nor reach the mountains in height" (Qur'an 17:36-37).

2.9 FORBIDDEN IS TO HOLD GOD'S COMMANDS IN LOW ESTEEM

Forbidden is hold God's commands in low esteem or make the lawful things unlawful. The Qur'an could be described as an embodiment of; 1) Besides the fact that it is worthy of receiving honor as a great book of guidance for humanity, it confers great favors on those who receive it, 2) It is well guarded, precious in itself, and well preserved in its purity, 3) None but clean shall touch it— clean in body, mind, thought, and intention; only unbiased readers can achieve real contact with its full meaning, 4) It is a revelation from the Lord of the Worlds, and therefore, universal for all. One may ask—How can one ignore it or treat it with contempt or refuse to allow it to improve one's life and that of humanity as a whole?

The believers are assured, "That this is indeed a Qur'an most honorable, in a Book well-guarded, which none shall touch but those who are clean: a

Revelation from the Lord of the Worlds. Is it such a message that you would hold in light esteem, and have you made it your livelihood that you should declare it false?" (Qur'an 56:77-82).

God is the sole lawgiver for people and therefore, even His messengers cannot declare a lawful thing as unlawful. Citing an incident from his family life, the Messenger was reminded that he cannot declare unlawful to eat, which God has made lawful, for any reason. God tells the Messenger (and the believers) that, "O Prophet! Why hold you to be forbidden that which Allah has made lawful to you? You seek to please your consorts, but Allah is Oft-Forgiving, Most Merciful" (Qur'an 66:1).

2.10 FORBIDDEN IS TO FOLLOW THE WAY OF THE HYPOCRITES
God condemns those believers who neglect their duties; their duties towards their Lord and their duties towards people "So woe to the worshipers who are neglectful of their prayers, those who (want but) to be seen (of men) but refuse (help even in) neighborly needs" (Qur'an 107:4-7).

Since, "the hypocrites will be in the lowest depths of the Fire; no helper will you find for them—" (Qur'an 4:145), the believers are forbidden to adopt the way of the hypocrites. It was narrated by Abu Hurairah that Allah's Messenger[PBUH] said, "The signs of a hypocrite are three: whenever he speaks, he tells a lie; and whenever he promises, he breaks his promise; and whenever he is entrusted, he betrays (proves himself to be dishonest)" (Sahih Bukhari: 8.73.117).

3
DEEDS AGAINST PEOPLE ARE FORBIDDEN

God gave people the faculty of reasoning and wisdom so that they could control and manage their selfish desires with reason. However, some people use their intellect to justify the fulfillment of their self-interests and arrogance. In the sight of God, such people are the lowest of the low, "We have indeed created man in the best of molds; then do We abase him (to be) the lowest of the low—except such as believe and do righteous deeds, for they shall have a reward unfailing" (Qur'an 95:4-6).

Reason and wisdom tell us that broadcasting false news to the public and defaming people by sarcasm, suspiciousness, spying, or speaking ill of others cannot be proper human traits. Likewise, one can humiliate oneself by being greedy or by being unkind to an orphan and the needy. It can't be proper to mistreat an orphan or refuse to feed a hungry person. Earning one's living by corruption, cut-throat rivalry, backbiting, and hoarding are forbidden in Islam. In short, the believers must be honest and should not follow the ways of the unbelievers in any of their daily activities. Specific commands that forbid the believers from such deeds, which are against human dignity, are given below.

3.1 Forbidden is to broadcast false news or tell lies

All news or reports especially if coming from unknown persons, must be investigated to assure their truth. If false news is assumed to be true and spread around, much harm can be done of which one may have to repent afterword. Scandals or slander of all kinds are therefore condemned.

The believers are forbidden to broadcast false news or tell lies,

"O you who believe! If a wicked person comes to you with any news, ascertain the truth, lest you harm people unwittingly and afterwards become full of repentance for what you have done" (Qur'an 49:6).

3.2 Forbidden is to laugh at or be sarcastic to others

Mutual ridicule ceases to be fun when there is arrogance, selfishness or malice behind it. One may laugh with people, to share in the happiness of life but one may never laugh at people in contempt or ridicule. In many things, the others may be better than ourselves. Since no body is perfect or can think to be better than others, it is forbidden to laugh or be sarcastic to others.

God commands the believers, "O you who believe!

1. Let not some men among you laugh at others; it may be that the (latter) are better than the (former).
2. Nor let some women laugh at others; it may be that the (latter) are better than the (former):

3. Nor defame nor be sarcastic to each other, nor call each other by (offensive) nicknames:..." (Qur'an 49:11).

3.3 FORBIDDEN IS TO SUSPECT, SPY, OR SPEAK ILL OF OTHERS

Defamation may consist in speaking ill of others by the spoken or written word, or in acting in such a way as to suggest a charge against some person whom we are not in a position to judge. A cutting, biting remark or taunt of sarcasm as well as an offensive nickname could be used to defame others. In any case there is no point in using offensive nicknames or names that suggest some real or fancied defect.

God commands the believers, "O you who believe!

1. Avoid suspicion as much (as possible), for suspicion in some cases is a sin,
2. And spy not on each other,
3. Nor speak ill of each other behind their backs.

Would any of you like to eat the flesh of his dead brother? Nay, you would abhor it. But fear Allah, for Allah is Oft-Returning, Most Merciful" (Qur'an 49:12).

3.4 FORBIDDEN IS TO HUMILIATE ONESELF BY BEING GREEDY

To the greedy, their capital or accumulated wealth is more important than help-ing people. Thus, they degrade themselves by not subscribing to such human value as helping orphans and the needy. Even at our own valuation, if we are favored with prosperity, do we think of the fatherless children, or the strug-gling poor? On the contrary, too many people are but ready to embezzle the helpless orphan's inheritance and to waste their own wealth in worthless activi-ties instead of supplying people's real needs.

Greedy people as described in the Qur'an are, "Now, as for man, when his Lord tried him, giving him honor and gifts, then says he, (puffed up), 'My Lord has honored me.' But when He tried him, restricting his subsistence for him, then he says (in despair), 'My Lord has humiliated me!'

1. Nay, nay! But you honor not the orphans!
2. Nor do you encourage one another to feed the poor!
3. And you devour inheritance—all with greed,
4. And you love wealth with inordinate love" (Qur'an 89:15-20).

3.5 FORBIDDEN IS TO BE UNKIND TO THE ORPHAN AND NEEDY

Judging future from the past, God has been good to the believers in their past experience, therefore they should also trust His goodness in the future. Citing three facts from the Messenger's life, the believers are told how God helps them. Therefore, as a token of gratitude, they should be kind to the orphans or the weaker members of their society. The Messenger treated all orphans with affection and respect, setting an example to his contemporaries, who frequently took advantage of the helpless position of orphans, and looked upon them as subordinate creatures to be repressed and kept in their place. Such an attitude has been common throughout history. Contrarily, helpless members of our society should be treated as a sacred trust, whether they are orphans, or dependants, or anybody unable to assert themselves, either because of age, sex, social rank, unusual circumstance, or any other cause whatever.

God asks the Messenger, "Did He not find you an orphan and give you shelter (and care)? And He found you wandering, and He gave you guidance. And He found you in need, and made you independent.

1. Therefore, treat not the orphan with harshness,
2. Nor repulse the petitioner (unheard),

But the bounties of your Lord— proclaim!" (Qur'an 93:6-11).

3.6 FORBIDDEN IS TO DENY THE DAY OR FEEDING THE POOR

Only those who deny faith and the accountability of their deeds, treat the helpless people with contempt and lead arrogant and selfish lives. The charity and love which feeds the indigent is a noble form of virtue, which is beyond the reach of those who are so callous as even to discourage, forbid or even look down upon the virtue of charity and kindness to others.

God asks, "See you one who denies the Judgment (to come)?

1. Then such is the (man) who repulses the orphan (with harshness),
2. And encourages not the feeding of the indigent" (Qur'an 107:1-3).

3.7 FORBIDDEN IS TO BE UNGRATEFUL LOVERS OF WEALTH

People who neither have received guidance nor do they do good deeds are surely ungrateful to their Lord, Who created them and sustains them, and sends His blessings and favors at all times. The ingratitude may be shown by thoughts, words and deeds—by forgetting or denying God and His goodness, by misusing His favors or by injustice to others. Rather, they themselves prove the charge of treason against them by their conduct and deeds. What an evil choice they make in committing treason against their own Benefactor by being violently in love of wealth and worldly gains.

After swearing, God tells people that:

1. "Truly man is to his Lord ungrateful,
2. And to that (fact) he bears witness (by his deeds),
3. And violent is he in his love of wealth.

Does he not know, when that which is in the graves is scattered abroad and that which is (locked up) in (human) breasts is made manifest, that their Lord had been well-acquainted with them, (even to) that Day" (Qur'an 100:6-11).

3.8 FORBIDDEN IS THE CUT-THROAT RIVALRY FOR WEALTH

The passion for seeking an increase in wealth, position, the number of followers or supporters, etc., may affect an individual just as it may affect whole societies or nations. People's rivalry and competition may aggravate situations. Up to a certain point it may be good and necessary, but when it leaves no time for improvement of society or for working righteousness and doing good deeds, then it will be of no use. People should never forget that they shell be held responsible for every kind of joy they indulge in; whether it was false pride or delight in things of no value, or things evil, or the legitimate enjoyment they kept within reasonable bounds.

God warns people that,

1. "The mutual rivalry for piling up (the good things of this world) diverts you (from the more serious things) until you visit the graves.

But nay, you soon shall know (the reality). Again, you soon shall know! Nay, were you to know with certainty of mind, (you would beware!)
You shall certainly see Hellfire! Again, you shall see it with certainty of sight!

2. Then, shall you be questioned that Day about the joy (you indulged in)!" (Qur'an 102:1-8).

3.9 FORBIDDEN IS CORRUPTION, BACKBITING OR HOARDING

Three evils are here condemned in the strongest terms: These are 1) scandal mongering, talking or suggesting evil of men or women by word, behavior, mimicry, sarcasm, or insult; 2) insulting people behind their back, even if the things suggested are true, but the motive is evil; 3) piling up wealth, not for service or use to those who need it, but in miserly hoards, as if such hoards can prolong the miser's life or give him immortality. Therefore, the believers neither pile up wealth nor they are scandalmongers or backbiters.

God tells people in *Surah Al-Humazah* that, "Woe to every (kind of) scandalmonger and backbiter, Who piles up wealth and lays it by, thinking that his wealth would make him last for ever! By no means! He will be sure to be thrown into that which Breaks to Pieces, And what will explain to you that which Breaks to Pieces? (It is) the Fire of (the wrath of) Allah kindled (to a blaze)" (Qur'an 104:1-6).

3.10 FORBIDDEN IS TO FOLLOW THE WAY OF UNBELIEVERS

The believers hold fast to their faith, because they know it is true. Contrarily, those who reject faith, cling hard to their worldly interests. Such people are free to do whatever they like, but they should not force their interests on the believers by favor, force, or fraud.

The believers are commanded to tell the unbelievers, "Say: 'O you that reject Faith!

1. I worship not that which you worship, nor will you worship that which I worship.
2. And I will not worship that which you have been wont to worship, nor will you worship that which I worship.
3. To you be your Way, and to me mine'" (Qur'an 109:1-6).

4
DEEDS AGAINST PUBLIC WELFARE ARE FORBIDDEN

God tells people in *Surah Al-Layl* that, "Verily, We take upon Ourselves to guide (Humanity)" (Qur'an 92:12). Therefore, the believers should not hold God's commands in low esteem and make unlawful, those things that were made lawful by Him. The believers should not indulge in things forbidden, e.g., making mischief in the land, breaking mutual ties by misappropriating each other's property, or bribing judges. Similarly, the believers should not be fraudulent or deceive others by their oaths. They should give full measure with justice when they deal with others. Specific commands that forbid the believers from such deeds that are against public welfare are given below:

4.1 FORBIDDEN IS TO BE FRAUDULENT— GIVE FULL MEASURE

The Messenger[PBUH] quotes God as saying: "My servants, I have forbidden Myself injustice and have made it forbidden among you, so do not be unjust to one another" (Sahih Muslim: 32.6246). A just society comes into existence only through the implementation of the divine law individually and in the society. God tells people in *Surah Hud*: "O my people! Give full measure and weigh fairly, and defraud not people their things, and do not act corruptly in the land, making mischief" (Qur'an 11:85). God also commands people in *Surah Al-Shuara*: "And follow not the bidding of the extravagant—who make mischief in the land, and mend not (their ways)" (Qur'an 26:151-152).

God tells people in *Surah Al-Mutaffifin*, that "Woe to those that deal in fraud—those who, when they have to receive by measure from men, exact full measure, but when they have to give by measure or weight to men, give less than due. Do they not think that they will be called to account on a Mighty Day?" (Qur'an 83:1-5).

4.2 FORBIDDEN IS TO USURP OR BRIBE AWAY ONE'S PROPERTY

Besides the three primal physical needs of people — for food, drink, and sex, which are apt to make them greedy, there is a fourth greed in the society, the greed of wealth and property. Generally, honest people are content if they restrain from robbery, theft, or embezzlement. Besides these there are two more types of greed—one is where one uses one's own property for corrupting others like judges or those in authority, as to obtain some material gain from private or from public property, even under the cover of the law. Another form of greed is where we use our own property for vain or frivolous uses. All these type of greed needs to be properly managed and eliminated.

As commanded, the believers do not misappropriate their property nor use it to bribe judges,

1. "And do not eat up your property among yourselves for vanities,
2. nor use it as bait for the judges, with intent that you may eat up wrongfully and knowingly a little of (other) people's property" (Qur'an 2:188).

4.3 FORBIDDEN IS TO SQUANDER WEALTH LIKE THAT OF SATAN

For the believers, God's worship is linked up with kindness—to parents, kindred, those in want, those who are far from their homes though they may be total strangers to them. It is not mere verbal kindness but they have certain rights which must be fulfilled. Natural resources which God has provided people are to be shared and used properly—never to be wasted. Spendthrift are not merely fools but they belong to Satan's family. Satan himself fell by his ingratitude to God. So, those who misuse or squander their provisions are also ungrateful to God.

God commands people to, "... But squander not (your wealth) in the manner of a spendthrift. Verily spendthrifts are brothers of the Evil Ones; and the Evil One is to his Lord (himself) ungrateful" (Qur'an 17: 26-27)

4.4 FORBIDDEN IS EVEN TO LOOK AT THE WEALTH OF OTHERS

Human mission in life is not to collect perishable things of this world but to flourish humanity as God has commanded people. Too many material things do not bring happiness. Even the temporary pleasure that they may give will never match the perpetual happiness which contentment and helping others brings. The Messenger, in his human love and sympathy, may grieve over a certain class of people who are puffed up with false notions and do not listen to the divine message. The Prophet and the believers are asked not to worry about such people but be kind to each other.

There is no flaw in God's plan, and it must prevail. Therefore,

1. "Strain not your eyes. (Wistfully) at what We have bestowed on certain classes of them,
2. Nor grieve over them: but lower your wing (in gentleness) to the believers" (Qur'an 15:88).

4.5 FORBIDDEN IS TO USE ONE'S OATHS TO DECEIVE PEOPLE

The believers know that using oaths to deceive others for material gains is forbidden in Islam. This is to avoid its evil consequences: 1) to others; if they had not been deceived, they might have walked firmly on the Path, but now they lose faith, and perhaps commit like frauds for which you,— 'who deceive others' will be responsible; 2) to yourself, you have not only gone wrong yourself; but have set others on the wrong path; and deserve double penalty— evil consequence in this world and in the Hereafter.

God commands the believers, "And take not your oaths to practice deception between yourselves, with the result that someone's foot may slip after it was firmly planted, and you may have to taste the evil (consequences) of having hindered (men) from the path of Allah and a mighty wrath descend on you" (Qur'an 16:94).

4.6 FORBIDDEN IS TO USE OATHS TO KEEP BACK FROM VIRTUE

The believers do not make oaths in the name of God, as an excuse for not doing the right thing when it is pointed out to them, or for refraining from doing something which will bring people together. If someone is swayed by anger or passion or mere caprice, God knows one's inmost heart, and right conduct, and He does not demand obstinacy or quibbling from people. For this reason, the thoughtless oaths, without any intention or a bad intention behind them, should be expiated by an act of charity.

God commands the believers to honor their oaths,

1. "And make not Allah's (name) an excuse in your oaths against doing good, or acting rightly, or making peace between persons; for Allah is One Who hears and knows all things.
2. Allah will not call you to account for thoughtlessness in your oaths, but for the intention in your hearts; and He is Oft-Forgiving, Most Forbearing" (Qur'an 2:224-225).

4.7 FORBIDDEN IS TO MARRY UNBELIEVING WOMEN OR MEN

Marriage is a most intimate relationship, and the mystery of sex finds its highest fulfillment in the presence of spiritual harmony. If religion is at all a real influence in life, a difference in this vital matter must affect the lives of both more profoundly than differences of birth, race, language, or position in life. It is therefore only right that the parties to be married should have the same spiritual outlook. Besides, religion defines human mission in life and teaches human values. People start a new human community with marriage and if the purpose and preferences in life of both partners match each others then their life will be easy and smooth.

Therefore, the believers are commanded not to marry the unbelievers,

1. "Do not marry unbelieving women (idolaters), until they believe: A slave woman who believes is better than an unbelieving woman, even though she allures you.
2. Nor marry (your girls) to unbelievers until they believe: A man slave who believes is better than an unbeliever, even though he allures you.

9

Unbelievers do (but) beckon you to the Fire. But Allah beckons by His Grace to the Garden (of bliss) and forgiveness, and makes His Signs clear to mankind: That they may receive admonition" (Qur'an 2:221).

The believers recite, learn, practice and teach what God has revealed to guide people. They remember what God commands and never violate His commands in their daily activities. They are content with what God has given them and never desire to violate His commands in seeking the pomp and glitter of this life. God's grace and His love is more important to them than material goods of this world.

For those who stray from His Path, God's grace is ever present: it seeks to reclaim them and bring them back to the Path. If someone resists, and follows his own lusts, a point is reached when his case becomes hopeless. God's grace does not then reach him, and he is abandoned to his pride and arrogance. The believers neither follow their example or advice nor seek their company.

God commands the believers, "And recite (and teach) what has been revealed to you of the Book of your Lord: none can change His Words, and none will you find as a refuge other than Him.

1. And keep your soul content with those who call on their Lord morning and evening, seeking His Face;
2. and let not your eyes pass beyond them, seeking the pomp and glitter of this Life;
3. nor obey any whose heart We have permitted to neglect the remembrance of Us, one who follows his own desires, whose case has gone beyond all bounds" (Qur'an 18:28).

Islam advocates the establishment of justice and human brotherhood. This cannot be achieved except under divine guidance. Those who fail to implement it by their own efforts and sacrifice, are not true to God. Such disloyalty or cowardice is not even good for them from a worldly point of view. With what face can they meet their friends after their disgraceful conduct? Their excuse for not fighting in God's Way is that it is not right to fight with kith and kin. On the other hand, it is a case of either subduing evil or being subdued by evil and if evil gets the upper hand, it is not likely to respect ties of kith and kin. Therefore, it is very important that the believers should earnestly seek to understand the Qur'an and implement its commands individually and in the society.

If Islam is not implemented and evil gets the upper hand, under such situation God asks, "Then, is it to be expected of you, if you were put in authority,

1. that you will do mischief in the land,
2. And break your ties of kith and kin?

Such are the men whom Allah has cursed for He has made them deaf and blinded their sight. Do they not then earnestly seek to understand the Qur'an, or are their hearts locked up by them. Those who turn back as apostates after Guidance was clearly shown to them— the Satan has instigated them and busied them up with false hopes" (Qur'an 47:22-25).

4.10 FORBIDDEN IS TO SPREAD CHOAS AND MISCHIEF IN LAND

In prayers, one must avoid any arrogance or show, or vanity of requests or of words. If excess is condemned in all things, it is especially worthy of condemnation when one goes humbly before one's Lord. The believer, who prays with humility and earnestness finds it easy to repent, reform and practice righteousness. He does not, like the wicked, upset the order to introduce evil or mischief into it.

God commands the believers to,

1. "Call on your Lord with humility and in private: for Allah loves not those who trespass beyond bounds.
2. Do no mischief on the earth, after it has been set in order, but call on Him with fear and longing (in your hearts):

for the Mercy of Allah is (always) near to those who do good" (Qur'an 7:55-56).

Chapter 7

What God Commands People

(Believers Live as God Commands)

The Contract between people and God consists of three sets of obligations that the believers have to fulfill during their lives on earth. These
obligations are about (1) belief and worship, (2) individual character and livelihood, and (3) society and justice. The Divine Contract consists of people's
obligations to God and their obligations to themselves and to God's creation,
including their fellow people. This contract is a single and complete whole,
each part being of equal importance. To ignore any part of the contract is to
reject it altogether. The believers have committed themselves to serve God by
implementing His commands in managing their affairs and in helping to build
a just human society in the world.

God commands the believers to spend what is surplus to their basic
needs. The best way to spend is for the welfare of the orphans and the needy.
Honoring one's oaths is mandatory in Islam, and oaths should not be taken
against doing something good in the future. Usury by which people profit by
exploiting the needy is also forbidden.

1
BELIEVERS— ENTER INTO ISLAM COMPLETELY

The believers enter into Islam completely and live their lives as commanded.
They learn to be righteous and practice their religion sincerely. They establish
and guard their prayers. They spend in God's Way, fast during the month of

Ramadan, and perform Hajj. They earn an honest living and eat what is lawful and good. They honor their oaths and promises.

The Messenger and the believers believe in God's revelations. They forgive and overlook those who wish to corrupt them. They do not follow their own selfish desires. The believers have a common goal in life so they strive together to do good deeds.

1.1 BELIEVE IN GOD, HIS ANGELS, BOOKS AND MESSENGERS

The believers believe in God, His revelations, His Angels and His Messengers. It is not for the believers to make distinction between any of God's Messengers. They honor them all equally. The believers learn what God commands in the Qur'an and implement those commands in their lives and in their societies. They admit their mistakes, repent and keep on improving their character and behavior:

God tells people about the Messenger and the believers as,

"The Messenger believes in what has been revealed to him from his Lord, as do the men of faith. Each one (of them) believes in Allah, His angels, His books, and His messengers. 'We make no distinction (they say) between one and another of His messengers.' And they say: 'We hear, and we obey. (We seek) Your forgiveness, our Lord, and to You is the end of all journeys'" (Qur'an 2:285).

1.2 GOD DOES NOT BURDEN PEOPLE BEYOND THEIR LIMITS

The believers know that God does not expect them to perform beyond their limits and they will be rewarded exactly according to their efforts. God assures them that, "On no soul does Allah place a burden greater than it can bear. It gets every good that it earns. (The believers try their best, and they supplicate:)

1. 'Our Lord! Condemn us not if we forget or fall into error.
2. Our Lord! Lay not on us a burden like that which You did lay on those before us.
3. Our Lord! Lay not on us a burden greater than we have strength to bear. Blot out our sins, and grant us forgiveness. Have mercy on us. You are our Protector; Help us against those who stand against Faith'" (Qur'an 2:286).

1.3 BELIEVERS REALIZE THEIR FAITH WITHIN THEIR HEARTS

The believers not only have faith, but they realize their faith within their hearts. The chief objects of their faith are God, His Messengers, and His revelations. To all these, believers must give a home in their heart. The Angels can not be seen and realized as God can be realized, Who is nearer to people than their jugular vein, and the Day of Judgment is when they will be rewarded for their deeds. People who go on changing sides again and again can have no real faith at any time. Their motives are mere worldly double dealing. They cannot really expect God's grace or forgiveness.

God commands the believers, "O you who believe!

Believe in Allah and His Messenger, and the scripture that He has sent to His Messenger and the scripture that He sent to those before (him). Any who denies Allah, His angels, His books, His messengers, and the Day of Judgment, has gone far, far astray. Those who believe, then reject Faith, then believe (again) and (again) reject Faith, and go on increasing in Unbelief—Allah will not forgive them nor guide them on the Way. To the hypocrites give the glad tidings that there is for them (but) a grievous penalty" (Qur'an 4:136-138).

1.4 BELIEVERS MAKE NO DISTINCTION AMONG MESSENGERS

The believers believe in God and His messengers and make no distinction between any of His messengers. Contrarily, unbelief takes various forms. Some of which are— 1) The denial of God and His revelations; 2) Nominal belief in God and His messengers, one which is partial, due to racial pride, which does not allow recognition of any messengers outside a specific race; and 3) A nominal belief in universal revelation, so hedged around with peculiar doctrines of exclusive salvation which amounts to a denial of God's universal love for all humanity and all creation. All three amount to unbelief, for they really deny God's universal love and care.

God tells people that, "Those who deny Allah and His messengers, and (those who) wish to separate Allah from His messengers, saying: 'We believe in some but reject others'—and (those who) wish to take a course midway, they are in truth (equally) unbelievers, and we have prepared for unbelievers a humiliating punishment. To those who believe in Allah and His messengers and make no distinction between any of the messengers, we shall soon give their (due) rewards, for Allah is Oft-Forgiving, Most Merciful" (Qur'an 4:150-152).

1.5 BELIEVERS FOLLOW ISLAM TRULY — NOT THEIR DESIRES

The believers practice Islam sincerely. They do not follow the whispering of Satan or their own selfish desires. People will make excuses to resist the appeal of God if they are not sincere in their faith. This cannot be accepted. The decision in all questions belongs to God. If the believers are true to Him, they wait for His decision and they do not expect Him to wait for theirs .

God commands the believers to, "O you who believe!

Enter into Islam whole-heartedly, and follow not the footsteps of the evil one, for he is to you an avowed enemy. If you backslide after the clear (Signs) have come to you, then know that Allah is Exalted in Power, Wise" (Qur'an 2:208-209).

1.6 EACH PERSON HAS A GOAL, SO STRIVE JOINTLY TO GOOD

Life is like a race in which all people zealously run forward to one goal. For the believers this goal is to do good and it is applied both individually and collectively.

God tells people that, "To each is a goal to which Allah turns him; then strive together (as in a race) towards all that is good. Wherever you are, Allah will bring you together, for Allah has power over all things" (Qur'an 2:148).

2

BELIEVERS— LEARN TO BE RIGHTEOUS

Islam is belief in the Hereafter and striving in God's Way. The believers believe in God, His angels, His books, His prophets, and the Last Day. They believe in all of the messengers without distinction or discrimination. Belief in the accountability for one's deeds makes people hardworking, vigilant, and responsible. The believers believe in God's revelation, pray and help others. They worship God and learn to be righteous. They study the Qur'an, follow it and refrain from all shameful deeds. During their struggle in life, they persevere with patience and seek God's help with patience and prayer.

2.1 BELIEVERS ARE RIGHTEOUS AND GOD FEARING PEOPLE

The believers obey what God commands, out of His love and the love of people. Their faith can be characterized as; 1) It is true and sincere, 2) It is confirmed by good deeds and deeds of charity, 3) It makes them good citizens who support community work and, 4) It converts them into patient and firm individuals who are unshaken in all circumstances.

God tells people about righteousness as, "It is not righteousness that you turn your faces towards east or west; but it is righteousness:

1. To believe in Allah and the Last Day, and the angels, and the Book, and the Messengers;
2. To spend of your substance, out of love for Him, for your kin, for orphans, for the needy, for the wayfarer, for those who ask, and for the ransom of slaves;
3. To be steadfast in prayer,
4. And practice regular charity;
5. To fulfill the contracts that you have made;
6. And to be firm and patient, in pain (or suffering) and adversity, and throughout all periods of panic.

Such are the people of truth, the God-fearing" (Qur'an 2:177).

2.2 BELIEVE IN REVELATION, LAST DAY AND THE CHARITY

Mentioning the behavior of the unbelievers among the People of the Book who took usury and devoured people's property, God has highlighted that the believers among them, like Muslims, believed in Him and all of His revelations. They established regular prayers, gave charity and believed in the Day of Judgment. Those people will be rewarded for their good deeds.

God tells people that "But those among them (the People of the Book), who are well grounded in knowledge, and the believers:

1. Believe in what has been revealed to you and what was revealed before you—

2. And (especially) those who establish regular prayer
3. And practice regular charity
4. And believe in Allah
5. And in the Last Day

To them shall We soon give a great reward" (Qur'an 4:162).

2.3 STUDY QUR'AN, PRAY AND REFRAIN FROM THE SHAMEFUL

Reciting the Qur'an implies: 1) rehearsing and proclaiming the divine Message for the benefit of humanity; 2) reading it to ourselves; 3) studying it to understand it as it should be understood. 4) meditating on it so as to accord our knowledge, life and desires with what God commands. When this is done, it turns into a real prayer, and the prayer purges the believers of anything shameful (such as: deed, plan, thought, motive or word) or that which could do injustice to others. Such prayer brings them nearer to God and His nearness motivates them to live their lives as He desires. This is the ultimate remembrance of God which is the greatest thing in life.

God asks the believers to,

1. "Recite what is sent of the Book by inspiration to you,
2. And establish regular prayer: for prayer restrains from shameful and unjust deeds;

And remembrance of Allah is the greatest (thing in life) without doubt, and Allah knows the (deeds) that you do" (Qur'an 29:45).

2.4 WORSHIP THEIR LORD AND SEEK HIS HELP WITH PATIENCE

Adoration of their Lord and patience are two of the most important characteristics of the believers. Adoration is the act of the highest and humblest reverence and worship. When people achieve that relationship with God, their faith produces works of righteousness. It is a chance given to them: will they then exercise their free will and take it? If they do, their whole nature will be transformed with the God's help to the best of humanity .

Patience, the other characteristic of the believers, implies; 1) the sense of being thorough, not hasty; 2) patience perseverance, constancy, steadfastness, firmness of purpose; 3) systematic as opposed to chance action; 4) a cheerful attitude of resignation and understanding of sorrow, defeat, or suffering as opposed to murmuring or rebellion but away from mere passivity or listlessness, by the element of steadfastness.

People are commanded to seek God's help with patience and prayer as, "O you people!

1. Adore your Guardian-Lord, Who created you and those who came before you, that you may become righteous" (Qur'an 2:21).
2. "Seek (Allah's) help with patient perseverance and prayer:

It is indeed hard, except to those who bring a lowly spirit— who bear in mind the certainty that they are to meet their Lord and that they are to return to Him" (Qur'an 2:45-46).

2.5 Persist in seeking help with patience and prayer
In the ups and downs of life, when difficulties and hardships confront people, and when difficulties and sufferings become long, it is patience that keeps the believer resolute and safe from disappointment, desperation, and frustration. Patience is a basic quality with which a person needs to shape his life in this world and in the next. It is patience that prepares people to tolerate hardships and difficulties in life. It gives hope and makes people wait for positive results, however long that may take. Patience increases self-confidence and assures people that difficulties and hardships will eventually disappear and that success and prosperity will appear again. Therefore, the coming of relief should be awaited with patience, peace, and conviction. People who are patient are not short tempered and arrogant, but calm and humble.

God commands the believers, "O you who believe!

1. Seek help with patient perseverance and prayer, for Allah is with those who patiently persevere.

2. And say not of those who are slain in the Way of Allah, 'They are dead.' Nay, they are living, though you perceive (it) not.

Be sure We shall test you with something of fear and hunger, some loss in goods or lives or the fruits (of your toil),

3. But give glad tidings to those who patiently persevere, who say, when afflicted with calamity: 'To Allah we belong, and to Him is our return.'

They are those on whom (descend) blessings from Allah, and mercy, and they are the ones that receive guidance" (Qur'an 2:153-157).

3
BELIEVERS— ESTABLISH AND GUARD THEIR PRAYERS

The believers accept their religion as the Truth; they reject all that is false and establish daily prayers. Why do the believers establish daily prayers? Various reasons mentioned in the Qur'an are; 1) because 'prayer restrains the believers from shameful and unjust deeds'; 2) 'things that are good, remove those that are evil'; and 3) the believers are commanded to pray so 'that they may have happiness'. Therefore, the believers study the Qur'an and learn all that God commands, and they refrain from all shameful deeds and sins. The believers pray at sunset and in the morning, afternoon, and the evening. Before the prayers, the believers wash themselves clean. After the prayers, they seek God's bounty and remember to follow His commands during their daily activities.

The believers guard their prayers; they leave off business and hasten to prayer on Friday and pray with moderate voice and with full attention. They can shorten their prayers during travel for security reasons.

3.1 WORSHIP GOD, ACCEPT TRUTH AND REJECT FALSEHOOD
The believers regularly pray five times a day. These prayers are obligatory for all Muslims. The morning prayer is singled out for separate mention, as special testimony is borne to the prayers of this hour by the angelic host. There

is also an optional prayer after midnight in the small hours of the morning. All prayers must be for God's help and support. As much as the believers may plan, their success depends on God's help. The believers are assured that falsehood must perish: for it is the opposite of truth and the truth must always prevail.

God commands the Messenger and the believers to,

1. "Establish regular prayers—at the sun's decline till the darkness of the night, and the morning prayer and reading: for the prayer and reading in the morning carry their testimony.
2. And pray in the small watches of the morning—(it would be) an additional prayer for you. Soon will your Lord raise you to a station of praise and glory!"
3. Say: 'O my Lord! Let my entry be by the gate of truth and honor, and likewise my exit by the gate of truth and honor, and grant me from Your presence an authority to aid (me).'
4. And say: 'Truth has (now) arrived, and falsehood perished, for falsehood is (by its nature) bound to perish" (Qur'an 17:78-81).

3.2 BELIEVERS GUARD THEIR PRAYERS AND REMEMBER GOD

The believers strictly guard their prayers, especially the middle one, to remember God in the midst of their daily activities. Depending on the situation, prayer can be offered on foot while on ground, but can be offered while riding as well.

God commands the believers to,

1. "Guard strictly your (habit of) prayers, especially the middle prayer; and stand before Allah in a devout (frame of mind).
2. If you fear (an enemy), pray on foot, or riding, (as may be most convenient),

But when you are in security, celebrate Allah's praises in the manner He has taught you, which you knew not (before)" (Qur'an 2:238-239).

3.3 PRAY AT SUNSET, IN MORNING, AFTERNOON, AND EVENING

Commands about the prayer in various situations are given in several places in the Qur'an. In Verse 29:45 about prayer, it has been mentioned that 1) 'prayer restrains from shameful and unjust deeds'. In Verse 11:114, about prayer, it has been mentioned that: 2) 'things that are good, remove those that are evil'. In Verse 20:130, it has been mentioned that: 3) the believers are commanded to pray so 'that you may have happiness'. In Verse 50:39-40 along with prayer, the believers are commanded to: 4) 'bear, then, with patience, all that they (unbelievers) say' and in Verse 52:48-49. 5) the believers are told, 'now await in patience the command of your Lord: for verily you are in Our eyes: and celebrate the praises of your Lord'. Details of these verses are given below:

1. "Recite what is sent of the Book by inspiration to you, 2. And establish regular prayer: for prayer restrains from shameful and unjust deeds; And remembrance of Allah is the greatest (thing in life) without doubt, and Allah knows the (deeds) that you do" (Qur'an 29:45).

2. "And establish regular prayers at the two ends of the day and at the approaches of the night. For those things that are good, remove those that are evil. In that is remembrance to those who remember (their Lord)" (Qur'an 11:114).

3. "Therefore, be patient with what they say, and celebrate (constantly) the praises of your Lord before the rising of the sun, and before its setting. Yea, celebrate them for part of the hours of the night and at the sides of the day that you may have happiness" (Qur'an 20:130).

4. "So (give) glory to Allah, when you reach eventide and when you rise in the morning—yea, to Him be praise in the heavens and on earth— and in the late afternoon and when the day begins to decline" (Qur'an 30:17-18).

5. "Bear, then, with patience, all that they say, and celebrate the praises of your Lord, before the rising of the sun and before (its) setting. And during part of the night, (also,) celebrate His praises, and (so likewise) after the postures of adoration" (Qur'an 50:39-40).

6. "Now await in patience the command of your Lord: for verily you are in Our eyes: and celebrate the praises of your Lord the while you

stand forth, And for part of the night you also praise Him, - and at the retreat of the stars" (Qur'an 52:48-49).

3.4 BELIEVERS CLEANSE THEMSELVES BEFORE THE PRAYER

The components of *Wudu* or ablution preparatory to prayers are 1) to wash the whole face with water, and 2) both hands and arms to the elbows, with 3) a little rubbing of the head with water, and 4) the washing of the feet to the ankles. In addition, following the practice of the Messenger, it is usual to wash the mouth, the throat, and the nose, before proceeding with the face. An alternative to *Wudu*, is *Tayammum,* or washing with clean sand or earth when water is not available or during illness or travel. To do *Tayammum,* one selects a place of clean earth, or a place where dust gathers. This may be a piece of furniture, or a carpet, or it may be the floor in one's home, or a place in open ground. It should be a clean place, where no impurity has fallen. One strikes twice with one's hands, shakes the dust and wipes one's hands, then shakes the dust and wipes one's face and one's arms after these strikes.

God commands the believers that, "O you who believe!

1. When you prepare for prayer, wash your faces, and your hands (and arms) to the elbows. Rub your heads (with water), and (wash) your feet to the ankles. If you are in a state of ceremonial impurity, bathe your whole body.
2. But if you are ill, or on a journey, or one of you comes from offices of nature, or you have been in contact with women, and you find no water, then take for yourselves clean sand or earth, and rub therewith your faces and hands.

Allah does not wish to place you in a difficulty, but to make you clean, and to complete His favor to you, that you may be grateful" (Qur'an 5:6).

3.5 LEAVE OFF BUSINESS AND HASTEN TO PRAYER ON FRIDAY

The believers, attend the weekly meeting of congregation on Friday in a central mosque of each locality. This is to show unity by sharing in common public worship, preceded by a *Khutbah* or a speech, in which the speaker offers advice or guidance on some aspect of righteous living.

The believers are commanded to, "O you who believe!

1. When the call is proclaimed to prayer on Friday (the Day of Assembly), hasten earnestly to the remembrance of Allah,
2. And leave off business (and traffic). That is best for you if you but knew" (Qur'an 62:9).

3.6 AFTER PRAYERS SEEK GOD'S BOUNTY AND REMEMBER HIM

The believers are encouraged to attend to their daily activities after the prayer is completed. They are to remember and act as God commands during their efforts to seek His bounty. This is the only way to prosper, because prosperity is not only measured by the provisions of life but also the health of the mind and of the spirit,

God commands the believers that,

1. "When the prayer is finished, then you may disperse through the land and seek of the bounty of Allah:
2. And celebrate the praises of Allah often (and without stint), that you may prosper" (Qur'an 62:10).

3.7 PRAY WITH MODERATE VOICE, NOT LOUD NOR A WHISPER

All prayers should be pronounced with earnestness and humility, whether in congregation or private. Such an attitude is not consistent with an over-loud pronunciation of the words, though in public prayers the permissible loudness is naturally higher than in the case of private prayer. The recitation in public prayers should neither be so loud as to attract the hostile notice of those who do not believe nor so low in tone as not to be heard by the whole congregation.

The believers are commanded to, "Say: 'Call upon Allah, or call upon Al Rahman (the Most Compassionate). By whatever name you call upon Him, (it is well), for to Him belong the most beautiful names. Neither speak your prayer aloud, nor speak it in a low tone, but seek a middle course between'" (Qur'an 17:110).

3.8 NEITHER PRAY INTOXICATED NOR IN CEREMONIAL IMPURITY

For prayers it is only right that the believers should collect their whole mind and approach God in a spirit of reverence. So it is not appropriate to approach prayer either in a state of intoxication or in a dazed state of mind on account of drowsiness or some other cause. While praying, the believers should know and understand exactly what they are saying in their prayers.

The believers are commanded as, "O you who believe!

1. Approach not prayers with a mind befogged, until you can understand all that you say,
2. Nor in a state of ceremonial impurity (except when traveling on the road), until after washing your whole body.
3. If you are ill, or on a journey, or one of you comes from offices of nature, or you have been in contact with women, and you find no water, then take for yourselves clean sand or earth, and rub therewith your faces and hands.

For, Allah does blot out sins and forgive again and again" (Qur'an 4:43).

3.9 SHORTENING OF PRAYERS IS PERMISSIBLE DURING TRAVELS

The believers are given permission to shorten their prayers when they are on a journey. The practice of the Messenger shows that the existence of danger is not an essential condition: it is merely mentioned as a possible incident.

The believers are commanded that, "When you travel through the earth, there is no blame on you if you shorten your prayers for fear the unbelievers may attack you: for the unbelievers are unto you open enemies" (Qur'an 4:101).

4

BELIEVERS— SPEND IN GOD'S WAY

There is neither a reason to disbelieve nor a reason to refuse spending in God's Way. Charity or helping others has a great reward. As such, the believers spend their God-given bounties in His Way before the Day comes when no bargaining will avail, nor will friendship or intercession. Compared to people, the material things are of no value. As such, the believers give in charity, those good things that they have honorably earned.

Since helping the needy is an obligation, people should not spoil their charity by boasting or by giving it to be seen by others. That is why secrecy is permitted during deeds of charity, justice, and peace.

4.1 NO REASON IS FOR THE UNBELIEF AND DENYING CHARITY

Whenever power or wealth or influence or any good thing is transferred from one person or group of persons to another, it involves added responsibilities to the persons receiving these advantages. They must be more zealous in real charity and all good works, for that is a part of the evidence which they give of their faith and gratitude. Besides their good deeds, under the general divine law, carry their own reward.

The believers, therefore,

1. "Believe in Allah and His Messenger,
2. And spend (in charity) out of the (substance) whereof He has made you heirs.

For those of you who believe and spend (in charity) — for them is a great reward.

3. What cause have you why you should not believe in Allah? —

And the Messenger invites you to believe in your Lord and has indeed taken your Covenant if you are men of faith.

He is the One Who sends to His servant manifest Signs that He may lead you from the depths of darkness into the light, and verily Allah is to you Most Kind and Merciful.

4. And what cause have you, why you should not spend in the Cause of Allah? —

For to Allah belongs the heritage of the heavens and the earth. Not equal among you are those who spent (freely) and fought before the victory (with those who did so later). Those are higher in rank than those who spent (freely) and fought afterwards. But to all has Allah promised a goodly (reward). And Allah is well-acquainted with all that you do" (Qur'an 57:7-10).

4.2 Charity and helping others have a great reward

All that people spend in God's cause is a beautiful loan to Him. It is excellent in many ways: 1) It shows a beautiful spirit of self-denial; 2) In other loans there may be a doubt as to its safety or any return thereon. Here, God Himself assures its return manifold. If believers' goal is to please God, then they cannot turn away from His Cause.

God asks the believers, "Who is he that will loan to Allah a beautiful loan, which Allah will double unto his credit and multiply many times? It is Allah that gives (you) want or plenty, and to Him shall be your return" (Qur'an 2:245).

"Who is he that will loan to Allah a beautiful loan? For (Allah) will increase it manifold to his credit, and he will have (besides) a liberal reward" (Qur'an 57:11).

4.3 Spend God-given bounties in his way before death

God's bounties to people include mental and spiritual as well as material things. People are to spend or give away a part of their bounties in charity, or employ them in good deeds, but they cannot hoard. Good deeds include everything that advances the welfare of one that is in need, whether a neighbor or a stranger, or that which is spent for the welfare of society or even for the welfare of the person himself. But it must be for real welfare without any admixture of baser motives, such as vain glory, or false indulgence, or encouragement of idleness or playing off one person against another.

God commands the believers, "O you who believe!

1. Spend out of (the bounties) We have provided for you, before the Day comes when no bargaining (will avail), nor friendship nor intercession.
2. Those who reject Faith (by not spending) they are the wrong-doers.

Allah! There is no god but He, the Living, the Self-subsisting, Eternal. No slumber can seize Him nor sleep. His are all things in the heavens and on earth. Who is there that can intercede in His presence except as He permits? ..."
(Qur'an 2:254-255).

4.4 COMPARED TO PEOPLE, MATERIAL THINGS ARE OF NO VALUE

The test of charity is: do you give something that you value greatly, something that you love? If you give your life in a Cause, that is the greatest gift one can give. If you give yourself, that is, your personal efforts, your talents, your skill, your knowledge, that comes next in degree. If you give your earning, your property, your possessions, that is also a great gift. God loves that there should be no selfish motive behind an act of charity, and there is no act of charity, however small, but it is well within His knowledge.

God tells people that, "By no means shall you attain righteousness unless you give (freely) of that which you love, and whatever you give, of a truth, Allah knows it well" (Qur'an 3:92).

4.5 CHARITY IS FROM HONEST EARNINGS AND GOOD THINGS

According to an often quoted saying, 'Charity covers a multitude of sins.' Such a statement is strongly disapproved in Islam. Charity has value only if 1) something good and valuable is given, 2) which has been honorably earned or acquired, or 3) which is produced in nature. Some skills or talents are God-given: and it is the highest kind of charity to teach them or share their products. Contrarily, some professions or services may be tainted, if these tend to do moral harm. Anything from these professions cannot be offered as charity.

God commands the believers, "O you who believe!

1. Give of the good things that you have (honorably) earned, and of the fruits of the earth that We have produced for you;
2. 2. And do not even aim at getting anything that is bad, in order that out of it you may give away something, when you yourselves would not receive it except with closed eyes.

And know that Allah is free of all wants and worthy of all praise" (Qur'an 2:267).

4.6 CHARITY IS AN OBLIGATION SO SPOIL IT NOT BY BOASTING

A very high standard is set for charity. 1) It must be in God's Way. 2) It must expect no reward in this world. 3) It must not be followed by reminders to the act of charity. 4) No annoyance or harm be caused to the recipient by boasting about it. Such behavior is near to those who reject faith.

God commands the believers, "O you who believe!

Cancel not your charity by reminders of your generosity or by injury— like those who spend their substance to be seen of men, but believe neither in Allah nor in the Last Day. They are in parable like a hard, barren rock on which is a little soil. On it falls heavy rain that leaves it (just) a bare stone. They will be able to do nothing with aught (anything) they have earned. And Allah guides not those who reject faith" (Qur'an 2:264).

4.7 SECRECY IS PERMITTED IN CHARITY, JUSTICE AND PEACE

Usually secrecy is for evil ends, or for questionable motives. The person seeking secrecy is ashamed of himself and knows that if his acts or motives became known, he will make himself odious. Islam therefore disapproves of secrecy and enjoins openness in all consultations and doings. But there are three things or situations where secrecy is permissible or even recommended. These three things are the acts of charity, of justice and of peace making.

God tells the believers that, "In most of their secret talks there is no good, but if one exhorts to a deed of charity or justice or conciliation between men, (secrecy is permissible). To him who does this, seeking the good pleasure of Allah, We shall soon give a reward of the highest (value)" (Qur'an 4:114).

5
BELIEVERS— FAST AND PERFORM HAJJ

Fasting is prescribed for the believers as it was prescribed for those in the past so that they may learn self-restraint. The believers are also commanded to perform Hajj if they can afford it. During Hajj, there should be no obscenity, wickedness, or wrangling.

5.1 FASTING IS PRESCRIBED TO TEACH PEOPLE SELF-RESTRAINT

The Muslim fast is not meant for self-torture. Although it is stricter than other fasts, it also provides alleviations for special circumstances. If it were merely a temporary abstention from food and drink, it would be curative to many people, who habitually eat and drink to excess. The instincts for food, drink, and sex are strong in animal nature, and temporary restraining from all these enables people's attention to be directed to their duties associated with the human mission of being God's Trustee on earth.

God tells the believers that, "O you who believe!

Fasting is prescribed for you as it was prescribed for those before you, that you may (learn) self-restraint" (Qur'an 2:183).

5.2 COMPLETE THE *HAJJ* AND *'UMRA* ONCE IN YOUR LIFETIME

The *Hajj* is the complete pilgrimage, of which the major rites are performed during the first twelve or thirteen days of the month of *Dhu al Hijjih*. The *Umra* is a less formal pilgrimage at any time of the year. In either case, the intending pilgrim commences by putting on a garment of two pieces- unsown cloth when a person is at some distance yet from *Makkah*. The putting on of the pilgrim garb (*ihram*) is symbolical of renouncing the vanities of the world. Once a person is wearing *ihram*, until the end of the pilgrimage, one must not wear any other clothes, or ornaments, anoint one's hair, use perfume, hunt, or do other prohibited acts. The completion of the pilgrimage is symbolized by the shaving of the head for men and the cutting off of a few locks of hair of the women, and then taking off the *ihram* and resuming normal way of being dressed.

God commands the believers that, "And complete the *Hajj* or *'Umra* in the service of Allah. But if you are prevented (from completing it), send an offering for sacrifice, such as you may find, and do not shave your heads until the offering reaches the place of sacrifice. And if any of you is ill or has an ailment in his scalp (necessitating shaving), (he should) in compensation either fast, or feed the poor, or offer sacrifice; and when you are in peaceful conditions (again), if any one wishes to continue the 'Umra on to the Hajj, he must make an offering, such as he can afford, but if he cannot afford it, he should fast three days during the Hajj and seven days on his return, making ten days in all. This is for those whose household is not in (the precincts of) the Sacred Mosque. And fear Allah, and know that Allah is strict in punishment" (Qur'an 2:196).

5.3 No obscenity, wickedness or wrangling during Hajj

The right conduct and honest provisions should cover all of the daily activities of the believers. Legitimate trade is allowed, in the interest of both the honest trader and customer, who can thus meet his own expenses, and the needs of pilgrims. However, there should be no abnormal profit taking. Good honest trade is a service to the community and therefore a form of serving or worshipping God.

God tells the believers that, "For Hajj are the months well known. If any one undertakes that duty therein, let there be no obscenity, nor wickedness, nor wrangling in the Hajj. And whatever good you do, (be sure) Allah knows it. And take a provision (with you) for the journey, but the best of provisions is right conduct. So fear Me, O you that are wise" (Qur'an 2.197).

"It is no crime in you if you seek of the bounty of your Lord (during pilgrimage). Then when you pour down from (Mount) Arafat, celebrate the praises of Allah at the sacred monument, and celebrate His praises as He has directed you, even though before this you went astray. Then pass on at a quick pace from the place whence it is usual for the multitude so to do, and ask for Allah's forgiveness. For Allah is Oft-Forgiving, Most Merciful" (Qur'an 2.198-199).

6
Believers— Eat the Lawful and Good

Islam encourages everyone to work hard to earn one's livelihood. In Islam, work is equated with worship. Anas bin Malik narrated: "We were with the Prophet (on a journey), and the only shade one could have was the shade made by one's own garment. Those who fasted did not do any work, and those who did not fast (being exempt from fasting because of the journey) served the camels, brought water to them, and treated the sick and wounded. So the Prophet[PBUH] said, 'Today, those who were not fasting took all the reward'" (Sahih Bukhari 4.52.140). Anas bin Malik also narrated: "The Messenger^{PBUH} said, 'There is none among the Muslims who plants a tree or sows a seed and then a bird or a person or an animal eats from it, but it is regarded as a charitable gift from him'" (Sahih Bukhari 3.39.513).

Striving hard to earn one's livelihood is a form of God's worship. An honest earning is called 'the bounty of your Lord' in the Qur'an. Ibn 'Abbas narrated: "Ukaz, Majanna, and Dhul-Majaz were marketplaces in the pre-Islamic period of ignorance. When Islam came, Muslims felt that marketing there might be a sin. So, the divine inspiration came: 'It is no crime in you if you seek of the bounty of your Lord' (Qur'an 2:198)" (Sahih Bukhari 2.26.822).

6.1 Eat of lawful and good, avoid evil or the shameful
All well regulated societies lay down reasonable limitations on what one can or cannot consume. These become enforceable on all loyal members of any given society, and show what is lawful in that society. Any food which is pure, clean, wholesome, nourishing, and pleasing to taste is good.

Concerning an honest living, God commands: "O people! Eat of what is on earth, lawful and good, and do not follow the footsteps of Satan (to earn your living), for he is to you an avowed enemy. For he commands you what is evil and shameful and that you should say of Allah that of which you have no knowledge" (Qur'an 2:168-169).

6.2 Eat the good things that God has provided for you
Foods which cause disgust to any refined person are forbidden in Islam. For example, carrion or meat of a dead animal and blood as articles of food fall into such category. So would swine's flesh as the swine lives on rubbish. Even if the swine are fed artificially on clean food, the prohibition remains: 1) that they are filthy animals in other respects and the flesh of filthy animals taken as food affects the eater; 2) that swine's flesh has more fat than muscle building material; and 3) that it is more liable to disease than other kind of meats. As to the food dedicated to idols or false gods, it is clearly not right for the servants of One God to take it.

God commands the believers, "O you who believe!

1. Eat of the good things that We have provided for you, and be grateful to Allah if it is Him you worship.
2. He has only forbidden you dead meat, and blood, and the flesh of swine, and that on which any other name has been invoked besides that of Allah.

But if one is forced by necessity, without willful disobedience, nor transgressing due limits, then he is guiltless. For Allah is Oft-Forgiving, Most Merciful" (Qur'an 2:172-173).

6.3 ENJOY THE LAWFUL AND GOOD BUT AVOID THE UNLAWFUL

Not following what God commands is like rejecting faith. This has been elaborated by giving three examples of the lawful: 1) Good and lawfully acquired foods including which is obtained by hunting, 2) the food of the People of the Book and 3) lawfully married good women of the People of the Book—

God tells the Messenger that, "They ask you what is lawful to them (as food). Say—

1. 'Lawful unto you are (all) things good and pure and what you have taught your trained hunting animals (to catch) in the manner directed to you by Allah. Eat what they catch for you, but pronounce the name of Allah over it, and fear Allah, for Allah is swift in taking account.
2. This day are (all) things good and pure made lawful unto you. The food of the People of the Book is lawful unto you, and yours is lawful unto them.
3. (Lawful unto you in marriage) are (not only) chaste women who are believers, but chaste women among the People of the Book revealed before your time—when you give them their due dowers, and desire chastity, not lewdness, nor secret intrigues.

If any one rejects faith (and not following what Allah commands is like rejecting faith), fruitless is his work, and in the Hereafter he will be in the ranks of those who have lost" (Qur'an 5:4-5).

6.4 DRINKING AND GAMBLING ARE SINFUL AND FORBIDDEN

Getting something too easily or getting a profit without working, is the basic principle why gambling is forbidden in Islam. The believers obey the commands of God which are always reasonable, instead of following superstitions, which are irrational, or seeking undue stimulation in intoxicants or undue advantage in gambling. To some there may be temporary excitement or pleasure in these, but that is not the way either of prosperity or of piety.

God tells the Messenger that,

1. "They ask you concerning wine and gambling. Say: 'In them is great sin, and some benefit, for men; but the sin is greater than the benefit'. ..." (Qur'an 2:219).
2. "O you who believe! Intoxicants and gambling, (dedication of) stones, and (divination by) arrows, are an abomination, - of Satan's handwork: eschew such (abomination), that you may prosper.

Satan's plan is (but) to excite enmity and hatred between you, with intoxicants and gambling, and hinder you from the remembrance of Allah, and from prayer: will you not then abstain?" (Qur'an 5:90-91).

6.5 DISHONEST EARNINGS ARE PROHIBITED TO THE BELIEVERS

Food that has been earned by concealing the truth, cheating, lying, or fraud has been forbidden to the believers. So is the illegal use of another's property and bribing judges for this purpose is forbidden.

God commands the believers that:

1. "Those who conceal Allah's revelations in the Book, and purchase for them a miserable profit— they swallow into themselves nothing but fire; ..."
2. "And do not eat up your property among yourselves for vanities, nor use it as bait for the judges, with the intent that you may eat up wrongfully and knowingly a little of (other) people's property" (Qur'an 2:174, 188).

7

BELIEVERS— HONOR THEIR COMMITMENTS

God commands the believers to spend that which is beyond their needs, and the best thing for someone to do is doing good for orphans and the needy. Honoring oaths is mandated in Islam, and oaths should not be taken against doing good in the future. Usury by which people profit by exploiting the needy is forbidden in Islam. Contrarily giving away excess wealth in charity carries a great reward.

7.1 CONSIDER SPENDING WHAT IS IN EXCESS OF YOUR NEED

Hoarding wealth or any material thing is of no use either to ourselves, or to any one else. Wealth should be spent to satisfy our personal needs. The remaining wealth must be spent in good works or in charity.

About charity, God tells the Messenger that, "… They ask you how much they are to spend (in charity). Say: 'What is beyond your needs.' Thus does Allah make clear to you His Signs in order that you may consider (their bearing) on this life and the Hereafter. …" (Qur'an 2:219-220).

7.2 GOD KNOWS INTENTIONS SO DO THE BEST FOR ORPHANS

For orphans the best rule is to keep their property, household, and accounts separate, lest there should be a temptation to obtain a personal advantage through mixing an orphan's property with their own property. In managing an orphan's affairs, the test is: what is the best in the orphan's affairs? If the guardian does fall into temptation, even if the legal system does not detect it, he is sinning in God's sight and that should keep him straight.

Concerning Orphans, God tells their Guardians as, "… They ask you concerning orphans. Say: 'The best thing to do is what is for their good. If you mix their affairs with yours, they are your brethren, but Allah knows the man who means mischief from the man who means good. And if Allah had wished, He could have put you into difficulties. He is indeed Exalted in Power, Wise" (Qur'an 2:220).

7.3 HONOR NOT YOUR OATHS MADE AGAINST DOING GOOD

Islam disapproves of thoughtless oaths, while insists that proper intentional oaths should be scrupulously observed. Thoughtless oaths, if there is no intention behind them, can be expiated by an act of charity. Again the believers are not to make an oath in the name of God as an excuse for not doing the right thing, especially when it becomes clear to them or for refraining from doing something which will bring people together. God knows people's inmost hearts, and their conduct. What He demands from them is neither obstinacy nor quibbling.

God commands the believers that, "And make not Allah's (name) an excuse in your oaths against doing good, or acting rightly, or making peace between persons, for Allah is One Who hears and knows all things. Allah will not call you to account for thoughtlessness in your oaths, but for the intention in your hearts; and He is Oft-Forgiving, Most Forbearing" (Qur'an 2:224-225).

7.4 TRADE IS NOT USURY; PROFIT NOT BY EXPLOITING NEEDY

Usury is condemned and prohibited in the strongest possible terms in Islam. According to Islamic teachings any excess on capital is interest (*riba*). No distinction is accepted insofar as prohibition is concerned, between reasonable and exorbitant rates of interest, and thus what came to be regarded as the difference between usury and interest.

Legitimate trade and industry increases the prosperity and stability of communities, a dependence on usury merely encourages a race of idlers, cruel blood-suckers, and worthless fellows who do not know their own good and therefore are akin to a mad person.

God tells people that, "Those who devour usury will not stand except as stands one whom the Evil One by his touch has driven to madness. That is because they say: 'Trade is like usury,' but Allah has permitted trade and forbidden usury. Those who, after receiving direction from their Lord, desist shall be pardoned for the past; their case is for Allah (to judge). But those who repeat (the offence) are companions of the Fire: They will abide therein (forever)" (Qur'an 2:275).

7.5 Give up usury; charity carries a greater reward

Whereas usury is deprived of all blessing, giving away excess wealth in charity carries a great reward in the form of an increase in the prosperity and stability of communities. The contrast between charity and unlawful grasping of wealth is evident. For the liberation of debtors who are unjustly dealt with and oppressed, the creditors are asked: 1) to give up claims arising out on account of usury, and 2) to give time for the payment of capital if needed or 3) to write off the debt altogether as an act of charity.

God tells the believers that, "Allah will deprive usury of all blessing but will give increase for deeds of charity, for He loves not creatures ungrateful and wicked.

1. Those who believe, and do deeds of righteousness, and establish regular prayers and regular charity will have their reward with their Lord. On them shall be no fear, nor shall they grieve.

O you who believe!

2. Fear Allah, and give up what remains of your demand for usury if you are indeed believers" (Qur'an 2:276-278).

Chapter 8

Believers—Submit to God's Will
(Believers Abide By What God Desires)

The objective of the believers in life is the implementation of the Way of Islam. A strong moral character, honest efforts, patience and dedication are required to overcome the difficulties that can befall one in attempting to achieve this objective. The believers are neither afraid of difficulties nor of death, as nothing happens without God's Will. Being aware of their mission of righteousness for humanity, the believers hold together in unity and discipline. They keep on improving their character and behavior, enforce justice, propagate virtue, and discourage vice. Since God loves those who do good deeds, the believers are rewarded in this life and will be bestowed with an even greater reward in the next life.

1
BELIEVERS— FOLLOW THE GUIDANCE

All people are required to submit to the will of their Creator. God asks, "Do they seek for other than the religion of Allah while all creatures in the heavens and on earth have, willing or unwilling, bowed to His will, and to Him shall they all be brought back" (Qur'an 3:83). Since the unbelievers like to misguide people and desire that all of us should be corrupted by following our selfish desires, God advises the believers to follow His commands and not befriend the unbelievers in such a way as to start following their selfish desires and forgetting their commitment to follow what God commands. Be sure that arrogant people who love to be praised for what they have not done will not escape the consequences of their arrogance.

1.1 ISLAM IS THE ORIGIN OF ALL DIVINE RELIGIONS SINCE ADAM

Divine truth is manifest, and all people that are good, true, sane and normal accept it with joy. For God's love is inescapable as is nature's environment, which a person cannot ignore. All of nature adores God, and Islam asks for nothing peculiar or sectarian; it asks that people should follow their true nature and make their will conformable to the Divine Will as seen in nature, history, and revelation. Its message is universal.

God commands the believers to, "Say: 'We believe in Allah and in what has been revealed to us and what was revealed to Abraham, Isma'il, Isaac, Jacob, and the tribes, and in (the books) given to Moses, Jesus, and the prophets from their Lord. We make no distinction between one and another among them, and to Allah do we bow our will (in Islam)" (Qur'an 3:84).

1.2 NONE IS BURDENED BEYOND WHAT ONE CAN BEAR OR DO

When the believers are sincere in their faith and conduct, they realize how far from perfection they are, and then they humbly pray to God for the forgiveness of their sins. They feel that God imposes no burden on someone which one cannot bear, and with this realization in their hearts and in the confession of their lips, they go to Him and ask for His help and guidance. God assures the believers that He will accept from them their righteous deeds which they have honestly performed according to their ability.

God assures the believers that, "On no soul does Allah place a burden greater than it can bear. It gets every good that it earns, and it suffers every ill that it earns..." (Qur'an 2:286).

1.3 BELIEVERS SUBMIT THEIR WILL TO GOD WITH PATIENCE

Some essential attributes of the believers are: 1) their humility before God makes them receptive, and prepares them to listen and then follow what God commands; 2) their fear of God, which is akin to His love, touches their heart and penetrates their soul; 3) they are not afraid of anything in life, they take their trials patiently, and they progress in their righteousness with constancy; 4) their prayer turn into a real communion with God, which provides them strength and confidence; and 5) their gratitude to God is shown by their acts of charity to their fellow-creatures.

God tells the believers that, "To every people did We appoint rites (of sacrifice) that they might celebrate the name of Allah over the sustenance He gave them from animals (fit for food). But your God is One God: submit then your wills to Him (in Islam); and

1. You give the good news to those who humble themselves—
2. To those whose hearts when Allah is mentioned are filled with fear,
3. Who show patient perseverance over their afflictions,
4. (Who) keep up regular prayer, and
5. (Who) spend (in charity) out of what We have bestowed upon them" (Qur'an 22:34-35).

About the purpose of animal sacrifice, God tells that, "It is not their meat nor their blood, that reaches Allah: it is your piety that reaches Him: He has thus made them subject to you, that you may glorify Allah for His Guidance to you and proclaim the good news to all who do right" (Qur'an 22:37). Besides, sharing meat with their fellow-men, animal sacrifice is a symbol of thanksgiving to God.

1.4 UNBELIEVERS DESIRE TO RUIN - BE NOT THEIR INTIMATE

The members of a believing community, at any time or age, is a mixture of sincere people, hypocrites and the wavers. Therefore it is important that people should know the criterion of sincerity in Islam. There are people, Muslim and non-Muslim, who have friendships with the enemies of Islam: they do not hesitate for the sake of their own selfish interests to be treacherous to their own religion and people. They spread doubt and suspicions against religion and prevent people from adopting it. That is why believers should not, under any circumstances and for any motive, have relations of love and friendship with the unbelievers and hypocrites who are actively hostile to Islam.

God commands the believers that, "O you who believe! Take not into your intimacy those outside your ranks. They will not fail to corrupt you. They only desire your ruin. Rank hatred has already appeared from their mouths. What their hearts conceal is far worse. We have made plain to you the Signs if you have wisdom" (Qur'an 3:118).

1.5 PENALTY TO THOSE WHO EXULT OR TAKE UNDUE CREDIT
Worldly smart people may cause mischief and misery to others, and enjoy any glory it may bring them. They may trample down the Truth and set up false standards of worship but take credit for virtues they do not possess and apparent successes that come in spite of their deceptions.

God has warned the believers to be away from such people and, "Think not that those who exult in what they have brought about, and love to be praised for what they have not done, - think not that they can escape the penalty. For them is a penalty grievous indeed" (Qur'an 3:188).

2
BELIEVERS— NEVER PERSIST IN WRONG

To be forgiven people have to repent. Every incident of acknowledgment, regret, and efforts not to repeat mistakes again impact human character. That is why the repentance improves one's behavior and transforms them into hard-working and honest individuals who when joined together form a just community. By hard work and good deeds they overcome their weaknesses and earn God's forgiveness. Honest efforts also increase one's productive efficiency, provide people with honorable earnings, and make a community prosperous. God commanded the Messenger to, "Say, O people! I am only a plain Warner to you. Then (as for) those who believe and do good, they shall have forgiveness and an honorable sustenance" (Qur'an 22:49-50).

2.1 BELIEVERS REGRET THEIR SINS, REPENT AND DO GOOD
The wise people regret their misdeeds, repent, and do good deeds as God commands. They ask for His forgiveness and mend their ways immediately afterwards.

God tells people about the believers as,

1. "Except for those that repent (even) after that,

2.   And make amends; for verily Allah is Oft-Forgiving, Most Merciful.

But those who reject Faith after they accepted it, and then go on adding to their defiance of Faith— never will their repentance be accepted, for they are those who have gone astray" (Qur'an 3:89-90).

2.2 BELIEVERS PERSIST NOT BUT REPENT- ASK FORGIVENESS

The believers never persist in the wrong they have done but repent and God forgives those who repent. With repentance, the believers keep on improving their character and behavior. That is why believers are of the best behavior and strive for the betterment of the society with their good deeds.

Again, God tells people about the believers as,

1.   "And those who, having done something to be ashamed of, or wronged their own souls, earnestly bring Allah to mind and ask for forgiveness for their sins—and who can forgive sins except Allah?—and
2.   Are never obstinate in persisting knowingly in (the wrong) they have done" (Qur'an 3:135).

2.3 BELIEVERS ARE THE BEST IN CONDUCT AND STRIVE UNITED

The believers fear God and inculcate human values in their self and in society. The fear is of many kinds: 1) the abject fear of the coward; 2) the fear of an ignorant person concerning an unknown danger; 3) the fear of a person who wishes to avoid harm to himself and his dear ones; and 4) the fear of doing something which is not pleasing to God. The believers cultivate the fear of God. The fear of unknown dangers and the fear of failures to save from harm may be necessary; but these are not the fear of God. The fear of a coward is a feeling which indicates a lack of faith or trust in God. The remedy of which is 'to hold fast by their faith, all together'— be not divided, and remember God with gratitude.

God commands the believers, "O you who believe!

1.   Fear Allah as He should be feared, and
2.   Die not except in a state of Islam.

3. And hold fast, all together, by the rope that Allah (stretches out for you), and be not divided among yourselves; and

4. Remember with gratitude Allah's favor on you;

For you were enemies, and He joined your hearts in love, so that by His Grace, you became brethren. And you were on the brink of the Pit of Fire, and He saved you from it. Thus does Allah make His Signs clear to you that you may be guided" (Qur'an 3:102-103).

3
BELIEVERS—ENJOIN GOOD AND FORBID EVIL

The believers and their leaders are always honest and trustworthy. They are charitable, they are never angry, and they forgive people. They enjoin the doing of good and forbid what is the evil. They acknowledge that God has created everything for a purpose. They are conscious about the things around them and keep trying to harness the natural resources God has created for humanity.

3.1 BELIEVERS AND THEIR LEADERS ARE EVER TRUSTWORTHY

The Messenger and the believers are never false to their trust. The general principles declared here are of eternal value: 1) that the messenger of God never acts from unworthy motives; 2) those who act from such motives are at the lowest edge of humanity; 3) neither a messenger of God nor the believers are to be judged by the same standard as that of a greedy person; 4) people are of various grades in God's eyes, and they should try to understand and appreciate such grades. A dishonest person is neither fit to be a leader nor a believer.

God tells people that, "No prophet could (ever) be false to his trust. If any person is so false, he shall on the Day of Judgment restore what he misappropriated; then every soul shall receive its due, whatever it earned— and none shall be dealt with unjustly" (Qur'an 3:161).

3.2 GIVE CHARITY, RESTRAIN ANGER, AND FORGIVE PEOPLE

Seven attributes of the believers are highlighted here. These attributes are: 1) that they do not devour usury but fear God; 2) they fear the fire that is prepared for the unbelievers; 3) they obey their messenger and what God commands; 4) they seek forgiveness and Paradise from their Lord; 5) they spend freely in charity; 6) they control their anger; and 7) they forgive all people.

God commands the believers that, "O you who believe!

1. Devour not usury, doubled and multiplied, but fear Allah that you may (really) prosper.
2. Fear the fire that is prepared for those who reject Faith,
3. And obey Allah and the Messenger that you may obtain mercy.
4. Be quick in the race for forgiveness from your Lord and for a Garden whose width is that (of the whole) of the heavens and of the earth, prepared for the righteous—
5. Those who spend (freely), whether in prosperity, or in adversity,
6. Who restrain anger, and
7. Pardon (all) men—for Allah loves those who do good" (Qur'an 3:130-134).

3.3 BELIEVERS STRIVE TO ENJOIN GOOD AND FORBID EVIL

An Islamic society is happy, untroubled by conflicts, strong, united and prosperous. This is so, because it invites all people to— all that is good, enjoins the right; and forbids the wrong.

God commands the believers that, "Let there arise out of you a band of people inviting to all that is good, enjoining what is right, and forbidding what is wrong; they are the ones to attain felicity" (Qur'an 3:104).

3.4 BELIEVERS REMEMBER AND THINK OF GOD'S CREATION

The believers never forget God and His commands under any circumstance— personal, social, economic, or other. Their aim is to earn their salvation without which their life would be that of a miserable, contemptible creature in the midst of the beauties and wonders of Nature.

God describes the believers as, "Men who celebrate the praises of Allah, standing, sitting, and lying down on their sides, and contemplate the (wonders of) creation in the heavens and the earth, (with the thought): 'Our Lord! Not for nothing have You created this! Glory to You! Give us salvation from the penalty of the Fire'" (Qur'an 3:191).

4
BELIEVERS—PERSEVERE WITH PATIENCE

People are surely being tried and tested in their lives on earth. The believers overlook other people's faults, try to overcome their own weaknesses, and trust God. That is why they neither lose heart nor despair. They are patient who persevere and strengthen each other in their struggle through life.

4.1 PEOPLE ARE SURELY TRIED AND TESTED IN THEIR LIVES
How do believers succeed in life? They know that they will be tried not only in wealth and possessions but also in their personal talents, knowledge, opportunities, and the opposites—in fact everything that happens to them and makes up their personality is a means for their testing. So is their faith; they will have to put up with many insults from those who do not share it. The believers persevere patiently and guard against evil to succeed in their trials.

The believers are told that, "You shall certainly be tried and tested in your possessions and in your personal selves, and you shall certainly hear much that will grieve you from those who received the Book before you and from those who worship many gods. But if you persevere patiently and guard against evil— then that will be a determining factor in all affairs" (Qur'an 3:186).

4.2 BELIEVERS IGNORE PEOPLE'S FAULTS AND TRUST GOD
Addressing the Messenger, God advised him and the believers about the best social behavior which one could not acquire without God's Mercy. Such behavior embodies: 1) overlooking other's faults and 2) praying for their forgiveness; 3) mutual consultation in community affairs; and 4) taking action for community welfare while putting one's trust in God.

God tells the Messenger that, "It is part of the Mercy of Allah that you do deal gently with them; were you severe or harsh-hearted, they would have broken away from about you:

1. So pass over (their faults),
2. And ask for (Allah's) forgiveness for them;
3. And consult them in affairs (of moment).
4. Then, when you have taken a decision, put your trust in Allah. Allah loves those who put their trust (in Him)" (Qur'an 3:159).

4.3 BELIEVERS DO NOT LOSE HEART NOR DO THEY DESPAIR

History tells us the stories of many civilizations that disappeared due to injustice in their societies. Only the societies built on truth and justice last and prosper in the end. If there are setbacks, the believers must not be discouraged, lose heart or give up the struggle. Faith means hope, activity, and striving steadfastly on to the goal of establishing justice in society.

God tells the believers that, "Many were the Ways of Life that have passed away before you. Travel through the earth, and see what was the end of those who rejected Truth. Here is a plain statement to men, a guidance and, instruction to those who fear Allah! So lose not heart, nor fall into despair, for you must gain mastery if you are true in Faith" (Qur'an 3:137-139).

4.4 BE PATIENT, PERSEVERE AND STRENGTHEN ONE ANOTHER

Patience is one of the most important attributes of a believer without which it is rather impossible for someone to win in life. Broadly, it also means perseverance, constancy, self-restraint, and refusing to be cowed down. These virtues are to be exercised by the believers themselves, and they are to set an example, so that others may vie with them in the society. In this way the believers strengthen each other and bind their mutual relations closer, in their common service to God for peace and prosperity in this world and success in the Hereafter.

God commands the believers as, "O you who believe!

1. Persevere in patience and constancy; vie in such perseverance;
2. Strengthen each other;
3. And fear Allah that you may prosper" (Qur'an 3:200).

Chapter 9

Believers—Serve God and Humanity
(Believers Worship God and Promote Humanity)

The believers spend their lives fulfilling their obligations towards God and His people. The importance of obligations towards people is stressed in *Surah Al-Nisa*. Besides establishing prayer, fasting, and paying *Zakat* (obligatory charity), Muslims are obligated to take an active part in the struggle to establish justice for all in every circumstance. Muslims are also obligated to fight in self-defense and against injustice, discrimination and oppression. For a believer who is interested in his salvation, believing in God, praying five times a day, fasting in the month of Ramadan, paying *Zakat*, and performing Hajj once in a lifetime may not be enough. He has to take part actively in the establishment of social justice, and he has to fulfill all of his moral, social, and financial obligations towards his relatives, orphans, the poor, and other people. The believers should always remember that God may forgive all sins that relate to their duties towards Him, but He may not forgive anything that is due to another person until that person is ready to forgive it. Hence, a balance between these duties must be restored before one can truly claim to lead an Islamic life.

1
BELIEVERS—THEIR MISSION AND DUTIES

An important part of the human mission is to serve God and one's family members. The believers worship God and are kind to their parents. Although the believers love their parents, they do not obey them in unbelief. To complete their mission, the believers obey God, the Messenger, and their honest leaders. They discharge their obligations honestly and treat each other with justice and fairness.

1.1 HUMAN MISSION IS TO SERVE GOD AND FAMILY MEMBERS

It is part of human duty to serve God by not associating others with Him, by worshiping Him alone, and by implementing His law. Serving one's family is to deal with one's relatives and those who come in contact with them with justice and generosity and be helpful to them without any discrimination.

In *Surah Al-Nisa,* people are told:

1. "Serve Allah, and join not any partners with Him.
2. And do good— to parents, kinsfolk, orphans, those in need, neighbors who are near, neighbors who are strangers, the companion by your side, the wayfarer (you meet), and what your right hands possess: For Allah loves not the arrogant, the vainglorious—
3. (Nor) those who are miserly or enjoin miserliness on others, or hide the bounties that Allah has bestowed on them, for We have prepared for those who resist Faith a punishment that steeps them in contempt; -
4. Nor those who spend of their substance to be seen of men but have no faith in Allah and the Last Day.

If any take the Satan for their intimate, what a dreadful intimate he is!" (Qur'an 4:36-38).

1.2 WORSHIP NONE BUT GOD AND BE KIND TO YOUR PARENTS

It was narrated by Ibn Mas'ud that a man asked the Prophet what are the best deeds. The Prophet[PBUH] said: (1) to perform the prayers at their stated fixed times, (2) To be good and dutiful to one's own parents. (3) And to participate in Jihad in Allah's Cause (Sahih Bukhari: 9.93.625)." This *hadith* points to three major areas of human activity, which are— developing a good relation with the Creator, developing good relation among people and defending human rights and human values.

God has specifically asked the believers to honor their parents. Not only respect but cherishing kindness and humility to parents is also commanded. This command is bracketed with the command to worship the One True God: Parental love is a type of divine love: nothing that one does can ever really compensate for that which one has received. One's spiritual advancement is tested by this—A person who is rude or unkind to those who unselfishly brought him/her up cannot expect God's forgiveness.

God tells the believers that, "Your Lord has decreed that

1.   You worship none but Him,
2.   And that you be kind to parents. Whether one or both of them attain old age in your life, say not to them a word of contempt, nor repel them, but address them in terms of honor. And, out of kindness, lower to them the wing of humility, and say: 'My Lord! Bestow on them Your Mercy even as they cherished me in childhood.'

Your Lord knows best what is in your hearts. If you do deeds of righteousness, verily He is Most Forgiving to those who turn to Him again and again (in true penitence)" (Qur'an 17:23-25).

1.3 Be kind to parents but obey them not in unbelief

No matter what, the believers cannot disobey God, even if the command is from their parents, leaders or employers. Where duty to man conflicts with the duty to God, there is something wrong, and the believers should obey God rather than man. But even in this instance, it does not mean that they should be arrogant or insolent. To parents and those in authority, believers must be kind, considerate, and courteous even when they are commanded things which they should not do and then disobedience becomes their highest duty. Worship of things other than God is the worship of wrong things— things which are alien to one's true knowledge, and things that go against one's own nature as created by God.

God tells the believers that,

1.   "And We (Allah) have enjoined on man (to be good) to his parents. In travail upon travail did his mother bear him, and in years twain was his weaning.
2.   (hear the command), 'Show gratitude to Me and to your parents'. To Me is (your final) goal.

But if they strive to make you join in worship with Me things of which you have no knowledge, obey them not;

3.   Yet bear them company in this life with justice (and consideration),

4. And follow the way of those who turn to me (in love).

In the end, the return of you all is to Me, and I will tell you the truth (and meaning) of all that you did" (Qur'an 31:14 15).

1.4 BE KIND TO PARENTS AND THANK GOD FOR HIS MERCY

God commands the believers to be kind, considerate, and courteous to their parents. They should pray for them and be grateful to God for His favor that He has bestowed upon them and on their parents. They also pray for the ability to do such deeds that He may approve of. The spiritual advancement of believers is also tested by their treatment of parents—A person who is unkind to their parents, cannot expect God's forgiveness and His mercy.

God tells the believers that,

1. "We have enjoined on man kindness to his parents:

In pain did his mother bear him, and in pain did she give him birth. The carrying of the (child) to his weaning is (a period of) thirty months. At length, when he reaches the age of full strength and attains forty years,

2. He says, 'O my Lord! Grant me that I may be grateful for Your favor that You has bestowed upon me and upon both my parents and that I may work righteousness such as You may approve and be gracious to me in my issue. Truly have I turned to You, and truly do I bow (to You) in Islam.'

Such are they from whom We shall accept the best of their deeds and pass by their ill deeds. (They shall be) among the companions of the Garden, a promise of truth that was made to them (in this life)" (Qur'an 46:15-16).

1.5 OBEY GOD, THE MESSENGER AND THE HONEST LEADERS

Since Islam makes no distinction between sacred or secular affairs, it expects governments to be imbued with righteousness. Therefore, Islam expects Muslims to respect the authority of such governments for otherwise there cannot be any order or discipline in society.

God commands the believers as, "O you who believe!

1. Obey Allah, and obey the Messenger, and those charged with authority among you.
2. If you differ in anything among yourselves, refer it to Allah and His Messenger, if you do believe in Allah and the Last Day: That is best and most suitable for final determination" (Qur'an 4:59).

1.6 DISCHARGE YOUR OBLIGATIONS HONESTLY WITH JUSTICE

The aim of divine guidance is to serve human interest, to help people build a happy life in a community characterized by trust and justice. The believers must be trustworthy and justice should be achieved at all levels, within the family, the local community, the social hierarchy, and the political system. According to a sacred *hadith* God says: "My servants, I have forbidden Myself injustice and have made injustice forbidden among you. Therefore, do not act unjustly to one another" (Sahih Muslim 32.6246).

God commands the believers that,

1. "Allah does command you to render back your trusts to those to whom they are due,
2. And when you judge between man and man, that you judge with justice.

Verily, how excellent is the teaching that He gives you! For Allah is He Who hears and sees all things" (Qur'an 4:58).

2
BELIEVERS —ADMIT MISTAKES AND REFORM

The believers have entered into a contract with God to live their lives according to the guidelines described in the Qur'an. Implementation of all what God commands is required, "O you who believe! 'Enter into Islam wholeheartedly'; and follow not the footsteps of the Satan; for he is to you an avowed enemy" (Qur'an 2:208).

The believers fulfill all obligations to their Lord and His Creation. They believe in Him, His angels, His books, His prophets, and the Hereafter. They believe in all His messengers without distinction. They establish prayers and practice regular charity. The believers are humble, just, and righteous. They are conscious of their weaknesses, try to improve their character and behavior as God commands, and they trust Him in order to succeed.

2.1 FULFILL OBLIGATIONS TO YOUR LORD AND HIS CREATION

In *Surah Al-Nisa*, people are commanded to serve God, associate none with Him, and show kindness and affection to parents. They are kind to relatives, orphans, and the needy. They are considerate to their neighbors, their companions, wayfarers, and those who are under their protection. In their dealings with others, people should not be proud or boastful. They should neither hoard wealth nor encourage others to be stingy. It is also stressed that people should be careful of their duty to God, under Whose name they claim their rights from one another.

God commands people as, "O mankind!

1. Reverence your Guardian-Lord, Who created you from a single person, created of like nature his mate, and from them twain scattered (like seeds) countless men and women;
2. Fear Allah, through whom you demand your mutual (rights), and (reverence) the wombs (that bore you),

For Allah ever watches over you" (Qur'an 4:1).

2.2 HYPOCRITES CAN NOT BE BELIEVERS WITHOUT REPENTANCE

There is nothing more hateful in Islam than hypocrisy. This is due to the fact that hypocrites are not only perpetual liars, but also think that they can easily fool people without being noticed. They see themselves perfectly shielded by their intellect. Hypocrites claim to be believers when they truly do not believe. Thus, they try to deceive God and make fun of His Knowledge and Power. It was narrated by 'Abdullah bin 'Amr that the Prophet[PBUH] said: "Whoever has the following four (characteristics) will be a pure hypocrite, and whoever has one of the following four characteristics will have one characteristic of hypocrisy unless and until he gives it up. 1) Whenever he is entrusted, he betrays. 2) Whenever he speaks, he tells a lie. 3) Whenever he makes a covenant, he proves treacherous. 4) Whenever he quarrels, he behaves in a very imprudent, evil, and insulting manner" (Sahih Bukhari 3.43.639).

Even the hypocrites can obtain God's forgiveness, on four accounts: 1) sincere repentance which purifies their mind; 2) amendment of their conduct, which purifies their life; 3) steadfastness and devotion to God, which strengthens their faith and protects them from evil temptations; and 4) sincerity in their religion, which makes them a full member of the Muslim brotherhood.

God warns people that, "The hypocrites will be in the lowest depths of the Fire; no helper will you find for them, except for those who repent, mend (their lives), hold fast to Allah, and purify their religion as in Allah's sight. If so they will be (counted) with the believers, and soon will Allah grant to the believers a reward of immense value" (Qur'an 4:145-146).

2.3 Believers avert evil with good and avoid vain speach
Christians and Jews who recognized that Islam was logical and a natural development of God's revelations given in the past, welcomed and accepted Islam. They also rightly claimed that they had always been Muslims. In this sense, Adam, Noah, Abraham, and Jesus had all been Muslims. Since they followed the earlier divine law and then accepted Islam, their credit will be twofold because they persevered in righteousness, averted evil with good, spent in charity and did not encourage idle talk or foolish arguments about things sacred.

God tells people that, "Those to whom We sent the Book before this (the Qur'an)—they do believe in this (revelation). And when it is recited to them, they say: 'We believe therein, for it is the truth from our Lord. Indeed, we have been Muslims (bowing to Allah's Will) from before this.' Twice will they be given their reward,

1. For that they have persevered,
2. That they avert evil with good, and
3. That they spend (in charity) out of what We have given them.
4. And when they hear vain talk, they turn away there from and say: 'To us our deeds and to you yours; peace be to you; we seek not the ignorant.'

It is true you will not be able to guide every one whom you love, but Allah guides those whom He will, and He knows best those who receive guidance" (Qur'an 28:52-56)

2.4 PARADISE IS FOR THE HUMBLE, JUST AND RIGHTEOUS PEOPLE

The believers are humble, just and do good deeds. They are neither arrogant nor mischief makers but submit to God's Will. It is the fruit of their righteousness and good deeds that will win in the end.

God tells the believers that, "That House of the Hereafter We shall give to those who intend not high-handedness or mischief on earth, and the end is (best) for the righteous. If any does good, the reward to him is better than his deed, but if any does evil, the doers of evil are only punished (to the extent) of their deeds" (Qur'an 28:83-84).

2.5 PARADISE IS FOR REFORMERS WHO REPENT AND DO GOOD

The believers know that it is humanly not possible to be perfect in character and behavior but they keep trying to improve themselves by: 1) turning away from evil in sincere repentance; 2) making sure that their life is good and righteous by following what God commands; 3) their intentions and good deeds are motivated by God's fearing love; and 4) they give up their whole heart and self in devotion to Him.

God promises such believers that, "And the Garden will be brought near to the righteous—no more a thing distant. (A voice will say:) 'This is what was promised for you, for every one

1. Who turned (to Allah) in sincere repentance,
2. Who kept (His law),
3. Who feared (Allah) Most Gracious unseen,
4. And brought a heart turned in devotion (to Him).

Enter you therein in peace and security; this is a Day of Eternal Life.'" (Qur'an 50:31-34).

3

BELIEVERS—STAND FIRM FOR JUSTICE

The believers know that transgressing God's Limits will lead people to the fire of Hell. That is why they take care of orphans and restore their property to them. They also arrange the distribution of inheritance with justice as God commands. Further, they know that being unjust is one of the most heinous social crimes. Therefore, they stand firm for justice, and they make sure to be a witness for justice as well. They speak truth, measure things with justice, and honor promises. God tells them that being active in a good cause is always better for the believers. The believers should even migrate to escape injustice if required.

3.1 TRANSGRESSING GOD'S LIMITS LEADS PEOPLE TO THE FIRE

After describing the rules that apply to the distribution of wealth after the death of a person, God tells people that, limits set by Him should strictly be followed as far as the rights of individuals are concerned. People who fail to do justice to others will surely be admitted to Hell for punishment.

God tells people that,

1. "Those are limits set by Allah. Those who obey Allah and His Messenger will be admitted to Gardens with rivers flowing beneath, to abide therein (forever), and that will be the supreme achievement.
2. But those who disobey Allah and His Messenger and transgress His limits will be admitted to a Fire, to abide therein, and they shall have a humiliating punishment" (Qur'an 4:13-14).

3.2 TAKE CARE OF ORPHANS AND RESTORE THEIR BELONGINGS

Justice to orphans is enjoined, and three things are specifically mentioned as temptations in the way of a guardian: 1) He must not postpone restoring all his/her ward's property when the time comes. 2) The property restored must be of equal value to the property received. 3) If property is managed together, then strictest probity is insisted when the separation takes place.

God commands the believers that, "To orphans restore their property (when they reach their age), nor substitute (your) worthless things for (their) good ones. And devour not their substance (by mixing it up) with your own, for this is indeed a great sin" (Qur'an 4:2).

3.3 GIVE TO KINDRED THEIR DUE BUT SQUANDER WEALTH NOT
In Islam, God's worship is linked with kindness—to parents, kindred, those in want, those who are far from their homes though they may be total strangers. It is not mere verbal kindness. They have certain rights which must be fulfilled. All charity, kindness and help depend on one's own resources. There is no merit if we merely spend out for idle show or ruin our families by extravagant expenses at various functions and parties. The command, 'squander not your wealth' is more relevant to no one but to present day Muslims.

God commands the believers that,

1. "And render to the kindred their due rights, as (also) to those in want and to the wayfarer,
2. But squander not (your wealth) in the manner of a spendthrift.

Verily spendthrifts are brothers of the evil ones, and the Evil One is to his Lord (Himself) ungrateful. And even if you have to turn away from them in pursuit of the Mercy from your Lord that you do expect, yet speak to them a word of easy kindness" (Qur'an 17:26-28).

3.4 GIVE THEIR DUE TO KINDRED, THE NEEDY AND WAYFARER
Generally people have unreasonable behavior during adversity, when they lose all heart, and in affluence they are puffed up and unduly elated. In prosperity, people should realize that it is not their merit that makes them deserving of God's bounty but it is given to them out of His abundant generosity. In adversity they should remember that their suffering is brought on by their own folly and sin, and humbly pray for His grace and mercy. God gives provisions to every one, in greater or lesser measure according to His own plan and to test or try the believers. The believers do not seek to benefit from the property of others but spend in charity which is profitable in both worlds.

God asks people that, "See they not that Allah enlarges the provision and restricts it, to whomsoever He pleases? Verily, in that are Signs for those who believe.

1. So give what is due to kindred, the needy, and the wayfarer.
2. That is best for those who seek the countenance of Allah, and it is they who will prosper.

That which you lay out for increase through the property of (other) people will have no increase with Allah, but that which you lay out for charity, seeking the countenance of Allah, (will increase). It is these who will get recompense multiplied" (Qur'an 30:37-39).

3.5 BELIEVERS ARE MANDATED DISTRIBUTION OF INHERITANCE

Inheritance is to be distributed among both male and female members of the family, and that relatives who have no legal shares, orphans and indigent people are not to be treated harshly if present at the division. People responsible for dividing the estate should have the same fear in their minds as they would have for their own estates if they had left a helpless family behind.

God tells the believers that, "From what is left by parents and those nearest related, there is a share for men and a share for women, whether the property be small or large, a determinate share. But if at the time of division other relatives or orphans or poor are present, feed them out of the (property), and speak to them words of kindness and justice. Let those (disposing of an estate) have the same fear in their minds as they would have for their own if they had left a helpless family behind. Let them fear Allah and speak words of appropriate (comfort). Those who unjustly eat up the property of orphans, eat up a fire into their own bodies. They will soon be enduring a blazing Fire" (Qur'an 4:7-10).

3.6 CORRUPTION AND INJUSTICE ARE MOST HEINOUS CRIMES

To waste any property is wrong, whether people hold it in trust, it is in their name, it belongs to the community, or it belong to individuals over whom they have control. Wasting or misappropriating property or national resources may also cause our own destruction. People are encouraged to increase their wealth by traffic and trade and not by corruption and injustice.

God commands the believers, "O you who believe!

1. Eat not up your property among yourselves in vanities, but let there be among you traffic and trade by mutual good will:
2. Nor kill (or destroy) yourselves, for verily Allah has been to you Most Merciful! If any do that in rancor and injustice, soon shall We cast them into the Fire—and easy it is for Allah.

If you (but) eschew the most heinous of the things that you are forbidden to do, We shall expel out of you all the evil in you, and admit you to a Gate of great honor" (Qur'an 4:29-31).

3.7 STAND FIRM FOR JUSTICE AND BE A WITNESS FOR JUSTICE

Justice is God's attribute and to stand firm for justice is to be a witness for Him, even if it is detrimental to one's own interest or the interests of those who are near and dear to him. Islamic justice calls for one's inner most motives and intentions because believers are to act as in the presence of God at all times, whom all things, acts, and motives are well known.

God commands the believers, "O you who believe!

1. Stand out firmly for justice, as witnesses to Allah, even as against your-selves, or your parents, or your kin, and whether it be (against) rich or poor: for Allah can best protect both.
2. Follow not the lusts (of your hearts), lest you swerve, and if you distort (justice) or decline to do justice, verily Allah is well-acquainted with all that you do" (Qur'an 4:135).

3.8 SPEAK OUT AND MEASURE JUSTLY AND HONOR PROMISES

There must be controls and constraints in life. These apply to one's attitudes, hopes, intentions, actions, and relations with other people. There is a moral law, which is for people's own good to follow. They should deal justly and rightly with others, and they should not think too much of themselves thereby forgetting others. God commands the believers so that they may remember to behave properly at all times.

God commands the believers,

1. "...; Give measure and weight with (full) justice; -

No burden do We place on any soul, but that which it can bear; -

2. Whenever you speak, speak justly, even if a near relative is concerned;
3. And fulfill the Covenant of Allah:

Thus does He command you, that you may Remember" (Qur'an 6:152).

3.9 STRIVE FOR JUSTICE OR AGAINST OPPRESSION IN SOCIETY

God's reward is promised to all people of faith but there are degrees among the believers. Some of them are naturally lazy - they do the minimum that is required of them. There are some who are weak in will and are easily frightened. But there are people who are so strong in will and so firm in faith that they are determined to conquer every obstacle, whether in their own physical self or in the external world around them. In the time of jihad, when believers give all they have, even their lives for a common cause, they must be accounted better than those who sit at home, even though they have goodwill to the cause and carry out some duties in its aid. There is a special reward for the self-sacrifice of the believers in the form of higher ranks and special forgiveness from God.

God tells the believers that, "Not equal are those believers who sit (at home) and receive no hurt and those who strive and fight in the Cause of Allah with their goods and their persons. Allah has granted a grade higher to those who strive and fight with their goods and persons than to those who sit (at home). Unto all (in faith), Allah has promised good, but those who strive and fight has He distinguished above those who sit (at home) by a special reward" (Qur'an 4:95).

3.10 BELIEVERS MIGRATE TO ESCAPE INJUSTICE & OPPRESSION

Migration from places where Islam is being prosecuted and oppressed is commanded to believers. Obviously, the duty of Muslims is to leave such places, even if it involves forsaking their homes. They should join and strengthen a Muslim community among whom they could live in peace and with whom they could help in fighting the evil around them. A believer's duty is not only to enjoin good but also to prohibit evil. Therefore, one must shun evil company where ever they cannot put it down, and organize a position from which they can put a stop to it. If some one is unable to fight a good fight due to one's physical, mental, or moral incapacity, he must nevertheless guard himself against it. God's gracious mercy will recognize and forgive one's weakness if it is a real weakness, and not merely an excuse.

God tells the believers, "When angels take the souls of those who die in sin against their souls, they say: 'In what (plight) were you?' They reply: 'Weak and oppressed were we in the earth'. They say:

1. 'Was not the earth of Allah spacious enough for you to move your-selves away (from evil)?' Such men will find their abode in Hell, what an evil refuge—

Except those who are (really) weak and oppressed, men, women, and children who have no means in their power, nor (a guidepost) to their way. For these, there is hope that Allah will forgive, for Allah does blot out (sins) and forgive again and again.

2. He who forsakes his home in the Cause of Allah, finds in the earth many a refuge, wide and spacious. Should he die as a refugee from home for Allah and His Messenger, His reward becomes due and sure with Allah,

And Allah is Oft-forgiving, Most Merciful" (Qur'an 4:97-100).

4

BELIEVERS— ARE JUST AND ESTABLISH JUSTICE

Being God's trustee each one of us has specific duties and responsibilities to fulfill. Individuals have their own specific sphere of influence and they are like rulers within their respective areas. The Messenger defined seven classes of people who will enjoy God's shelter on the Day of Judgment. The first of these is a just ruler. It has been reported by Abu Hurairah that the Messenger[PBUH] of

God said: "Seven are (the persons) whom Allah will give protection with His shade on the Day when there would be no shade but that of Him, (and they are): a just ruler..." (Sahih Muslim 5.2248). So, all believers are the just rulers in their own specific area of influence.

Justice for all is the foundation and mainstay of Humanity. God has provided guidance and the means to establish justice in society. The believers are commanded to avoid fraud and to give full measure with justice. They are not to collect wealth through fraud or corruption and they are not to hoard wealth thinking that it will make them immortal.

4.1 JUSTICE IS THE FOUNDATION AND MAINSTAY OF HUMANITY
People should be honest and straight in their everyday activities, not only with other people, but with oneself in obedience to divine law. Justice is the central virtue and avoidance of both excesses and defects in conduct keeps humanity balanced just as the heavenly world is kept in balance by its physical laws.

God tells the believers that, " ... , He (Allah) has set up the balance (of justice), in order that you (people) may not transgress (due) balance. So establish weight with justice, and fall not short in the balance" (Qur'an 55:7-9).

4.2 GUIDANCE AND MEANS ARE GIVEN TO ESTABLISH JUSTICE
Three things are mentioned as blessings of God to humanity: they are the Book, the balance, and Iron, which stand as emblems of three things which hold society together. These are: 1) the revelation, which commands good and forbids evil; 2) justice, which gives each person its due; and 3) strong arm of the Law, which maintains sanctions for evildoers.

God tells people that, "We sent aforetime Our Messengers with Clear Signs and sent down with them the Book and the Balance (of right and wrong), that men may stand forth in justice; and We sent down Iron, in which is (material for) mighty war, as well as many benefits for mankind, that Allah may test who it is that will help, Unseen, Him and His messengers: For Allah is Full of Strength, Exalted in Might (and able to enforce His Will)" (Qur'an 57:25).

4.3 BELIEVERS GIVE FULL MEASURE - THEY DEAL NOT IN FRAUD

Fraud covers much more than short measure or a short weight. It is the spirit of injustice that is condemned— giving too little and asking too much. This may be shown in commercial dealings, where a person exacts a higher standard in his own favor than one is willing to concede. One must give in full what is due, whether one expects or wishes to receive full consideration from the other side or not.

God condemns the fraudulent people as, "Woe to those that deal in fraud—those who, when they have to receive by measure from men, exact full measure, but when they have to give by measure or weight to men, give less than due. Do they not think that they will be called to account on a Mighty Day" (Qur'an 83:1-5).

4.4 BELIEVERS GATHER NOT ILLEGAL WEALTH NOR HOARD IT

Three evils of human character are condemned here in the strongest terms for the believers to avoid: 1) scandal mongering, talking and suggesting evil of men or women by word, behavior, mimicry, sarcasm, or insult; 2) detracting people from their character behind their backs, even if the things suggested are true, but the motive is evil; 3) piling up wealth, not for use and service to those who need it, but in miserly hoards, as if such hoards can prolong the miser's life or give him immortality.

God tells in *Surah Al-Humazah*: "Woe to every slanderer and backbiter who piles up wealth and lays it by. Thinking that his wealth would make him last forever. By no means! He will be sure to be thrown into that which breaks to pieces" (Qur'an 104:1-4).

5

BELIEVERS— PLEAD NOT FOR THE CORRUPT

God commands the believers to plead neither on behalf of the corrupt nor for heinous sinners, including those who accuse others with one's own faults. The criminals may hide their crimes from people, but they cannot hide them from God. God asks people, 'these are the sort of men on whose behalf you may contend in this world, but who will contend with Him on their behalf on the Day of Judgment, or who will carry their affairs through'? Although God is Oft-Forgiving, Most Merciful, He rejects the repentance of those who go on sinning intentionally even after realizing the seriousness of their sins.

5.1 PLEAD NOT ON BEHALF OF CORRUPT OR HEINOUS SINNERS

Religion is a source of strength and not of weakness in all human affairs. If people have to struggle hard and suffer hardships, those without faith have to do the same, with the difference, that the believers are full of hope in God, whereas the faithless have nothing to sustain them.

People are blessed with souls as a trust from God and they have to guard their souls against all temptations. Those who surrender to crime or evil, betray this trust. People are warned against being deceived into being unjust, even if it may seem to them that they are helping their own people and not doing anything wrong, they are still being unjust to others.

God warns people that,

1. "We have sent down to you the Book in truth that you might judge between men as guided by Allah, so be not (used) as an advocate by those who betray their trust;

But seek the forgiveness of Allah, for Allah is Oft-Forgiving, Most Merciful.

2. Contend not on behalf of such as betray their own souls; for Allah loves not one given to perfidy and crime.

They (criminals) may hide (their crimes) from men, but they cannot hide (them) from Allah, seeing that He is in their midst when they plot by night, in words that He cannot approve; and Allah does compass round all that they do" (Qur'an 4:105-108).

5.2 NONE WILL PLEAD FOR THE CORRUPT ON THE JUDGMENT DAY

Pleading for the guilty will be of no use because in the end, every one is to be judged with justice by God Himself. The plots of sinners are fully known to God, and He can fully circumvent them if necessary. And if in His Wisdom He allows it, it is to further His own plan. Even out of evil He can bring good. The corrupt can save themselves only by repenting and reforming their conduct as God commands.

God asks people, who will contend on behalf of sinners on Judgment Day?

1. "Ah! These are the sort of men on whose behalf you may contend in this world, but who will contend with Allah on their behalf on the Day of Judgment, or who will carry their affairs through?
2. If any one does evil or wrongs his own soul but afterwards seeks Allah's forgiveness, he will find Allah Oft-Forgiving, Most Merciful" (Qur'an 4:109-110).

5.3 Accusing others with one's own fault is a heinous sin
People do a day's work to earn their livelihood: so in spiritual sense, whatever good or evil they do in this life, earns them good or evil in the life to come. Three cases of human behavior can be evaluated here: 1) If people do evil and repent, God will forgive; 2) if people do evil and do not repent, thinking to hide it, they are wrong; nothing is hidden from God and they shall suffer the full consequences in the life to come, because individual responsibility cannot be avoided; and 3) if people do evil, and blame someone else for it, their original responsibility remains, but they add to it the guilt of falsehood, which converts even a minor fault into a great sin and brands them even in this life with shame and ignominy.

God tells people that, "And if any one earns sin, he earns it against his own soul; for Allah is full of knowledge and wisdom. But if any one earns a fault or a sin and throws it on to one that is innocent, he carries (on himself, both) a falsehood and a flagrant sin" (Qur'an 4:111-112).

5.4 Denied is the repentance of one who keeps on sinning
Every incident of acknowledgment, regret, and effort not to repeat mistakes again impacts human character. That is why people's repentance improves their behavior and transforms them into hardworking and honest individuals who when joined together form a just community. To be forgiven, people have to repent and repent quickly. Delaying repentance shows insincerity and a lack of

resolve. Such behavior does not qualify for God's forgiveness and His mercy and therefore, it should be avoided.

God tells people that, "Allah accepts the repentance of those

1. Who do evil in ignorance and repent soon afterwards; to them will Allah turn in mercy, for Allah is full of knowledge and wisdom.

Of no effect is the repentance of those

2. Who continue to do evil, until death faces one of them, and he says, 'Now have I repented indeed,'
3. Nor of those who die rejecting Faith. For them have We prepared a punishment most grievous" (Qur'an 4:17-18).

6
BELIEVERS— BELIEVE AND DO GOOD DEEDS

The believers do not propagate evil talk, nor make news public before assuring its truth. The believers respond with a better greeting when greeted or return the same. Anyone who greets a believer with an Islamic greeting is assumed to be a Muslim. Secrecy is recommended in deeds of charity, justice and peace. Since the believers desire God's Mercy, they sincerely believe and do good deeds.

6.1 BELIEVERS PROTEST AND PROPAGATE AGAINST INJUSTICE
People can publicize a scandal of evil in many ways. 1) It may be idle sensation-mongering: which often leads to more evil by imitation, such as crimes glorified in cinema, or talked about shamelessly in a novel or drama. 2) It may be malicious gossip of a foolish, personal kind: which does no good but hurts another's feelings. 3) It may be slander or libel intended deliberately to cause harm to someone's reputation, or injure him/her in other ways, and is rightly punishable under all laws. 4) It may be a public rebuke or correction without malice. Out of these the first three are forbidden but a public complaint by a person who has suffered an injustice is allowed. Such person has every right to seek public redress.

God tells the believers that, "Allah loves not that evil should be noised abroad in public speech, except where injustice has been done, for Allah is He Who hears and knows all things" (Qur'an 4:148).

6.2 ASSURE THE TRUTH OF A NEWS BEFORE PUBLICIZING IT

Spreading gossip should be restrained especially during times of war or public panic. False news causes needless alarm. News, either true or false can also encourage the enemy. The proper way is to direct all such news quietly to those who are in a position to investigate it. They can then assure its authenticity and take suitable measures. Not to do so is to fall directly into the snares of evil.

God commands the believers that, "When there comes to them some matter touching (public) safety or fear, they divulge it. If they had only referred it to the Messenger or to those charged with authority among them, the proper investigators would have tested it from them (direct). Were it not for the Grace and Mercy of Allah unto you, all but a few of you would have followed Satan" (Qur'an 4:83).

6.3 RESPOND WITH A BETTER GREETING OR RETURN THE SAME

Fighting for a good cause mandates that mutual love and cordiality should always be cultivated among people. Fighting is an essential necessity to defend oneself, but cultivating mutual love and respect in daily human intercourse is a normal need. Further, people should always extend kindness and courtesy among themselves and return a good deed or a word in a better way or at least in the same terms. All people are creatures of the same One God and shall be brought together before Him in the end.

God commands the believers that, "When a greeting is offered you, meet it with a greeting still more courteous, or (at least) of equal courtesy. Allah takes careful account of all things" (Qur'an 4:86).

6.4 ASSUME ONE A MUSLIM WHO GREETS IN AN ISLAMIC WAY

When people travel either for jihad or for trade or any other activity which is done honestly, it counts as a service in God's cause. In war or in peace, people are apt to catch some worldly advantage by assuming themselves as superior in faith than others. This is not right. A believer, if he is really in God's service, has abundant and richer rewards in spiritual terms. Therefore, a righteous person should give others the benefit of doubt and treat them as having good intentions.

God commands the believers, "O you who believe! When you go abroad in the Cause of Allah, investigate carefully, and say not to anyone who offers you a salutation: 'You are none of a believer!' coveting the perishable goods of this life. With Allah are profits and spoils abundant. Even thus were you yourselves before, till Allah conferred on you His favors. Therefore, carefully investigate, for Allah is well aware of all that you do" (Qur'an 4:94).

6.5 HAVE FAITH AND DO GOOD IF YOU DESIRE GOD'S MERCY

Personal responsibility is stressed again and again in Islam. In this, faith as well as right conduct are implied. Faith is not an external thing; it begins with an intention or an act of will, and if true and sincere, it affects the whole individual self and leads to right conduct. If people do evil, they must suffer the consequence, unless God's mercy comes to their help. Salvation does not depend on merely believing in such religion which promises salvation because someone else has borne away people's sins or on being born in a certain race of chosen people.

God confirms that, "Not your desires nor those of the People of the Book (can prevail):

1. Whoever works evil will be requited accordingly. Nor will he find, besides Allah, any protector or helper.
2. If any do deeds of righteousness, be they male or female, and have faith, they will enter Heaven, and not the least injustice will be done to them" (Qur'an 4:123-124).

Chapter 10

Believers— Fulfill Their Obligations
(Believers Conscientiously Strive Hard)

God commands people to reflect, "Do you not see that Allah has subjected to your use all things in the heavens and on earth and has made His bounties flow to you in exceeding measure, seen and unseen? Yet, there are among people those who dispute about Allah without knowledge and without guidance, and without a Book to enlighten them. ... It is We Who have placed you with authority on earth and provided you therein with means for the fulfillment of your life: ..." (Qur'an 31:20; 7:10). Why has God established people with authority on earth, and why has He provided all that they need for the fulfillment of their lives? God describes the purpose behind creation by saying, "Then We made you heirs in the land after them to see how you would behave" (Qur'an 10:14). People have the assignment of being God's trustee on earth in order to evolve a system of life according to the dictates of their Lord and not according to their own selfish desires.

Therefore, God's trustees are "Those who, if We (Allah) establish them in the land, establish regular prayer and give regular charity, enjoin the right and forbid wrong: ..." (Qur'an 22:41). This makes it obligatory on each one of us that we should keep up the prayers, pay *Zakat* (obligatory charity), enjoin what is good, and forbid what is evil. This is the only option we have if we want to succeed in life. Otherwise our fate may not be any different from those destroyed societies we read about in history. God warns us in *Surah Al-Infal*, "And guard yourselves against a chastisement that cannot fall exclusively on those of you who are wrongdoers, and know that Allah is severe in punishment" (Qur'an 8:25).

1
BELIEVERS—FOLLOW DIVINE LAW

Life on earth is governed by Divine Law. The Law is to forgive people, to command what is right, and turn away from the ignorant. The Law is to learn what God commands and to commit no shameful deeds. The Law is to seek God's protection from Satan, and the Law is to serve God like Abraham did—to repent, and amend one's behavior, and to invite people to the 'Way of their Lord' with wisdom.

Islam sets up controls in human life, defines them with clarity, and imparts in them an authority derived from God, ensuring that they remain well respected, observed, and obeyed. They are not subject to changing tendencies or temporary interests that may be given prominence by an individual, a group, a nation, or a generation. Human interest lies in observing them even though an individual, a community, a nation, or a whole generation may feel otherwise, for it is God Who knows best, while people have, at best, an incomplete knowledge and biased reasoning. These controls and constraints are what is termed by God here as 'obligations'. He commands those who believe in Him to guard and remain true to these obligations. Therefore, the believers worship God, give charity, and fulfill all of their other obligations as God commands to the best of their ability and understanding.

1.1 FORGIVE, DO WHAT IS RIGHT AND IGNORE THE IGNORANT
Since it is humanly impossible to be perfect in character and behavior, the believers: 1) forgive each others' mistakes; 2) they guide people on how to reform; 3) they are not discouraged by those who cannot appreciate the need to improve their conduct; and 4) they seek refuge in God when evil thoughts assail their minds.

This is because God commands the believers to,

1. "Hold to forgiveness;
2. Command what is right;
3. But turn away from the ignorant.
4. If a suggestion from Satan assails your (mind), seek refuge with Allah, for He hears and knows (all things)" (Qur'an 7:199-200).

1.2 BELIEVERS ESCHEW EVIL— WORSHIP IT NOT AND REPENT

There is always a danger that evil may seize people even if they approach it out of mere curiosity. If they take an interest in it, they may become its worshippers or slaves. The wise people eschew it altogether, and enroll themselves among the servants of God. Such people choose the best meaning of what He commands and follow it in their lives. For example, it is permitted within limits to punish those who do wrong, but the nobler course is to "Repel evil that which is best: ..." (Qur'an 23:96).

God gives good news to, "Those who eschew evil, and fall not into its (evil's) worship, and turn to Allah (in repentance), for them is good news. So announce the good news to My servants— those who listen to the Word (revelation) and follow the best (meaning) in it. Those are the ones whom Allah has guided, and those are the ones endued with understanding" (Qur'an 39:17-18).

1.3 BELIEVERS ALWAYS SEEK GOD'S PROTECTION FROM SATAN

Evil has no authority or influence over those who put their trust in God. It is good to express that trust in outward actions and a formal expression of it ie—'I seek Allah's protection from Evil' helps us. Reading the Qur'an and its understanding should be an earnest desire of the believers to know and understand what God desires from them to do and how they should behave or act. People are weak at best and they should seek strength for their will in God's help and protection.

God commands the believers that, "When you do read the Qur'an, seek Allah's protection from Satan, the rejected one. No authority has he over those who believe and put their trust in their Lord. His authority is over those only who take him as patron and who join partners with Allah" (Qur'an 16:98-100).

1.4 SERVE GOD LIKE ABRAHAM— REPENT AND MAKE AMENDS

Abraham was a model, and an example for imitation for the believers. He was an *Ummah* or an institution in himself, standing alone against the world. The divine Unity has been the cornerstone of Truth for all time. In this respect, Abraham is the model and fountainhead for humanity and its descendents all over the world. Abraham was born among a people who worshipped stars. He was among them but not with them in their religion. He suffered persecution and was forced to leave his home and his people. He settled in the land of Canaan.

God tells the believers to repent, reform and follow the way of Abraham,

1. "But verily your Lord—to those who do wrong in ignorance, but who thereafter repent and make amends— your Lord, after all this, is Oft-Forgiving, Most Merciful.

Abraham was indeed a model, devoutly obedient to Allah (and) True in Faith, and he joined not gods with Allah. He showed his gratitude for the favors of Allah, Who chose him and guided him to a Straight Way. And We gave him good in this world, and he will be, in the Hereafter, in the ranks of the righteous. So We have taught you the inspired (message),

2. 'Follow the ways of Abraham, the True in Faith, and he joined not gods with Allah'" (Qur'an 16:119-123).

1.5 INVITE PEOPLE TO THE WAY OF THEIR LORD WITH WISDOM

The believers must invite all to God's Way, which is without doubt— for the benefit of Humanity, with wisdom and discretion, meeting them on their own ground and convincing them with examples from their own knowledge and experience. Preaching and arguments must be presented in the most courteous and gracious way, so that the hearer may know, 'that this person is sincerely motivated by his goodwill for people without any selfish desires or gains'. The preacher should not look for immediate results. People's inner thoughts are known best to God and no one knows how the seed of God's Word may germinate in a person's mind.

In any struggle, believers restrain themselves and are patient. Patience does not give an advantage to the adversary but the advantage is with the patient one, who does not lose their temper or forget their own principles of conduct. Concluding the situation, the believers are told that they should not yield to human passion, anger or impatience, and that they should go on with constancy doing good all around them because God is always with them.

God commands the believers to,

1. "Invite (all) to the Way of your Lord with wisdom and beautiful preaching; and argue with them in ways that are best and most gracious:

For your Lord knows best, who have strayed from His path, and who receive guidance.

2. And if you do punish, then punish with the like of that with which you were afflicted; but if you show patience, that is indeed the best (course) for those who are patient.
3. And be patient, for your patience is but from Allah.
4. Nor grieve over them, and distress not yourself because of their plots,

For Allah is with those who restrain themselves and those who do good" (Qur'an 16:125-128).

1.6 BELIEVERS GUARD AGAINST EVIL & FULFILL THEIR DUTIES
There must be controls and constraints in life. These apply to people's attitudes, hopes, intentions, actions, and relations with other humans. These controls and constraints also govern a person's relations with other living or non-living things that exist in the world. Further, there must be controls and constraints to govern human life and the human relationship with God from which all other relationships are derived. God commands the believers, "O you who believe! Fulfill (all your) obligations. ..." (Qur'an 5:1).

1.7 BELIEVERS PRAY, GIVE CHARITY & FOLLOW GOD'S WAY
It is not right that the believers should be in an intimate association with those to whom religion is either a subject of mockery or at best is nothing but a plaything. Their association with them will sap the earnestness of their faith and make them cynical and insincere.

God tells the believers in *Surah Al-Maidah* that "Your (real) protectors are (no less than) Allah, His Messenger, and the (fellowship of) believers—

1. Those who establish regular prayers and regular charity,

2.   And they bow down humbly (in following all what Allah commands with dedication).

As to those who turn (for friendship) to Allah, His Messenger, and the (fellowship of) believers—it is the fellowship of Allah that must certainly triumph" (Qur'an 5:55-56).

2
BELIEVERS— UNITE TO SERVE GOD

God created jinns and men, both endowed with free will, so they may serve Him alone. This requires that they be sincere, join no one with Him in worship, and do not split their religion into various groups fighting with one another. In fact, the believers are commanded to make peace between the fighting parties. What is God's servitude? It is that, 'they should believe in God and His messengers and live as He commands'. They should follow the truth and be sincere in their intentions and deeds. Since guidance is such that those who reject it will be in Hell, the believers serve God sincerely.

2.1 GOD CREATED JINN AND MEN THAT THEY MAY SERVE HIM

Both jinns and humans are created to serve God. Then what is His Servitude? It is to manage our lives on earth as He commands in the Qur'an. God is the source and center of all power and goodness and our progress depends on putting ourselves into accord with His Will and follow what He commands. It is not for His benefit but for our own benefit in this world as well as in the Hereafter.

God tells people that, "I have only created jinns and men that they may serve Me. No sustenance do I require of them, nor do I require that they should feed Me. For Allah is He Who Gives (all) Sustenance, Lord of power— Steadfast (forever)" (Qur'an 51:56-58).

2.2 BELIEVE IN GOD AND HIS MESSENGERS, LIVE AS HE LIKES

The believers sincerely believe in God and His Messengers and they testify the truth and spend in charity. Four attributes of the believers are: 1) the Prophets who teach, 2) the sincere lovers of truth, 3) the witnesses who testify and 4) the righteous who do deeds of charity. The witnesses are not only martyrs, but all those who carry the banner of truth against all odds and positions of danger, whether by pen, speech, deed or council.

God tells the believers that,

1. "For those who give in charity, men and women, and loan to Allah a beautiful loan, it shall be increased manifold (to their credit), and they shall have (besides) a liberal reward.
2. And those who believe in Allah and His messengers— they are the sincere (lovers of truth), and the witnesses (who testify), in the eyes of their Lord:

They shall have their reward and their light. But those who reject Allah and deny Our Signs— they are the companions of Hellfire" (Qur'an 57:18-19).

2.3 GOD FAVORED YOU WITH FAITH, BE TRUE AND SINCERE

Islam in itself is a precious privilege. By accepting it, the believers confer no favor on its preacher or any community. If the acceptance is from heart, it is a great favor done to those who accept—that the Light of God has entered their hearts and they have received guidance.

God tells the Messenger that, "They impress on you as a favor that they have embraced Islam.

1. Say, 'Count not your Islam as a favor upon me.
2. Nay, Allah has conferred a favor upon you that He has guided you to the Faith, if you be true and sincere'" (Qur'an 49:17).

2.4 NEITHER JOIN OTHERS WITH GOD, NOR SPLIT INTO SECTS

None of the created things have any superiority over another, either among themselves or other created things. God has created things in a certain way. People are created innocent, true, inclined to do what is right, just and endued with an understanding about their own position as God's trustee on earth and about God's goodness, wisdom and power. This is their true nature as the true nature of a lamb is to be gentle or of a horse is to be swift. But people are also being influenced by customs, superstitions, selfish desires and false teachings. This may make them quarrelsome, unclean, false, and slavish who are inclined towards what is wrong and forbidden. Such people are turned aside from the love of their fellow people, and the worship of one true God—their Creator. The religion tries to cure this crookedness and restore human nature to what it should be under the Will of God— their Creator. This may be achieved by: 1) God's fear, 2) Repentance, 3) His worship, 4) Rejecting false gods or selfish desires, and 5) Being sincere to one's faith.

God commands people, "So (O People) set your face steadily and truly to the Faith. (Establish) Allah's handiwork according to the pattern on which He has made mankind. No change (let there be) in the work (wrought) by Allah. That is the standard Religion, but most among mankind understand not. (Therefore, O People)

1. You turn back in repentance to Him,
2. And fear Him.
3. Establish regular prayers, and
4. Be not among those who join gods with Allah—
5. Those who split up their religion, and become (mere) sects—each party rejoicing in that which is with itself" (Qur'an 30:30-32).

2.5 THE BELIEVERS MAKE PEACE BETWEEN FIGHTING PARTIES

The enforcement of the Muslim Brotherhood is the greatest social ideal of Islam and Islam cannot be completely realized until this ideal is achieved. Therefore, it is expected that the Muslim community should act justly and try to settle their quarrels, for peace is better than fighting. But if one party is determined to be the aggressor, the whole force of the community should be brought to bear on it. The essential condition is that there should be perfect fairness and justice; for Islam takes account of every just and legitimate interest of both parties without separating spiritual from temporal matters.

God commands the believers that,

1. "If two parties among the believers fall into a quarrel, make peace between them: ...

2. The believers are but a single brotherhood, so make peace and recon-
    ciliation between your two (contending) brothers, and fear Allah that
    you may receive Mercy" (Qur'an 49:9-10).

2.6 GUIDANCE TRANSFORMS THE WORST PEOPLE TO THE BEST

People are given the faculty of discrimination between right and wrong. If then
they reject truth and right, in the presence of their free will, then it is the worst
mistake which they commit. This must bring its own punishment, whether they
belong to the children of Abraham, or those redeemed by Christ, or whether they
go by mere light of nature and reason. Honor in the sight of God is not due to a
race or professions of faith, but to sincere and righteous conduct and deeds. God
tells people, "O mankind! We created you from a single (pair) of a male and a
female, and made you into nations and tribes, that you may know each other (not
that you may despise each other). Verily the most honored of you in the sight of
Allah is (he who is) the most righteous of you. ..." (Qur'an 49:13).

God warns people that,

1. "Those who reject (truth) among the People of the Book and among
    the polytheists will be in Hellfire to dwell therein (forever). They are
    the worst of creatures.
2. Those who have faith and do righteous deeds—they are the best of
    creatures" (Qur'an 98:6-7).

3

BELIEVERS— ADORE THEIR LORD

The believers adore their Lord, strive hard in His Way, and do good deeds. They
understand that He is very near to them and knows what is in every person's
heart. God is present among people wherever they may be, and He is merciful
to those who believe and fear Him. God created people and ordained laws. He
guides them and knows well who is rightly guided and does good deeds, as well
as the one who denies the truth and forbids others from praying. God is the
One and Only, the Eternal and Absolute. Forgetting Him makes people forget
their own selves, and thus they degenerate into rebellious transgressors.

3.1 GOD CREATED PEOPLE, ORDAINED LAW & GAVE GUIDANCE

The story of creation is wonderful and continuous. There are numerous processes by which people contemplate in glorifying God's name. Firstly, it is He who brought us into being. Secondly, He endowed us with forms and faculties exactly suited to what is expected of us, and to the environment in which our life will be cast, giving to everything due order and proportion. Thirdly, He has ordained laws and decrees by which we can develop ourselves and fit into His scheme of evolution for all His creation. Fourthly, He gives us guidance, so that we may not be subjected to some casual laws. Under divine guidance, exercising their reason and will, people can become the best of Humanity.

God commands the believers that, "Glorify the name of your Guardian-Lord Most High, Who has created, and further, given order and proportion, Who has ordained laws and granted guidance" (Qur'an 87:1-3).

3.2 GOD IS THE ONE AND ONLY, THE ETERNAL AND ABSOLUTE

People have a tendency to conceive of God after their own pattern. This tendency has existed throughout history among all people. People believed in many gods and lords of various kinds. Polytheism is opposed to the truest and most profound conception of life. For Unity in Design, Unity in fundamental facts of existence, proclaim the Unity of a Maker.

God commands people to, "Say: 'He is Allah, the One and Only, Allah, the Eternal, Absolute. He begets not, nor is He begotten, and there is none like unto Him'" (Qur'an 112:1-4).

3.3 GOD KNOWS WHO IS GUIDED AND WHO DENIES THE TRUTH

Human arrogance leads to two results: 1) self-destruction through self-misguidance; 2) a false example or false guidance to others. The righteous person must therefore test human guidance by questions like, "Is there God's guidance behind it?" or "Does it lead to righteousness?" Denying God and His Truth answers the first question in the negative, and the conduct which does not follow the eternal principles of what is Right, is not righteous. The ungodly people refuse to face the truth. If they are compelled, they deny even what is clear to a reasonable person, and turn their backs.

God does confirm that He knows the guided and unguided people

1. "See you one who forbids— a votary when he (turns) to pray?
2. See you if he is on (the road of) guidance— or enjoins righteousness?
3. See you if he denies (truth) and turns away?
4. Does not he know that Allah does see?" (Qur'an 96:9-14).

3.4 GOD LET THOSE WHO FORGET HIM FORGET THEMSELVES

People should not forget the presence or existence of God. Forgetting God is to forget the only eternal reality. Since we are only reflected realities, how can we understand or do justice to or remember ourselves, when we forget the very source of our being? Besides, the fear of God is akin to His love; for it means the fear of offending Him or doing anything wrong that will forfeit His Good Pleasure. It is God's fear (or *Taqwa*), which implies—self-restraint, guarding ourselves from all sin, injustice, and—the positive doing of 'deeds of righteousness'.

God commands people to do their self-evaluation and accountability, "O you who believe!

1. Fear Allah, and let every soul look to what (provision) he has sent forth for the morrow.
2. Yea, fear Allah, for Allah is well-acquainted with (all) that you do.
3. And you be not like those who forgot Allah, and He made them forget their own souls! Such are the rebellious transgressors" (Qur'an 59:18-19).

3.5 ADORE YOUR LORD, STRIVE IN HIS WAY AND DO GOOD

Islam gives freedom and full play to people's faculties of every kind. It is universal, and claims to date from Adam: father Abraham is mentioned as the great ancestor of those whom Islam was first taught. Since the Messenger is a guide and witness among the believers, the believers ought to be witnesses among people. The best witness to God's Truth are the believers who show its light in their lives.

God says, "O you who believe!

1. Bow down, prostrate yourselves, and adore your Lord; and do good that you may prosper.
2. And strive in His Cause as you ought to strive, (with sincerity and under discipline).

He has chosen you and has imposed no difficulties on you in religion; it is the cult of your father Abraham. It is He Who has named you Muslims, both before and in this (revelation), that the Messenger may be a witness for you, and you be witnesses for mankind!

1. So establish regular prayer,
2. Give regular charity,
3. And hold fast to Allah!

He is your Protector— the Best to protect and the Best to help" (Qur'an 22:77-78).

3.6 GOD IS VERY NEAR AND KNOWS EVEN WHAT PEOPLE THINK

God created people, and gave them their limited free will. God knows the inmost desires and motives of people even better than they know themselves. He is nearer to a person than his/her own jugular vein. As the blood stream is the vehicle of life and consciousness, the phrase 'nearer than the jugular vein' means that God knows more truly the innermost state of people's feeling and consciousness than they do themselves.

God tells people that, "It was We Who created man, and We know what dark suggestions his soul makes to him, for We are nearer to him than (his) jugular vein. Behold, two (guardian angels) appointed to learn (his doings) learn (and note them), one sitting on the right and one on the left. Not a word does he utter but there is a sentinel by him ready (to note it). And the stupor of death will bring truth (before his eyes): 'This was the thing which you were trying to escape!'" (Qur'an 50:16-19).

3.7 GOD IS PRESENT AMONG PEOPLE WHEREVER THEY MAY BE

Secrecy is a relative and limited term. There is nothing hidden or unknown to God. He is present everywhere and He knows all, whether open or hidden. Usually secrecy implies fear or distrust, plotting or wrongdoing. But all is open before God's sight.

God asks people, "See you not that Allah does know (all) that is in the heavens and on earth? There is not a secret consultation between three, but He makes the fourth— among them, nor between five but He makes the sixth— nor between fewer nor more but He is with them, where so ever they be. In the end will He tell them the truth of their conduct on the Day of Judgment, for Allah has full knowledge of all things" (Qur'an 58:7).

3.8 GOD IS MERCIFUL TO THOSE WHO BELIEVE AND FEAR HIM

Addressing the People of the Book who have also believed in Islam, God assures them that any wrong they may have committed through ignorance or misconception in their previous religion will be forgiven as they have seen the new Light and followed it. The qualifying behavior for God's Mercy is that they fear Him, believe in His Messenger, then He will enable them to follow His Path.

God assures the believers, "O you that believe!

1. Fear Allah,
2. And believe in His Messenger,

And He will bestow on you a double portion of His Mercy. He will provide for you a light by which you shall walk (straight in your path), and He will forgive you (your past sins), for Allah is Oft-Forgiving, Most Merciful" (Qur'an 57:28).

4

BELIEVERS— REFLECT ON THE QUR'AN

The Qur'an is guidance for people who fear God. Such people read the Qur'an by the name of their Lord Who taught them reading and writing with the pen. People read the Qur'an as much as it may be easy for them to read in one sitting. The Qur'an is guidance and a path to your Lord wherein people learn to distinguish good from evil. This information benefits all those among people who fear God, but it does not benefit the unbelievers. The believers recite, learn and reflect on, and follow what God commands of them in the Qur'an. The revelation of the Qur'an began in the Night of Power as God's mercy for those who believe, worship Him, and give charity.

4.1 THE QUR'AN IS A GUIDANCE AND A PATH TO YOUR LORD
The Qur'an was revealed stage by stage as situations demanded and at the time of revelation of *Surah Al-Insan*, it was still at one of the earlier stages. Persecution, abuse, and false charges were being leveled against the Messenger (and the believers) and he was bidden to stand firm and do his duty. In general, they were advised: 1) to be patient; 2) not to worry about what sinners say; and 3) remember God. These commands now apply to the believers, who face difficulties in the way of truth during their lives.

The Messenger and the believers are told that, "It is We Who have sent down the Qur'an to you by stages.

1. Therefore, be patient with constancy to the command of your Lord,
2. And hearken not to the sinner or the ingrate among them.
3. And celebrate the name of your Lord morning and evening and part of the night; prostrate yourself to Him, and glorify Him a long night through" (Qur'an 76:23-26).

4.2 THE QUR'AN DISTINGUISHES BETWEEN GOOD AND EVIL
The revelation or the divine truth leads people to the goal of their lives: it separates Good from Evil. The believers believe in it and do righteous deeds. It is not mere play or amusement, but it helps them in the main issues of their lives.

God tells people that, "Behold this is the Word (the Qur'an) that distinguishes (Good from Evil). It is not a thing for amusement" (Qur'an 86:13-14).

4.3 THE QUR'AN PROFITS ONLY THOSE— WHO FEAR GOD
God's Message is for all people; but particular and personal admonition is due only to those in whose hearts is the fear of God. Admonition is useless to those

who run away from it or dishonor it. They are the unfortunate ones who prepare their own ruin. The Divine Message is not a new law, nor have the vanity and short duration of this world been preached for the first time. The divine truth has been renewed and reiterated again and again throughout history for human good and the progress of humanity.

God tells the believers that, "And We will make it easy for you (to follow) the simple (Path). Therefore, give admonition in case the admonition profits (the hearer).

1. The admonition will be received by those who fear (Allah), but it will be avoided by those most unfortunate ones who will enter the Great Fire, in which they will then neither die nor live.
2. But those will prosper who purify themselves, and glorify the name of their Guardian-Lord, and (lift their hearts) in prayer.

Nay (behold), you prefer the life of this world, but the Hereafter is better and more enduring. This is in the books of the earliest (revelation)— the books of Abraham and Moses" (Qur'an 87:8-19).

4.4 THE QUR'AN GUIDES THOSE WHO FEAR GOD'S WARNING
People may have doubts about the Day of Judgment and the Hereafter. The Messenger's task is not to force people to accept anything. His duty is only to deliver the Message of the Qur'an, admonish those who are ready to take advice and reform in order to develop themselves into those who are fit for the progress of humanity.

God commands the Messenger (and the believers) that, "We know best what they (unbelievers) say, and you are not one to overawe them by force. So admonish with the Qur'an such as fear My warning" (Qur'an 50:45).

4.5 THE QUR'AN IS A MERCY TO WORSHIPERS WHO DO GOOD
The Qur'an is a Book full of Wisdom, a guide to all people and to those who accept its guidance, a source of mercy leading them to their salvation. The righteous or the doers of good are distinguished here by three marks, that 1)

they yearn towards God in duty, love and prayer, 2) they love and serve their fellow-people in charity, and 3) they win peace and prosperity for themselves in the assured hope for the future. Such people will be blessed because they submit their will to God and receive His guidance. They will do well in this life and will achieve their goal in the Hereafter.

God tells people that, "These are verses of the Wise Book— a Guide and a Mercy to the Doers of Good—

1. those who establish regular prayer,
2. and give regular charity,
3. and have (in their hearts) the assurance of the Hereafter.

These are on (true) guidance from their Lord, and these are the ones who will prosper" (Qur'an 31:2-5).

4.6 BELIEVERS RECITE, LEARN AND REFLECT ON THE QUR'AN

The believers recite and try to understand and reflect on what God commands in the Qur'an to the best of their abilities and follow what God commands them. They take the revelation to their heart, ever seeking to get closer and closer to their Lord by prayer and in doing so, they move more and more to charity. They are not ashamed of giving charity openly but they do not do it to be seen. They try to help each other to the best of their ability.

God says about the righteous people that,

1. "Those who rehearse (recite, understand, and reflect on) the Book of Allah,
2. Establish regular prayer,
3. And spend (in charity) out of what We have provided for them, secretly and openly, hope for a commerce that will never fail,

For He will pay them their wages in full. Nay, He will give them (even) more out of His Bounty, for He is Oft-Forgiving and Most Ready to appreciate (service)" (Qur'an 35:29-30).

4.7 BELIEVERS READ THE QUR'AN BY THE NAME OF THEIR GOD

The lowly origin of the animal in people is to be developed by their Creator, to achieve its higher destiny as God's trustee through their intellectual, moral, and spiritual nature. No knowledge is withheld from people. Through the faculties freely given to them, they acquire it in such measure as outstrips their immediate understanding and leads them to strive for newer and higher objectives of Humanity.

God commands people, "Proclaim! (Or read!) In the name of your Lord and Cherisher, Who created—created man out of a (mere) leech-like clot of congealed blood:

1. Proclaim! And your Lord is Most Bountiful,
2. He Who taught (the use of) the pen—
3. Taught man that which he knew not" (Qur'an 96:1-5).

4.8 BELIEVERS STUDY THE QUR'AN AS MUCH AS MAY BE EASY

After giving a general command to acquire knowledge, the believers are told to acquire Qur'anic knowledge. In the Qur'an there is an admonish for the good of humanity. If people have the will, they can at once come for the Grace and Mercy of God, and obtain it. For believers, repentance and reforming themselves as God commands is the straight way to His nearness. God can be served in many ways. The believers must give some time to His devotion (as may be most easy and convenient to them) in various circumstances of health, travel, and during the performance of various duties. They must not violate His commands during their daily activities.

God commands the believers to,"…: Read, therefore, of the Qur'an as much as may be easy for you. He knows that there may be (some) among you in ill health, others traveling through the land, seeking of Allah's bounty, yet others fighting in Allah's Cause,

1. Read, therefore, as much of the Qur'an as may be easy (for you),
2. And establish regular prayer,
3. And give regular charity,
4. And loan to Allah a beautiful loan.

And whatever good you send forth for your souls, you shall find it in Allah's presence—yea, better and greater in reward, and you seek the Grace of Allah, for Allah is Oft-Forgiving, Most Merciful" (Qur'an 73:20).

5
BELIEVERS— FOLLOW THEIR MESSENGER

The Messenger guides people to believe and worship God, and the believers assist and honor him. They cherish him as their role model. He recites the Qur'an, sanctifies, and instructs them in scripture and wisdom. The Messenger has an exalted standard of character and guides the believers honestly in a message that has been revealed to him by the Lord of the Worlds.

5.1 MESSENGERS GUIDE PEOPLE WITH A TRUE DIVINE MESSAGE
Messengers are from God, the Creator of the Universe. If imposters arise, they would soon be found out. They could not carry out their fraud for ever. The messengers of God, however much they are persecuted, gain more and more power every day as did the Prophet of Islam, whose truth, earnestness, sincerity, and love for all were recognized as his life unfolded itself. The protection which the messengers of God enjoy in circumstances of danger and difficulty would not be available to imposters.

God tells people that, "That this (the Qur'an) is verily the word of an honored messenger. It is not the word of a poet—little it is you believe, nor is it the word of a soothsayer—little admonition it is you receive. (This is) a message sent down from the Lord of the Worlds.

And if the messenger were to invent any sayings in Our name, We should certainly seize him by his right hand, and We should certainly then cut off the artery of his heart. Nor could any of you withhold him (from Our wrath), but verily this is a message for the God-fearing" (Qur'an 69:40-48).

5.2 MESSENGERS GUIDE PEOPLE TO BELIEVE AND WORSHIP GOD
Messengers came to establish Faith in God and true worship. They can be viewed in three capacities: 1) as a witness to help the weak if they are oppressed

and check the strong if they are wrong; 2) as a giver of glad tiding of God's grace and His mercy to those who repent and live good lives; and 3) one who warns the sinners about the consequences of their sins. The believers, on the other hand, are to assist and honor the Messengers, and worship God by following what they command.

God tells the Messenger and the believers that, "We have truly sent you (O Messenger) as a witness, as a bringer of glad tidings and as a Warner,

1. In order that you (O people) may believe in Allah and His Messenger,
2. that you may assist and honor him (the Messenger),
3. And celebrate His (Allah's) praise morning and evening" (Qur'an 48:8-9).

5.3 THE MESSENGER RECITES, SANCTIFIES AND GUIDES PEOPLE

God is full Sovereign, and therefore cares for all His people and has been sending His prophets and messengers to them: So that: 1) they recite to people God's revelations; 2) they help purify and sanctify those who were steeped in superstition and wickedness; and 3) they give instructions in wisdom, both through Scriptures and the laws of nature which God has put in place.

God tells people that, "It is He Who has sent among the unlettered a messenger from among themselves

1. To rehearse to them His Signs,
2. To sanctify them, and
3. To instruct them in Scripture and Wisdom— although they had been before in manifest error" (Qur'an 62:2).

5.4 THE MESSENGER HAS AN EXCELLENT MORAL CHARACTER

The believers emulate the Messenger and try their best to behave in the best possible way when they deal without discrimination with others. The Messenger stated that the foremost purpose of his being sent to this world was for the purpose of perfecting human moral character and behavior. In the translation of Malik's Muwatta, it is mentioned that, "Yahya related to me that he had

heard that the Messenger[PBUH] said, 'I was sent only to perfect good character.'"
(Malik, Muwatta 47.1.8).

This has been testified in *Surah Al-Qalam*, in which God, addressing the
Messenger, says, "And (O Messenger:) you (stand) on an exalted standard of
character" (Qur'an 68:4).

Chapter 11

Believers—Excel in their Behavior
(Believers Behave as God Commands)

Like bricks joined together in a house, humans have to be strong in character and beautiful in behavior in order to contribute in accomplishing the divine trust of eliminating corruption from human society. As raw bricks of ugly mold cannot increase the strength and looks of a house, neither can an individual with a raw character full of ugly, selfish desires and undisciplined behavior strengthen the society. The logical outcome of believing in God and of worshiping Him is the growth of one's moral character and the refinement of their behavior, without which they cannot fulfill their responsibility of being God's trustee.

The believers described in *Surah Al-Sajdah* are those: "Their limbs do forsake their beds of sleep, the while they call upon their Lord in fear and hope, and they spend (in charity) out of the sustenance We have given them" (Qur'an 32:16). The believers are hardworking; they are not lazy, and they diligently attend to their duties towards God and their duties towards His creation. They are honest in their dealings and do not fulfill their needs and desires in wrong ways. However to err is human and people are likely to commit mistakes. In such situations, they call upon their Lord in fear and hope to repent and reform their behavior. The believers deal kindly with the unbelievers. They patiently persevere and try to nurture Islamic values individually and collectively in society. They strive hard to do good deeds to live within the prescribed limits of divine order.

1
BELIEVERS—REPENT AND REFORM

The believers are God's trustee and they fear accountability of their deeds in the Hereafter. They worship God and do not violate His commands. The believers are kind, deal among people with justice, and honor their promises. They are moderate, patient, and do not commit evil. They are neither miserly nor spendthrifts. The believers do not kill their children or anyone else, and they never come near adultery.

The believers state what is right and true, and obey God and His Messenger. They commit no crime or shameful deed, and they defend themselves when attacked. They place their hope in God and do not despair. The believers who confirm their belief by their good deeds are people of the best mold. They seek refuge from evil of all created things and from the mischief of Satan.

1.1 BELIEVERS ARE GOD'S TRUSTEE WHO FEAR THE HEREAFTER
On the day of Reckoning, no one can help another. Neither the most loving father will help his son nor will the son help his father. Each one will be judged, and rewarded or punished according to their own individual deeds. God commands people to fulfill their duties towards Him as well as towards His people and no one should be ignored.

People are told that all their activities will be judged one Day, "O mankind! Do your duty to your Lord, and fear (the coming of) a Day when no father can avail aught for his son, nor a son avail aught for his father. Verily, the promise of Allah is true: let not then this present life deceive you, nor let the chief Deceiver deceive you about Allah" (Qur'an 31:33).

1.2 BELIEVERS WORSHIP GOD AND VIOLATE NOT HIS COMMANDS
Real human freedom comes only if people stop worshiping false deities and their own selfish desires. This can only be achieved by worshiping the Creator of the Universe and by following His law. Citing an example from history, Luqman, a wise man of the past told his son about the biggest human failing and advised him not to join others with God but worship Him alone.

God tells people that, "We bestowed (in the past) wisdom on Luqman, (telling him): 'Show (your) gratitude to Allah. Any who is grateful does so to the profit of his own soul, but if any is ungrateful, verily Allah is free of all wants, worthy of all praise.' Behold, Luqman said to his son by way of instruction: 'O my son! Join not in worship (others) with Allah, for false worship is indeed the highest wrong-doing' (because it leads to slavery)" (Qur'an 31:12-13).

1.3 BELIEVERS ARE JUST, KIND AND HONOR THEIR PROMISES

Who are the believers? They deal among people with justice and are good to their relatives. They avoid all shameful deeds, injustice and rebellion. They honor their contracts, fulfill their oaths and never deceive people for any reason.

God commands people Justice, "Allah commands (people to deal with) justice,

1. The doing of good, and liberality to kith and kin, and
2. He forbids all shameful deeds,
3. And (He forbids) injustice,
4. And (He forbids) rebellion:

He instructs you, that you may receive admonition.

5. Fulfill the Covenant of Allah when you have entered into it (by saying that there is no god but Allah and Muhammad is His Messenger), and
6. Break not your oaths after you have confirmed them; indeed, you have made Allah your surety, for Allah knows all that you do. And be not like a woman who breaks into untwisted strands the yarn which she has spun, after it has become strong.
7. Nor take your oaths to practice deception between yourselves, lest one party should be more numerous (in profit or benefit) than another:

For Allah will test you by this, and on the Day of Judgment He will certainly make clear to you (the truth of) that wherein you disagree" (Qur'an 16:90-92).

1.4 BELIEVERS ARE PATIENT, MODERATE, JUST & RIGHTEOUS
Believers establish prayer, enjoin justice, forbid evil and are patient. They are never arrogant but moderate in pace and lower in voice.

A believing father advises his son in *Surah Luqam*, as, "O my son!
1. Establish regular prayer,
2. Enjoin what is just, and forbid what is wrong.
3. And bear with patient constancy whatever betide you;

For this, is firmness (of purpose) in (the conduct of) affairs.

4. And swell not your cheek (for pride) at men,
5. Nor walk in insolence through the earth:
For Allah loves not any arrogant boaster.
6. And be moderate in your pace,
7. And lower your voice;

For the harshest of sounds without doubt is the braying of the ass" (Qur'an 31:17-19).

1.5 BELIEVERS ARE HUMBLE AND GIVE MEASURE WITH JUSTICE
The believers never spoil another's property, they fulfill their promises and contracts, and give full measure. Since undue estimation of one's power or abilities leads people to many evils, the believers neither pursue that which is vain nor indulge in arrogance.

God advises the believers in *Surah Al-Isra*, that they should—

1. "Come not near to the orphan's property except to improve it, until he attains the age of strength,
2. And fulfill (every) engagement,
For (every) engagement will be enquired into (on the Day of Reckoning).
3. Give full measure when you measure, and weigh with a balance that is straight.

That is the most fitting and the most advantageous in the final determination.

4.   And pursue not that of which you have no knowledge,

For every act of hearing, or of seeing or of (feeling in) the heart will be enquired into.

5.   Nor walk on the earth with insolence,

For you cannot rend the earth asunder, nor reach the mountains in height.

Of all such things the evil is hateful in the sight of your Lord" (Qur'an 17:34-38).

1.6 BELIEVERS ARE MODERATE, NOT MISERLY OR SPENDTHRIFTS

The believers are neither so lavish as to make themselves destitute nor do they keep their resources from the just needs of those who have a right to their help. They keep a just measure between their capacity and other people's needs.

God commands them, "Make not your hand tied (like a miser's) to your neck, nor stretch it forth to its utmost reach, so that you become blameworthy and destitute. Verily, your Lord does provide sustenance in abundance for whom He pleases, and He provides in a just measure, for He does know and regard all His servants" (Qur'an 17:29-30).

1.7 BELIEVERS DO NOT KILL CHILDREN NOR COMMIT ADULTERY

The Arabs were addicted to female infanticide. In a society perpetually at war, a son was a source of strength while a daughter was a source of weakness. Even now infanticide is not unknown in other countries for economic reasons. This crime against children's lives is one of the greatest sins in Islam. Similar is the case of adultery. It is not only shameful in itself but it opens the doorway to many evils. Thus killing anyone and adultery are strictly forbidden to believers.

God commands the believers,

1. "Kill not your children for fear of want.

We shall provide sustenance for them as well as for you. Verily, the killing of them is a great sin.

2. Nor come near to unlawful sex, for it is a shameful (deed) and an evil, opening the road (to other evils).
3. Nor take life, which Allah has made sacred, except for just cause.

And if anyone is slain wrongfully, we have given his heir authority (to demand *Qisas* or to forgive), but let him not exceed bounds in the matter of taking life, for he is helped (by the law)" (Qur'an 17:31-33).

1.8 BELIEVERS ARE TRUE, OBEY GOD AND HIS MESSENGERS

The believers fear God and speak truth as far as they know. They are neither unreasonable nor beat around the bush, but go straight to that which is right, in deed as well as in word. This will make their conduct right and cure any defect that may be in their knowledge and character. By their striving directed straight to the goal, obeying God and His messenger, they will achieve great success and their mistakes, weaknesses and sins of the past will be forgiven.

For their success the believers are commanded as, "O you who believe! Fear Allah, and (always) say a word directed to the right, that He may make your conduct whole and sound and forgive you your sins. He that obeys Allah and His Messenger has already attained the highest achievement" (Qur'an 33:70-71).

1.9 BELIEVERS TRUST GOD, THE LAST DAY, AND DESPAIR NOT

What should be the attitude of the believers in life? They must trust God, and not take God's enemies to protect and befriend themselves, their families, or those who are near or dear to them. An excellent example to follow is the way of Abraham and his followers.

God tells people that like Abraham and his followers, the believers trust God, repent, seek His forgiveness and protection and they pray,

1. "... , Our Lord! In You do we trust and to You do we turn in repentance: to You is our final goal.
2. Our Lord! Make us not a trial for the unbelievers, but forgive us, our Lord! For You are the Exalted in Might, the Wise.

There was indeed in them (Abraham and his followers) an excellent example for you to follow—for those whose hope is in Allah and in the Last Day. But if any turn away, truly Allah is Free of all Wants, Worthy of all Praise" (Qur'an 60:4-6).

1.10 BELIEVERS WHO STRIVE HARD ARE THE BEST OF HUMANITY
The believers strive hard in God's Way and therefore are the best members of humanity. Such people can also save themselves from divine punishment because of their honest efforts.

God tells the believers: "O you who believe!
Shall I lead you to a bargain that will save you from a grievous penalty?

1. That you believe in Allah and His Messenger, and
2. That you strive (your utmost) in the Cause of Allah with your property and your persons.

That will be best for you (and Humanity), if you but knew" (Qur'an 61:10-11).

1.11 BELIEVERS WHO DO GOOD DEEDS ARE OF THE BEST MOLD
People have been created to behave as humans who respect all human values but their selfish desires often degrade them to an animal stature in morality.

God informs them in *Surah Al-Tin* that, "We have indeed created man in the best of molds. Then do We abase him (to be) the lowest of the low, except such as believe and do righteous deeds, for they shall have a reward unfailing. Then what can, after this, contradict you as to the judgment (to come)? Is not Allah the wisest of judges?" (Qur'an 95:4-8).

1.12 BELIEVERS SEEK REFUGE FROM EVILS OF ALL HUMAN ILLS

People are advised to seek God's Refuge from the evil of all created things and evil of all those who whisper evil ideas into the human mind to commit corruption and satisfy their own selfish desires.

God commands people to,

1. "Say: 'I seek refuge with the Lord of the Dawn from the mischief of created things, from the mischief of darkness as it overspreads, from the mischief of those who practice secret arts, and from the mischief of the envious one as he practices envy'" (Qur'an 113:1-5).

2. "Say: 'I seek refuge with the Lord and Cherisher of mankind, the King (or Ruler) of mankind, the God (or Judge) of mankind— from the mischief of the whisperer (of evil) who withdraws (after his whisper), who whispers into the hearts of mankind among jinn and among men'" (Qur'an 114:1-6).

2
BELIEVERS— DEAL KINDLY WITH UNBELIEVERS

The believers do not argue or dispute with the People of the Book but praise God and bear patiently with what the unbelievers say. They ignore those who swear lies and take sides with the unbelievers. Although the believers do not love unbelievers even if they are their near relatives, they are kind and just to those unbelievers who are not hostile to them.

2.1 BELIEVERS DO NOT DISPUTE WITH THE PEOPLE OF THE BOOK

Mere disputations with people about faith are futile and therefore should be avoided. Believers find true common ground in any interfaith work. They are kind, sincere and true in their discourse. Their main purpose is for the good of people and not merely for seeking selfish aims.

The believers are commanded to, "And you dispute not with the People of the Book, except with means better (than mere disputation), unless it be with those of them who inflict wrong (and injury). But say, 'We believe in the revelation that has come down to us and in that which came down to you; Our Allah and your Allah is One, and it is to Him we bow (in Islam)'" (Qur'an 29:46).

2.2 BELIEVERS ARE NOT DISCOURAGED BY WHAT DENIERS SAY
Believers are never discouraged by the propaganda of hypocrites and unbelievers. They face it with patience and prayer. Hence, it increases their faith.

God advises the believers in *Surah Qaf* to,

1. "Bear then with patience all that they (unbelievers) say, and
2. Celebrate the praises of your Lord before the rising of the sun and before (its) setting, and during part of the night (also) celebrate His praises, and (so likewise) after the postures of adoration" (Qur'an 50:39-40).

2.3 BELIEVERS IGNORE THOSE WHO SEEK HELP FROM DENIERS
Only hypocrites seek help from the unbelievers. Such people could never be reliable. God advises the believers to ignore them, "Turn not your attention to those who turn (in friendship) to such as have the wrath of Allah upon them? They are neither of you nor of them, and they swear to falsehood knowingly" (Qur'an 58:14).

2.4 BELIEVERS DO NOT LOVE UNBELIEVERS— EVEN NEAR KIN
Dealing among people with respect and justice is different from being affectionate to them. Although the believers deal with the unbelievers with justice and fairness, they do not love the unbelievers even if they are their close relatives.

God tells the believers that, "You will not find any people who believe in Allah and the Last Day loving those who resist Allah and His Messenger, even though they were their fathers, or their sons, or their brothers, or their kindred. ..." (Qur'an 58:22).

2.5 BELIEVERS ARE JUST & KIND TO FRIENDLY UNBELIEVERS
A believer should refrain from everything that might be helpful to the unbelievers during a conflict between the believers and unbelievers. However, the believers are encouraged to deal kindly and justly with those unbelievers who are not engaged in hostile activities against Islam or in the persecution of the believers.

God tells the believers in *Surah Al-Mumtahinah* that, "It may be that Allah will grant love (and friendship) between you and those whom you (now) hold as enemies... Allah forbids you not, with regard to those who fight you not for (your) Faith nor drive you out of your homes, from dealing kindly and justly with them, for Allah loves those who are just" (Qur'an 60:7-8).

"Allah only forbids you, with regard to those who fight you for (your) Faith, and drive you out of your homes, and support (others) in driving you out, from turning to them (for friendship and protection). It is such as turn to them (in these circumstances), that do wrong" (Qur'an 60:9).

3
BELIEVERS— EXCEL IN THEIR CHARACTER

The believers act according to God's commands in their daily activities. Since absence from work with a lame excuse is hypocrisy, the believers do not depart from their place of duty without permission. The believers respect individual privacy and nurture friendships among their relatives and friends. They make room in their assemblies for late comers.

Since things happen as decreed, the believers neither exult in prosperity nor despair during difficulties. Temptations, doubts, and vain desires do not deceive them. The believers heed not those rich people who are easy with their oaths, cruel in their behavior, and sinful in their lives. Surely people who are not covetous will be prosperous.

3.1 BELIEVERS LEAVE NOT WORK PLACE WITHOUT PERMISSION

Since absence from work without telling someone or with a lame excuse is hypocrisy, the believers do not depart from their place of duty without permission especially in those 'matters requiring collective action,' which could be anything that deals in the peace and prosperity of the community as a whole.

The believers are told that, "Only those are believers who believe in Allah and His Messenger. When they are with him on a matter requiring collective action, they do not depart until they have asked for his leave. Those who ask for your leave are those who believe in Allah and His Messenger; so when they ask for your leave, for some business of theirs, give leave to those of them whom you will, and ask Allah for their forgiveness, for Allah is Oft-Forgiving, Most Merciful. Deem not the summons of the Messenger among yourselves like the summons of one of you to another. Allah does know those of you who slip away under shelter of some excuse. Then let those beware who withstand the Messenger's order, lest some trial befall them or a grievous penalty be inflicted on them" (Qur'an 24:62-63).

3.2 BELIEVERS RESPECT INDIVIDUAL PRIVACY IN THEIR HOMES

The believers respect individual privacy even in their homes. God commands them in *Surah Al-Nur* "O you who believe! Let those whom your right hands possess and the (children) among you who have not come of age ask your permission (before they come to your presence) on three occasions: before morning prayer; the while you doff your clothes for the noonday heat; and after the late-night prayer. These are your three times of undress. Outside those times it is not wrong for you or for them to move about attending to each other. Thus does Allah make clear the Signs to you, for Allah is full of knowledge and wisdom" (Qur'an 24:58).

3.3 BELIEVERS NURTURE FRIENDSHIPS AMONG KINS AND FRIENDS

Nurturing friendship among relatives and other people is very much recommended in Islam—The believers are told that, "It is no fault in the blind, nor in one born lame, nor in one afflicted with illness, nor in yourselves that you should eat in your own houses, or those of your fathers, or your mothers, or your brothers, or your sisters, or your father's brothers or your father's sisters, or your mother's brothers, or your mother's sisters, or in houses of which the keys are in your possession, or in the house of a sincere friend of yours.

1. There is no blame on you, whether you eat in company or separately.
2. But if you enter houses, salute each other—a greeting of blessing and purity as from Allah. Thus does Allah make clear the Signs to you that you may understand" (Qur'an 24:61).

3.4 BELIEVERS MAKE ROOM IN ASSEMBLIES FOR LATE COMERS

In any meeting place, some adjustments are required, 1) for making room for additional participants and 2) for concluding the meeting. For conducting orderly meetings, the participants should abide by the instructions.

Hence the believers are told, "O you who believe!

1. When you are told to make room in the assemblies, (spread out and) make room. (Ample) room will Allah provide for you.
2. And when you are told to rise up, rise up. Allah will rise up, to (suitable) ranks (and degrees) those of you who believe and who have been granted knowledge. And Allah is well-acquainted with all you do" (Qur'an 58:11).

3.5 BELIEVERS EXULT NOT NOR DESPAIR, THEY JUST TRY HARD

God commands people who are boasting or despairing to reform themselves by telling them in *Surah Al-Hadid* that, although it is their duty to try their best and make efforts, success or failure is not the outcome of their efforts only. The law of nature which God has put in place or the *'Qadar'* effects the outcome or decree or *Taqdir*.

God tells people that, "No misfortune can happen on earth or in your souls but is recorded in a decree before We bring it into existence. That is truly easy for Allah, in order that you may not despair over matters that pass you by, nor exult over favors He bestowed upon you, for Allah loves not any vainglorious boaster— Such persons as are covetous and commend covetousness to men, and if any turn back (from Allah's Way), verily Allah is free of all needs, worthy of all praise" (Qur'an 57:22-24).

3.6 BELIEVERS ARE NOT DECEIVED BY THEIR SELFISH DESIRES

The believers neither follow temptation nor do their false desires deceive them. They believe in God and the Hereafter, never doubting the promises of His forgiveness, mercy and justice. They are not deceived by the whispering of the devil against what God has promised the believers.

Temptations, doubts and vain desires only deceive the hypocrites not the believers, "One Day will the Hypocrites— men and women— say to the Believers: 'Wait for us! Let us borrow (a Light) from your Light!' ... (Those without light) will call out, 'Were we not with you?' (The believers) will reply, 'True! But you led yourselves into temptation; you looked forward (to our ruin); you doubted (Allah's promise), and (your false) desires deceived you until there issued the command of Allah. And the Deceiver deceived you in respect of Allah'" (Qur'an 57:13-14).

3.7 Believers heed not theose who do not honor oaths

Normally the corrupt use oaths to deceive people and apply all types of illegal practices to slander them. God advises the believers to, "Heed not the type of despicable men— ready with oaths, a slanderer, going about with calumnies, (habitually) hindering (all) good, transgressing beyond bounds, deep in sin, violent (and cruel) — with all that, base-born— because he possesses wealth and sons" (Qur'an 68:10-14).

3.8 Believers are not covetous but prosperous at heart

A true believer always tries not to be covetous. This is so because God confirms that, "… And those saved from the covetousness of their own souls—they are the ones that achieve prosperity. And those who came after them say: 'Our Lord! Forgive us and our brethren who came before us into the Faith, and leave not in our hearts rancor (or sense of injury) against those who have believed. Our Lord! You are indeed Full of Kindness, Most Merciful'" (Qur'an 59:9-10).

4

Believers— Patiently Persevere

The believers patiently perform their duties and fear the Day of Judgment. They persevere in patience and put their trust in God. Since He commands the believers to be patient, they wait with patience for the judgment of their Lord. Neither can any difficulty shake their firmness and resolve, nor do they despair of God's mercy, but they continue to repent and reform their character and behavior to excel in Humanity.

The believers know that for every difficulty there is also a relief, so they strive hard and pray for God's help. They believe, do good deeds, and patiently strive and struggle for the Truth. When help from God arrives, the believers

praise Him and ask for His forgiveness. They pray and offer sacrifices to thank
God for His Mercy and His Bounty.

4.1 BELIEVERS PATIENTLY PERFORM DUTIES AND FEAR THE DAY
God created people to try and test them. He blessed them with various capa-
bilities and gave them guidance. Whether they are grateful or ungrateful to their
Lord depends on their will.

The grateful people are —

1. "They (who) perform (their) vows (daily activities serving Allah and
   Humanity),
2. And they fear a Day whose evil flies far and wide.
3. And they feed, for the love of Allah, the indigent, the orphan, and the
   captive—

(Saying), 'We feed you for the sake of Allah alone; no reward do we desire
from you, nor thanks. We only fear a Day of distressful wrath from the side of
our Lord.' But Allah will deliver them from the evil of that Day and will shed
over them a light of beauty and (blissful) joy.

4. And because they were patient and constant, He will reward them with
   a Garden and (garments of) silk" (Qur'an 76:7-12).

4.2 BELIEVERS PERSEVERE IN PATIENCE AND TRUST THEIR LORD
The believers' purpose in life is to worship God and do good deeds. No one
can be excused from this duty. Believers should refuse to be corrupted and if
circumstances are such that it is impossible at a certain situation or location,
they should move to another place. God's creation is wide enough to enable
people to find an alternate place to live but this requires will, patience and
constancy to achieve.

Addressing the believers God tells in *Surah Al-Ankabut* that, "O My servants who
believe! Truly, spacious is My Earth. Therefore, you serve Me— (and Me alone)!
Every soul shall have a taste of death; in the end, to Us shall you be brought back.

1. But those who believe and work deeds of righteousness—

to them shall We give a Home in Heaven, - lofty mansions beneath which flow rivers, - to dwell therein for ever; - an excellent reward for those who do (good)! —

2. Those who persevere in patience
3. And put their trust, in their Lord and Cherisher.

How many are the creatures that carry not their own sustenance? It is Allah Who feeds (both) them and you, for He hears and knows (all things)" (Qur'an 29:56-60).

4.3 BELIEVERS PATIENTLY PERSEVERE TO ACCOMPLISH SUCCESS
Patience is a human quality that is required to accomplish results in any good cause. The believers should, "Therefore patiently persevere, as did (all) messengers of inflexible purpose; and be in no haste about them (unbelievers). ..." (Qur'an 46:35).

4.4 BELIEVERS WAIT PATIENTLY FOR THEIR LORD'S JUDGEMENT
Reforming people and human society takes tremendous effort and time. Therefore, the believers are to keep making efforts patiently over a long period of time to accomplish results.

God commands the believers: "So wait with patience for the command of your Lord, and be not like the companion of the fish (Jonah) when he cried out in agony. Had not grace from his Lord reached him, he would indeed have been cast off on the naked shore in disgrace. Thus did his Lord choose him and make him of the company of the righteous" (Qur'an 68:48-50).

4.5 BELIEVERS LET NO ONE SHAKE THEIR FIRMNESS AND RESOLVE
The unbelievers seal up their hearts by deliberately rejecting the truth. Such people who reject the truth intentionally cannot be convinced to seek God's grace by repentance. It is already too late for them.

Even under such circumstances the believers are told to continue their efforts, "Verily, We have propounded for men in this Qur'an every kind of parable: But if you bring to them any Sign, the unbelievers are sure to say, 'You do nothing but talk vanities.' Thus does Allah seal up the hearts of those who understand not.

1. So patiently persevere, for verily the promise of Allah is true,
2. Nor let those shake your firmness who have (themselves) no certainty of faith" (Qur'an 30:58-60).

4.6 Believers despair not but keep continually improving

Since people have free will, perfection of their character and behavior without divine guidance is not humanly possible. What Islam teaches is an attitude that leads to a continual improvement in individual character and in society.

God asks the Messenger to tell people not to despair of His mercy but repent and reform following the best of what your Lord has revealed: God commands the Messenger to,

1. "Say: 'O my servants who have transgressed against their souls! Despair not of the Mercy of Allah, for Allah forgives all sins, for He is Oft-Forgiving, Most Merciful.
2. Turn you to your Lord (in repentance), and bow to His (Will), before the penalty comes on you; after that, you shall not be helped.
3. And follow the best of (the courses) revealed to you from your Lord before the penalty comes on you of a sudden while you perceive not!'" (Qur'an 39:53-55).

4.7 Believers do good and are united for truth & petience

Time or the life-time is a divine gift bestowed on people by their Creator. At the end of their life, they will have nothing left if they were attending to their material needs only. This life will show profit only if they had Faith, lead a good life, and contributed to the uplift of humanity by doing good deeds for social welfare and by directing and motivating other people on the path of Truth and Constancy with patience and determination.

Who are the Believers?

Swearing by Time, God reaffirms in *Surah Al-Asr*, that "By (the) time (through the ages), verily man is in loss, except

1. Such as have Faith,
2. And do righteous deeds,
3. And (join together) in the mutual teaching of Truth,
4. And of Patience and Constancy" (Qur'an 103:1-3).

4.8 BELIEVERS DO NOT DISPARE BUT STRIVE PATIENTLY FOR RELIEF
Citing the example from the Messenger's life, God assures the believers that, 'with every difficulty there is relief' so they should not lose heart but keep striving and remember Him.

In *Surah Al-Inshirah*, God asks the Messenger, "Have We not expanded you your breast and removed from you your burden that did gall your back— and raised high the esteem (in which) you (are held)?

1. So, verily, with every difficulty, there is relief. Verily, with every difficulty there is relief.
2. Therefore, when you are free (from your immediate task), still labor hard, and to your Lord turn (all) your attention" (Qur'an 94:1-8).

4.9 BELIEVERS THANK GOD BY OFFERING SACRIFICES AND PRAYER
Since it is God who grants people blessings in life, He alone should be adored and thanked. Ungrateful people, who do not appreciate the striving of His Messengers or of righteous people for their contribution to humanity, leave nothing behind for posterity.

Addressing the Messenger God tells the believers, that they should thank Him in their prayers and by offering Him sacrifice. The believers should ignore their adversaries—

1. "To you (O Messenger) have We granted the fount (of abundance).
2. Therefore, to your Lord turn in prayer and sacrifice.
3. For he who hates you, he will be cut off (from future hope)" (Qur'an 108:1-3).

174

4.10 BELIEVERS PRAISE GOD & ASK FORGIVENESS FOR HIS HELP

The believers are conscious of their weaknesses. They seek God's Grace and their success is not due to their own efforts only, but it is also due to God's help and His mercy. That is why they celebrate their success by worshipping Him and asking for His forgiveness.

The believers are told, "When comes the help of Allah, and victory, and you do see the people enter Allah's religion in crowds,

1.   Celebrate the praises of your Lord,
2.   And pray for His forgiveness, for He is Oft-Returning (in Grace and Mercy)" (Qur'an 110:1-3).

5
BELIEVERS—ESTABLISH THE WAY OF ISLAM

God promises the believers, who do good deeds, that they will be provided with leadership in their communities. The believers guard their communities and enforce justice based on the principle that 'an injury begets an injury'. They also promote 'forgiveness' as a better option.

5.1 GOD PROMISES POWER —TO THE BELIEVERS WHO DO GOOD

Three things are promised to those who have faith and obey Divine Law: 1) They will be granted power and authority not for selfish purposes but to enforce Divine Law. 2) Their religion will be established to eradicate corruption and oppression and 3) they will live in peace and security.

The believers are assured that, "Allah has promised to those among you who believe and work righteous deeds that—

1.   He will of a surety grant them in the land inheritance (of power), as He granted it to those before them, that
2.   He will establish in authority their religion, the one that He has chosen for them, and that

3. He will change (their state), after the fear in which they (lived), to one of security and peace. ..." (Qur'an 24:55).

This has been promised by God on the following three conditions that,

1. ". ...'They will worship Me (alone) and not associate aught with Me.' If any do reject faith after this, they are rebellious and wicked.
2. So establish regular prayer and give regular charity and obey the Messenger that you may receive mercy.
3. Never think that the unbelievers are going to frustrate (Allah's plan) on earth:

Their (unbelievers') abode is the Fire— and it is indeed an evil refuge" (Qur'an 24:55-57).

5.2 GOD PROMISES HELP—TO THOSE WHO STRIVE IN HIS CAUSE

God has permitted people to defend themselves and their religion saying that, 'had He not checked one set of people by means of another, all monasteries, churches, synagogues, and mosques would have been destroyed. God has assured His help to all those who fight in His cause.

In *Surah Al-Hajj*, the believers are assured that, "Verily, Allah will defend (from ill) those who believe. Verily, Allah loves not any that is a traitor to faith or shows ingratitude.

1. To those against whom war is made, permission is given (to fight) because they are wronged— and verily Allah is most powerful for their aid—

(They are) those who have been expelled from their homes in defiance of right— (for no cause) except that they say, 'Our Lord is Allah.' Had not Allah check one set of people by means of another, there would surely have been pulled down monasteries, churches, synagogues, and mosques in which the name of Allah is commemorated in abundant measure.

2. Allah will certainly aid those who aid His (Cause)— for verily Allah is full of strength, exalted in might, (able to enforce His Will) (Qur'an 22:38-40).

5.3 BELIEVERS ENFORCE —THE WAY OF ISLAM IN THEIR LANDS
When the believers are established in the land, they adopt the way of Islam in their communities: 1) by establishing prayer; 2) by giving regular charity; 3) by enjoining the right; and, 4) by forbidding the wrong. The believers are: "those who, if We establish them in the land, establish regular prayer and give regular charity, enjoin the right and forbid wrong. With Allah rests the end of affairs" (Qur'an 22:41).

5.4 BELIEVERS ESTABLISH — JUSTICE AND THE RULE OF LAW
There are numerous situations when an individual has to stand up against an oppressor and seek redress for his own rights, for the rights of his kin, or for the rights of someone in the community or the community itself. When one stands up for rights, either on private or public grounds, it may be through processes of law, or by the way of private defense insofar as the law permits private action. In all cases one must not seek a compensation greater than the injury suffered. One can also take steps to prevent repetition, by physical or moral means; the best moral means would be to turn hatred into friendship by forgiveness and reconciliation. In such a case the reward is much greater, for it wins the pleasure of God.

God commands the believers to fight for their rights with patience, "And those who, when an oppressive wrong is inflicted on them, (are not cowed but) help and defend themselves. The recompense for an injury is an injury equal thereto (in degree):

1. But if a person forgives and makes reconciliation, his reward is due from Allah, for (Allah) loves not those who do wrong.
2. But indeed if any do help and defend themselves after a wrong (is done) to them, against such there is no cause of blame.

The blame is only against those who oppress men with wrongdoing and insolently transgress beyond bounds through the land, defying right and justice. For such there will be a penalty grievous. But indeed, if any show patience and forgive, that would truly be an exercise of courageous will and resolution in the conduct of affairs" (Qur'an 42:39-43).

6

BELIEVERS—STRIVE HARD IN RIGHTEOUSNESS

Denying accountability for their deeds makes people arrogant and untrustworthy. People need accountability to motivate them to perform righteously. The believers believe in the Hereafter with their heart and mind. They strive hard, correct their mistakes, and help one another. They know that accountability for their deeds is true, so they do not waste time in vanities. Only a heavy balance of good deeds will achieve salvation in the Hereafter. People are rewarded according to their striving, intentions and deeds. On the Day of Judgment, people will be sorted out by their deeds, and the righteous will be in the bliss of Paradise only due to their good deeds and God's Mercy.

6.1 DENIAL OF ACCOUNTABILITY — MAKES PEOPLE SINNERS

People are not self sufficient but arrogant. Their arrogance leads them to transgress all limits. Their arrogance will vanish if they refresh their memory about their lowly birth from a mere leech-like clot of congealed blood and about the accountability of their deeds in the Hereafter.

About human nature people are told that, "Nay, but man does transgress all bounds in that he looks upon himself as self-sufficient. Verily, to your Lord is the return (of all, for judgment)" (Qur'an 96:6-8).

6.2 ACCOUNTABILITY IS TRUE SO WASTE NOT TIME IN VANITIES

Various issues of life and accountability of one's deeds in the Hereafter are serious issues. All that we do in this life is important and will have an impact both in this world and in the Hereafter. Therefore, the believers should watch their behavior and deeds.

People should shun all frivolities, strive to be righteous and worship God because, "The (Judgment) ever-approaching draws near. No (soul) but Allah can lay it bare.

1. Do you then wonder at this recital, and will you laugh and not weep, wasting your time in vanities?
2. But you fall down in prostration to Allah, and adore (Him)" (Qur'an 53:57-62).

6.3 BELIEVERS BELIEVE IN THE HEREAFTER & ACCOUNTABILITY

God explains things in the Qur'an that guide the believers, state His attributes, and define their position and the world around them. God directs them to right conduct, away from evil. He gives good news of forgiveness and salvation to those people who believe and live as He commands.

God introduces people about His Guidance thus, ".... These are verses of the Qur'an, a book that makes (things) clear, a guide and glad tidings for the believers—

1. Those who establish regular prayer, and give regular charity,
2. And have (in their hearts) the assurance of the Hereafter (and the accountability of their deeds)" (Qur'an 27:1-3).

6.4 BELIEVERS WORK HARD, REPENT, REFORM AND ARE HELPFUL

The believers are hard working, not lazy. They prefer activity to idleness, and the service of God and His creatures to self indulgence. Believers are honest and deal with one another with justice and respect.

They admit their mistakes, repent, reform and help others, therefore, "As to the righteous, they will be in the midst of Gardens and Springs, taking joy in the things that their Lord gives them because before then they lived a good life.

1. They were in the habit of sleeping but little by night,

2. And in the hour of early dawn, they (were found) praying for forgiveness, and

3. In their wealth and possessions (was remembered) the right of the (needy), him who asked and him who (for any reason) was prevented (from asking)" (Qur'an 51:15-19).

6.5 PEOPLE WILL HAVE NOTHING BUT WHAT THEY STRIVE FOR

There are Laws of Nature which God has put in place—like 'people are only responsible for their own actions and they are rewarded only for what they do'. People must strive or they will gain nothing; and if they strive, the results will soon appear in sight and they will find their reward in full measure.

Therefore, God tells people that,

1. "…no bearer of burdens can bear the burden of another;
2. That man can have nothing but what he strives for;
3. That (the fruit of) his striving will soon come in sight.

Then will he be rewarded with a reward complete" (Qur'an 53:38-41).

6.6 PEOPLE WILL BE REWARDED ACCORDING TO THEIR DEEDS

God's attributes of forgiveness and mercy are unlimited. They come into action even without our own action. Our prayer helps us to bring our minds and wills as an offering to Him and is necessary for our own psychological good. He knows about everyone of us and thus we cannot even plead for ourselves. But if we try out of love for Him, to guard against evil, our striving is all that He asks for.

God knows best who it is that guards against evil,
"Yea, to Allah belongs all that is in the heavens and on earth: so that

1. He rewards those who do evil according to their deeds,
2. And He rewards those who do good with what is best.

Those who avoid great sins and shameful deeds, only (falling into) small faults—verily, your Lord is ample in forgiveness. He knows you well when He brings you out of the earth and when you are hidden in your mothers' wombs. Therefore justify not yourselves. He knows best who it is that guards against evil" (Qur'an 53:31-32).

6.7 A HEAVY BALANCE OF GOOD DEEDS ACHIEVES SALVATION

Good and bad deeds will be appraised in the Hereafter. The appraisal will consider all intentions, motives, temptations and the surrounding environment.

People with good deeds will be rewarded and those with evil deeds will be punished.

In the Hereafter, "(On) a Day whereon men will be like moths scattered about and the mountains will be like carded wool,

1. Then he whose balance (of good deeds) will be (found) heavy will be in a life of good pleasure and satisfaction,
2. But he whose balance (of good deeds) will be (found) light—will have his home in a (bottomless) pit. And what will explain to you what this is? (It is) a Fire blazing fiercely" (Qur'an 101:4-11).

6.8 PEOPLE WILL BE SORTED OUT BY THEIR DEEDS ON THE DAY
The righteous and evil people are mixed together in this world but in the Hereafter, they will be sorted out, and each grade of good and evil people will proceed in groups to receive their judgment. They will be shown the exact description of everything that they had thought, said or done in their lives on earth. Everything will be considered in taking the account and people will testify to it concerning themselves.

In the Hereafter, "On that Day will men proceed in companies sorted out to be shown the deeds that they (had done).

1. Then shall anyone who has done an atom's weight of good see it!
2. And anyone who has done an atom's weight of evil shall see it" (Qur'an 99:6-8).

6.9 THE RIGHTEOUS WILL BE IN PARADISE DUE TO THEIR DEEDS
One of the Laws of Nature which God has put in place is the doctrine of efforts and reward. According to this doctrine, the people only get rewarded for what they strive for.

Especially in the Hereafter, "And he (the righteous) will be in a life of Bliss in a Garden on high, the fruits whereof (will hang in bunches) low and near. You eat and you drink with full satisfaction because of the (good deeds) that you sent before you, in the days that are gone!" (Qur'an 69:21-24).

7

BELIEVERS— LIVE WITHIN DIVINE LIMITS

God curses those people who annoy Him and His Messenger by violating His
commands. He made Hell for those who forbid people to be kind to others and for
those who transgress the limits set by Him. Cursed people neither feed the poor
nor encourage others to do so. Hell is their destiny if they do not repent and reform
themselves. Lying and sinful people will be dragged to their final destination.

7.1 CURSED ARE THOSE WHO ANNOY GOD AND HIS PROPHETS
God and His angels honor and bless the Messenger as the greatest role model
for people. He took upon himself to suffer the sorrow and afflictions of this
life to guide people to the right way of life—to help believers achieve the best
of humanity.

The believers should, therefore bless and honor the Messenger,

1. "Allah and His angels send blessings on the Prophet: O you that
   believe! Send your blessings on him, and salute him with all respect.
2. Those who annoy Allah and His Messenger—Allah has cursed them in
   this world and in the Hereafter and has prepared for them a humiliating Punishment.
3. And those who annoy believing men and women undeservedly bear
   (on themselves) a calumny and a glaring sin" (Qur'an 33:56-58).

7.2 HELL IS FOR THE VIOLATORS OF LIMITS WHO FORBID GOOD
According to their evil deeds, people will be condemned to Hell because they
did not reform to live as their Lord desired— They forbade what was good and
transgressed divine limits.

Such people are told that, their "(Sentence will be:) 'Throw; throw into Hell
every contumacious rejecter (of Allah) — (Such as those),

1. Who Forbade what was good,
2. (Who) Transgressed all bounds,

3. (Who) Cast doubts and suspicions.
4. Who set up another god beside Allah: throw him into a severe Penalty'" (Qur'an 50:24-26).

7.3 Unbelieving misers will be led to the blazing fire

Unbelief and rebellion against the Merciful God dries up human values. They neither help nor feed those in need, but also hinder others from doing so. Such people will surely face the consequence of their cruelty both in this world and in the Hereafter.

In the Hereafter, "(The stern command will say): 'You seize him, and you bind him, and you burn him in the blazing Fire. Further, make him march in a chain, whereof the length is seventy cubits!

1. This was he that would not believe in Allah Most High
2. And would not encourage the feeding of the indigent'" (Qur'an 69:30-34).

7.4 Lying unbelievers will be draged by their forelock

God assures the believers' success in their struggle with the unbelievers. Addressing Abu Jahl, an unbeliever of Makkah, God warns him and the other unbelievers that if they desist not, they will have a humiliating defeat.

God warns, "Let him (Abu Jahl) beware! If he desists not, We will drag him by the forelock, a lying, sinful forelock! Then, let him call (for help) to his council (of comrades). We will call on the angels of punishment (to deal with him)! Nay, heed him not. But bow down in adoration, and bring yourself closer (to Allah)" (Qur'an 96:15-19).

Chapter 12

Women's—Rights and Obligations
(All People Have Similar Rights and Obligations)

There are various Signs in the creation of the Universe that do confirm that God is Exalted in Might and is full of Wisdom. If we believe this then we will try our best to follow His commands in raising our families and managing our communities. God reminds people in *Surah Al-Rum*, that, "Among His Signs is this, that He created you from dust; and then, - behold, you are human beings scattered (far and wide)! And among His Signs is this, that He created for you mates from among yourselves, that you may find peace with them, and He has put love and mercy between your (hearts): verily in that are Signs for those who reflect. And among His Signs is the creation of the heavens and the earth, and the variations in your languages and your colors: verily in that are Signs for those who know. And among His Signs is the sleep that you take by night and by day, and the quest that you (make for livelihood) out of His Bounty: verily in that are Signs for those who hearken" (Qur'an 30:20-23).

1
BELIEVERS— FEAR TO IGNORE GOD'S COMMANDS

Only belief in God and good deeds can assure one's salvation. God warns people that no one can save another, even the nearest of one's kin from God's punishment. Even His messenger Noah could not save his son because his son's conduct was unrighteous, nor was His messenger Lot able to save his wife. The angels who were sent to destroy Lot's people told Lot to leave the city behind and not turn back, but Lot's wife failed to follow this angelic advice and paid the consequence.

The drowning of Noah's son and the destiny of Lot's wife prove that only belief in God and good deeds can assure individual salvation. God told Noah that those who did wrong would be drowned and when: "Noah called upon his Lord, and said: 'O my Lord! Surely my son is of my family! And Your promise is true, and You are the just of judges!' He said: 'O Noah! He is not of your family, for his conduct is unrighteous. So ask not of Me that of which you have no knowledge! I give you counsel lest you act like the ignorant'" (Qur'an 11:45-46).

The believers are commanded to save themselves and their families from Hell. Transgressing divine limits will lead people to difficulties in the life of this world and will lead them to Hell in the next. Since God is merciful to people He guides them to lighten their difficulties. Strictly following His commands spares people from such difficulties. People should repent and reform to save themselves and their families from bad conduct and sins. Since repenting is not accepted by God from perpetual sinners, people should repent and mend their ways before it is too late. The believers should also beware of their kin's behavior but forgive and overlook their faults.

1.1 BELIEVERS TRY TO SAVE THEIR FAMILIES FROM THE FIRE
The family is the smallest unit of humanity. Parents have to inculcate human values in themselves and then in the members of their families. Since human conduct is the only criteria that distinguishes people from animals, they must carefully guard not only their own conduct, but the conduct of all those who are near and dear to them.

God commands the believers, "O you who believe! Save yourselves and your families from a Fire whose fuel is men and stones…" (Qur'an 66:6).

1.2 VIOLATION OF DIVINE LIMITS— LEADS PEOPLE TO THE FIRE
After describing the rules that apply to the distribution of inheritance after the death of an individual in *Surah Al-Nisa*, God tells people that,

1. "Those are limits set by Allah; those who obey Allah and His Messenger will be admitted to Gardens with rivers flowing beneath, to abide therein (forever), and that will be the supreme achievement.

2. But those who disobey Allah and His Messenger and transgress His limits will be admitted to a Fire, to abide therein: and they shall have a humiliating punishment" (Qur'an 4:13-14).

1.3 GOD IS MERCIFUL— HE GUIDES TO LIGHTEN DIFFICULTIES

The purpose of divine guidance is that it should become clear to people what is right and what is wrong. By following what God commands the believers become a candidate for His Mercy.

God tells the believers that, "Allah does wish to make clear to you and to show you the ordinances of those before you; and (He does wish to) turn to you (in mercy); and Allah is All-knowing, All-wise. Allah does wish to turn to you, but the wish of those who follow their lusts is that you should turn away (from Him)—far, far away. Allah does wish to lighten your (difficulties), for man was created weak (in flesh)" (Qur'an 4:26-28).

1.4 STRICTLY FOLLOWING GOD'S COMMANDS SPARES PEOPLE

Divine disrespect consists not only in the breach of religious rites, but even more vital is the defiance of the laws of nature which God has put in place. These laws relate to all human beings to whom justice and fairness are the basis of all their social duties. Breach of these laws has adverse consequences for individuals and society, in this life as well as in the Hereafter.

God asks in *Surah Al-Talaq* as to, "How many populations that insolently opposed the command of their Lord and of His messengers, did We not then call to account—to severe account? And We imposed on them an exemplary punishment. Then did they taste the evil result of their conduct, and the end of their conduct was perdition. Allah has prepared for them a severe punishment (in the Hereafter). Therefore, fear Allah, O you men of understanding who have believed!— for Allah has indeed sent down to you a message—" (Qur'an 65:8-10).

1.5 REPENT AND REFORM TO SAVE YOURSELF FROM THE FIRE

Repentance is a way to encourage and motivate people to improve their character and behavior and thus society. It also saves them from God's punishment for violating His law and helps them adjust their lives to what He commands.

He commands the believers that, "O you who believe! Turn to Allah with sincere repentance in the hope that your Lord will remove from you your ills and admit you to Gardens beneath which rivers flow— the Day that Allah will not permit to be humiliated the Prophet and those which who believe with him. ..." (Qur'an 66:8).

1.6 REPENTING IS NOT ACCEPTED FROM PERPETUAL SINNERS

In a society where sinning becomes fashion, people tend to repent on their death bed. Such repentance is not acceptable to God. This is because such repentance neither improves the individual's behavior nor reforms the society.

God tells people that, "Allah accepts the repentance of those

1. Who do evil in ignorance and repent soon afterwards; to them will Allah turn in mercy, for Allah is full of knowledge and wisdom.

Of no effect is the repentance of those

2. Who continue to do evil, until death faces one of them, and he says, 'Now have I repented indeed,'
3. Nor of those who die rejecting faith. For them have We prepared a punishment most grievous" (Qur'an 4:17-18).

2
BELIEVERS'— LIMITS IN MARRIAGE AND DIVORCE

Believing men do not marry unbelieving women. Married couples remain married honorably or separate equitably. God commands honest reconciliation efforts before completing the process of divorce, and these reconciliation efforts last three periods or three months. During the reconciliation process, wives live in their own homes. The waiting period before a woman can remarry ends with the end of the reconciliation period and the finality of the divorce. The waiting period for a widow is four months and ten days. No waiting period is required if the marriage is dissolved before its consummation. In this case, the payment of half of the dower is required. In any case, men are commanded to properly take care of their ex-wives or widows.

2.1 SINGLE BELIEVERS SHOULD MARRY OR REMAIN CHASTE

Single persons, either unmarried, divorced or widowed should get married. Marriage in Islam requires some sort of dower for the wife and financial resource to support one's family. If a person cannot afford that, he must wait and keep himself chaste. He is forbidden to find ways to satisfy his natural cravings outside marriage.

The believing men and women are told to,

1. "Marry those among you who are single or the virtuous ones among your-selves, male or female. If they are in poverty, Allah will give them means out of His Grace, for Allah encompasses all, and He knows all things.
2. Let those who find not the wherewithal for marriage keep themselves chaste until Allah gives them means out of His Grace. ..." (Qur'an 24:32-33).

2.2 MARRY NOT UNBELIEVERS- BELIEVING SPOUSES ARE BETTER

Celibacy is not necessarily a virtue but may be a vice and has been repudiated in Islam. On the other hand, marriage is very much recommended and organized around certain rules which need to be followed.

God tells the believers that,

1. "Do not marry unbelieving women (idolaters) until they believe: A slave woman who believes is better than an unbelieving woman, even though she allures you.
2. Nor marry (your girls) to unbelievers until they believe: A man slave who believes is better than an unbeliever, even though he allures you. ..."
3. "They ask you concerning women's courses. Say: 'They are a hurt and a pollution, so keep away from women in their courses, and do not approach them until they are clean. ..."
4. "Your wives are as a tilth unto you, so approach your tilth when or how you will, but do some good act for your souls beforehand; and fear Allah.

And know that you are to meet Him (in the Hereafter), and give (these) good tidings to those who believe" (Qur'an 2:221-223).

2.3 Believing women are not lawful for the unbelievers

Believing women are not lawful wives for unbelievers, nor are unbelievers lawful husbands for believing women. This law forbidding Muslim men or women to marry unbelieving women or men was enforced very early in Islam and made it necessary to ascertain the faith of female refugees coming to Madinah before giving them asylum.

God commands the believers as "O you who believe! When there come to you believing women refugees, examine (and test) them. Allah knows best as to their faith. If you ascertain that they are believers, then send them not back to the unbelievers. They (the believing women) are not lawful (wives) for the unbelievers, nor are the (unbelievers) lawful (husbands) for them. ..." (Qur'an 60:10).

2.4 Remain married honorably or part with equitably

The provision for divorce has been made only as an unavoidable necessity otherwise God does not approve that the marriage relationship that has been established between a man and a woman should ever break. It is narrated by Abdullah ibn Umar that the Prophet[PBUH] said: Of all the lawful acts the most detestable to Allah is the divorce (Abu Dawud: 12.2173). However, if separation does take place, it should only be after all possibilities of mutual reconciliation have been exhausted.

Addressing the Messenger God tells the believers: "O Prophet!

1. When you do divorce women, divorce them at their prescribed periods,
2. And count (accurately) their prescribed periods.
3. And fear Allah your Lord, and turn them not out of their houses.
4. Nor shall they (themselves) leave, except in case they are guilty of some open lewdness.

Those are limits set by Allah, and any who transgresses the limits of Allah does verily wrong his (own) soul. You know not if perchance Allah will bring about thereafter some new situation.

5. Thus when they fulfill their term appointed, either take them back on equitable terms or part with them on equitable terms.

And take for witness two persons from among you, endued with justice, and establish the evidence (as) before Allah. Such is the admonition given to him who believes in Allah and the Last Day. And for those who fear Allah, He (ever) prepares a way out" (Qur'an 65:1-2).

2.5 ISLAM HAS A SPECIFIC WAY TO BE FOLLOWED IN DIVORCE

Islam tries to maintain the married state as far as possible, especially where children are concerned. But it is against the restriction of liberty of both men and women in such vitally important matters as love and family life. Islam checks hasty action in divorce as far as possible, and leaves the door to reconciliation open at many stages. Even after divorce a suggestion of reconciliation is made to protect against thoughtless action. A period of waiting (*'iddah*) for three monthly courses is prescribed, in order to see if the marriage conditionally dissolved is likely to result any issue.

God commands the divorced wives and their ex-husbands that,

1. "Divorced women shall wait concerning themselves for three monthly periods. Nor is it lawful for them to hide what Allah has created in their wombs, if they have faith in Allah and the Last Day.
2. And their husbands have the better right to take them back in that period, if they wish for reconciliation.
3. And women shall have rights similar to the rights against them, according to what is equitable; but men have a degree (of advantage) over them. And Allah is Exalted in Power, Wise" (Qur'an 2:228).

2.6 FAMILY ARBITRATION IS TO ACHIEVE RECONCILIATION

An excellent plan for settling family disputes without too much publicity and mud-throwing, is through arbitration by family members. The arbiters from each family will know the weaknesses of both parties, and thus will be able with God's help to achieve a real reconciliation.

God tells the believers that, "If you fear a breach between them twain, appoint (two) arbiters, one from his family and the other from hers. If they wish for peace, Allah will cause their reconciliation, for Allah has full knowledge and is acquainted with all things" (Qur'an 4:35).

2.7 RECONCILIATION LASTS THREE PERIODS OR THREE MONTHS

If separation does take place between the husband and wife, it should only be after all possibilities of mutual reconciliation have been exhausted. This effort lasts three periods or three months. For normal women, the *iddah* is the three monthly courses after separation: if there are no courses or if the courses are in doubt, it is three calendar months. By that time it will be clear whether there is a pregnancy: if there is, the waiting period is extended until after the delivery.

God tells the believers that, "Such of your women as have passed the age of monthly courses, for them the prescribed period, if you have any doubts, is three months, and for those who have no courses (it is the same). For those who carry (life within their wombs), their period is until they deliver their burdens: And for those who fear Allah, He will make their path easy" (Qur'an 65:4).

2.8 WOMEN LIVE IN THEIR HOMES— DURING RECONCILIATION

A selfish man may, in the probationary period before the divorce becomes absolute, treat her badly and while giving her residence and maintenance, may so restrict it as to make her life miserable. This is forbidden. There is still hope of reconciliation, and even if it is not, the parting must be honorable. In case of pregnancy, there is an added responsibility and perhaps an added hope for reconciliation for both parents. In any case, no separation is possible until after the child is born. Even after birth, if no reconciliation between parents is possible, for welfare of the child the care of the mother remains the duty of the father, and there must be mutual council between parents in all truth and sincerity.

The believers are commanded that they should,

1. "Let the women live (in *'Iddah*) in the same style as you live, according to your means;
2. Annoy them not, so as to restrict them.
3. And if they carry (life in their wombs), then spend (your substance) on them until they deliver their burden.

4. And if they suckle your (offspring), give them their recompense and take mutual counsel together, according to what is just and reasonable. And if you find yourselves in difficulties, let another woman suckle (the child) on the (father's) behalf" (Qur'an 65:6).

2.9 DIVORCE BECOMES FINAL WHEN RECONCILIATION FAILS

Let no one think that the liberty given to men 'to divorce' can be used for their own selfish ends. If one uses the law for the injury of the weaker party, his own moral and spiritual nature suffers. The difficult questions of marital relations are often taken as a joke. But these questions profoundly affect our individual lives, the lives of our children, and the purity and welfare of society. This aspect of the situation should be considered again and again.

The believers are also commanded that, "When you divorce women, and they fulfill the term of their *'Iddah*, (The reconciliation or waiting period), either take them back on equitable terms or set them free on equitable terms.

1. But do not take them back to injure them (or) to take undue advantage. If any one does that, he wrongs his own soul.
2. Do not treat Allah's Signs as a jest, but solemnly rehearse Allah's favors on you and the fact that He sent down to you the Book and wisdom for your instruction. And fear Allah, and know that Allah is well-acquainted with all things.
3. When you divorce women, and they fulfill the term of their *'Iddah*, do not prevent them from marrying persons of their choice, if they mutually agree on equitable terms.

This instruction is for all among you who believe in Allah and the Last Day. That is (the course making for) most virtue and purity among you, and Allah knows, and you know not.

4. The mothers shall give suck to their offspring for two whole years, if the father desires to complete the term. But he shall bear the cost of their food and clothing on equitable terms. No soul shall have a burden laid on it greater than it can bear.

5. No mother shall be treated unfairly on account of her child, Nor father on account of his child. An heir shall be chargeable in the same way. If they both decide on weaning by mutual consent and after due consultation, there is no blame on them.
6. If you decide on a foster mother for your offspring, there is no blame on you, provided you pay (the mother) what you offered on equitable terms.

But fear Allah and know that Allah sees well what you do" (Qur'an 2:231-233).

2.10 THE WAITING PERIOD FOR WIDOW IS 4 MONTHS 10 DAYS
When the widows have fulfilled their waiting period after the death of their husbands, they are free to accept proposals for marriage or get married again.

God instructs the believers that, "If any of you die and leave widows behind, they shall wait concerning themselves four months and ten days.

1. When they have fulfilled their term, there is no blame on you (the guardian) if they dispose of themselves in a just and reasonable manner, and Allah is well-acquainted with what you do.
2. There is no blame on you if you (prospective husband) make an offer of betrothal or hold it in your hearts. Allah knows that you cherish them in your hearts, But do not make a secret contract with them except in terms honorable, nor resolve on the tie of marriage till the term prescribed is fulfilled. ... "(Qur'an 2:234-235).

2.11 NO WAITING PERIOD IF MARRIAGE IS NOT CONSUMMATED
Although no waiting period is required if the marriage is not consummated, the believing men are commanded to separate in a friendly manner by giving the parting women a suitable gift.

The believers are commanded that, "O you who believe! When you marry believing women and then divorce them before you have touched them, no period of 'Iddah have you to count in respect of them: So give them a present, and set them free in a handsome manner" (Qur'an 33:49).

2.12 HALF DOWER IS DUE IF MARRIAGE IS NOT CONSUMMATED

A divorce may happen before the consummation of marriage either before or after the fixation of a dower.

At least half of the dower is due if the dower has been fixed before such a divorce.

God tells the believers that,

1. "There is no blame on you if you divorce women before consummation or the fixation of their dower;

But bestow on them (a suitable gift), the wealthy according to his means, and the poor according to his means—a gift of a reasonable amount is due from those who wish to do the right thing.

2. And if you divorce them before consummation, but after the fixation of a dower for them,

Then the half of the dower (is due to them), unless they remit it or (the man's half) is remitted by him in whose hands is the marriage tie; and the remission (of the man's half) is the nearest to righteousness. Do not forget liberality between yourselves. For Allah sees well all that you do" (Qur'an 2:236-237).

2.13 BELIEVERS TAKE CARE OF THEIR EX-WIVES AND WIDOWS

God has commanded the believers to take care of their widows or ex-wives after their death or divorce for a reasonable period of time according to their means.

The believers are commanded that,

1. "Those of you who die and leave widows should bequeath for their widows a year's maintenance and residence,

But if they leave (the residence); there is no blame on you for what they do with themselves, provided it is reasonable. And Allah is Exalted in Power, Wise.

2. For divorced women (a one time provision should be paid) on a reasonable (scale). This is a duty on the righteous.

Thus does Allah make clear His Signs to you in order that you may understand" (Qur'an 2:240-242).

3
BELIEVERS— ARE KIND TO THEIR WIVES

Polygamy is permitted in Islam only if one can do justice—justice to his first wife and justice to his second, third, and fourth wife. Since it is not easy for a man to do justice, God advises men not to ignore anyone of one's wives. Marrying widows is encouraged for the care of the orphans, and it is forbidden to marry unwilling women or to be unkind to them. Marriage between some relatives is also forbidden.

3.1 MARRIAGE IS ENCOURAGED TO TAKE CARE OF ORPHANS
Since polygamy was already permitted in society, Verse 3 of *Surah Al-Nisa* was not sent to permit polygamy but to help solve the problem of the orphaned children of the Muslims who fell martyrs in the Islamic battles (this verse was revealed after the battle of Uhud): Saying, 'O Muslims, If you cannot fulfill the rights of the orphans in other ways, you may marry those widows who have orphans with them'.

This Verse was also revealed to solve the problem of grown up female orphans who were not given proper dower (*Mahr*) by their guardians who wanted to marry them. So they (guardians) were forbidden to marry the orphan girls unless they paid them an appropriate dower, otherwise, they were told to marry other women instead of them (Sahih Bukhari 4.51.025).

The believers are told that,

1. "If you fear that you shall not be able to deal justly with the orphans, marry women of your choice, two or three or four.

But if you fear that you shall not be able to deal justly (with them), then only one, or (a captive) that your right hands possess. That will be more suitable, to prevent you from doing injustice.

2. And give the women (on marriage) their dower as a free gift; but if they, of their own good pleasure remit any part of it to you, take it and enjoy it with right good cheer" (Qur'an 4:3-4).

3.2 BE JUST TO WIVES AND SETTLE YOUR AFFAIR AMICABLY

In Islam, the provision for divorce has been made only as an unavoidable necessity, therefore, all possibilities of mutual reconciliation should be attempted to save the marriage.

The believers are told that,

1. "If a wife fears cruelty or desertion on her husband's part, there is no blame on them if they arrange an amicable settlement between themselves; and such settlement is best; even though men's souls are swayed by greed. But if you do good and practice self-restraint, Allah is well-acquainted with all that you do.

2. You are never able to be fair and just as between women, even if it is your ardent desire: But turn not away (from a woman) altogether, so as to leave her (as it were) hanging (in the air). If you mend your ways, and practice self-restraint, Allah is Oft-forgiving, Most Merciful.

But if they disagree (and must part), Allah will provide abundance for all from His all-reaching bounty: for Allah is He that cares for all and is Wise" (4:128-130).

3.3 FORCED MARRIAGES AND MARITAL ABUSE ARE BANNED

God commands the believers to be kind and just to their wives and reminds them that, He has put a great deal of good even in those things which some one may dislike. On divorce, the believers are forbidden to ask back any gifts which they have given to their wives.

The believers are commanded that, "O you who believe!

1. You are forbidden to inherit women against their will,
2. Nor should you treat them with harshness,

That you may take away part of the dower you have given them,- except where they have been guilty of open lewdness;

3. On the contrary live with them on a footing of kindness and equity. If you take a dislike to them, it may be that you dislike a thing, and Allah brings about through it a great deal of good.
4. But if you decide to take one wife in place of another, even if you had given the latter a whole treasure for dower, take not the least bit of it back;

Would you take it by slander and manifest wrong? And how could you take it when you have gone in unto each other, and they have taken from you a solemn covenant?" (Qur'an 4:19-21).

3.4 MEN CANNOT MARRY SOME OF THEIR FEMALE RELATIVES

God has prohibited marriage among some relatives as well as with women who are already married. Except for these, all other women are lawful, provided one is seeking them in marriage, desiring chastity, not lust.

The believers are told that,

1. "And marry not women whom your fathers married, except what is past. It was shameful and odious, an abominable custom indeed.
2. Prohibited to you (for marriage) are

Your mothers, daughters, sisters, father's sisters, mother's sisters, brother's daughters, sister's daughters, foster mothers (who gave you suck), foster sisters, your wives' mothers, your step-daughters under your guardianship, born of your wives to whom you have gone in—no prohibition if you have not gone in, (those who have been) wives of your sons proceeding from your loins, and two sisters in wedlock at one and the same time, except for what is past, for Allah is Oft-Forgiving, Most Merciful.

3. Also (prohibited are) women already married, except those whom your right hands possess:

Thus has Allah ordained (prohibitions) against you. Except for these, all others are lawful, provided you seek (them in marriage) with gifts from your property, desiring chastity, not lust. Seeing that you derive benefit from them, give them their dowers as prescribed. But if after a dower is prescribed, you agree mutually (to vary it), there is no blame on you, and Allah is All-knowing, All-wise" (Qur'an 4:22-24).

3.5 GOD TURNS TO YOU IN MERCY AND GUIDES TO HIS WAY

God encourages believers to marry women captured during war telling that, 'you all belong to one human family' so wed them with the permission of their owners, and give them appropriate dowers.

The believers are told that, "If any of you have not the means wherewith to wed free believing women, they may wed believing girls from among those whom your right hands possess; and Allah has full knowledge about your faith. You are one from another; wed them with the leave of their owners, and give them their dowers, according to what is reasonable. They should be chaste, not lustful, nor taking paramours. When they are taken in wedlock, if they fall into shame, their punishment is half that for free women. This (permission) is for those among you who fear sin; but it is better for you that you practice self-restraint. And Allah is Oft-Forgiving, Most Merciful" (Qur'an 4:25).

4

BELIEVERS— AS SPOUSES AND PARENTS

Men are commanded to protect and support women and their families. They are also commanded to be just and kind with their wives, their children, and the orphans. Wives on their part are obedient and sincere to their husbands. They protect what Allah would have them protect in their husband's absence. A general rule which should be followed in family relationships is to, 'Know enemies among your kin, but forgive them.' God tells the believers in *Surah*

Al-Taghabun that, "O you who believe! Truly, among your wives and your children are (some that are) enemies to yourselves; so beware of them! But if you forgive and overlook and cover up (their faults), verily Allah is Oft-Forgiving, Most Merciful" (Qur'an 64:14).

4.1 MEN'S OBLIGATION IS TO PROTECT AND SUPPORT WOMEN
Husbands are commanded to look after their wives' affairs and protect their interests. They are also obligated to financially support the female members of their families: This is a general rule applicable to all family relationships between male and female members of a family. Since women have no financial responsibility, they receive less in inheritance than the male members of their family.

God tells the believers that, "Men (male members of a family) are the protectors and maintainers of their (women). (This is) because Allah has given the one (men) more (strength) than the other (women), and because they (men are obligated to) support them from their means. ... " (Qur'an 4:34).

4.2 WOMEN'S OBLIGATION IS LOYALTY AND ACCOMODATION
Wives are obedient and supportive to their husbands and they look after the interests of their husbands in their absence. The believing women are told that,

1. "... Therefore the righteous women (as wives) are devoutly obedient, and
2. (They) guard in (the husband's) absence what Allah would have them guard. ..." (Qur'an 4:34).

4. 3 THE MESSENGER'S WIVES' CONDUCT IS TO BE EMULATED
Addressing the Messenger's wives, God has highlighted the behavior traits which should be emulated by them (and all believing women) in their households.

The Messenger's wives are told that,
"O consorts of the Prophet! You are not like any of the (other) women. If you do fear (Allah),

1. Be not too complacent of speech, lest one in whose heart is a disease should be moved with desire,

2. But you speak a speech (that is) just,
3. And stay quietly in your houses,
4. And make not a dazzling display, like that of the former times of ignorance,
5. And establish regular prayer, and give regular charity,
6. And obey Allah and His Messenger.

And Allah only wishes to remove all abomination from you, you members of the (Prophet's) family, and to make you pure and spotless.

7. And recite what is rehearsed to you in your homes, of the revelations of Allah and His Wisdom:

For Allah understands the finest mysteries and is well-acquainted (with them)" (Qur'an 33:32-34).

4.4 MEN TREAT WIVES WITH JUSTICE AND ANNOY THEM NOT

Loosing one's temper, nagging, sarcasm, speaking ill of each other in other people's presence, reverting to past faults which should have been forgiven and forgotten - all this is forbidden in Islam. In all relationships people should know that God is watching over them. They should live their lives in His presence—realizing how foolish their little squabbles would appear in God's presence!

God tells the believing husbands that,

1. " ... As to those women on whose part you fear disloyalty and ill-conduct, admonish them (first), (next) refuse to share their beds, (and last) spank them (lightly).
2. But if they return to obedience, seek not against them means (of annoyance),

for Allah is Most High, great (above you all)" (Qur'an 4:34).

4.5 BE JUST TO YOUR WIVES, CHILDREN AND THE ORPHANS

Again and again it is stressed in Islam that individuals and the society should be just in their dealings with women, orphans, children, and all whose weakness requires special consideration. It has further been commanded that people should be very sensitive and honest in dealing with orphan females and widows with orphans to safeguard their rights.

Concerning women and orphans, God instructs the Messenger as, "They ask your instruction concerning the women. Say: 'Allah does instruct you about them.

1. And (remember) what has been rehearsed unto you in the Book concerning the orphans of women to whom you give not the portions prescribed, and yet whom you desire to marry, as
2. also (remember) concerning the children who are weak and oppressed—that you stand firm for justice to orphans.

There is not a good deed which you do, but Allah is well-acquainted therewith" (Qur'an 4:127).

4.6 Beware of kin—forgive and overlook their faults
Forgiving people is a divine attribute which is highly recommended to be followed by the believers. This is strongly recommended especially for the members of one's own family.

God tells the believers as, "O you who believe!

1. Truly, among your wives and your children are (some that are) enemies to yourselves: so beware of them!
2. But if you forgive and overlook, and cover up (their faults), verily Allah is Oft-Forgiving, Most Merciful" (Qur'an 64:14).

5
Believers— Shun all Social Crimes

Being unjust to others, prostitution, adultery, and homosexuality are some of the most heinous crimes. Adultery and falsely accusing chaste women are forbidden and are punishable by the law, and those who slander chaste women are cursed in life. Other significant crimes include being envious of others and eating unlawful foods. Gossip not proven by witnesses is considered to be a lie and serious misconduct. Entering other people's homes without permission and staring at each other are forbidden to both men and women. Singles are commanded to remain chaste, and they should be helped to get married.

Although outer covering garments are not required for older women, male and female believers are commanded to dress modestly. Women are also encouraged to emulate the conduct of the Messenger's wives. The believing women are not lawful wives for the unbelieving men and cannot be married to them. Family members are also commanded to honor their secrets as secrets.

5.1 PROSTITUTION, ADULTERY, HOMOSEXUALITY ARE SINS

Prostitution, adultery, and homosexuality are punishable crimes. In *Surah Al-Nur*, the believers are commanded that, "The woman and the man guilty of adultery or fornication, - flog each of them with a hundred stripes: Let not compassion move you in their case, in a matter prescribed by Allah, if you believe in Allah and the Last Day: and let a party of the believers witness their punishment" (Qur'an 24:2).

Homosexuality is a behavior that is morally unacceptable as it is an open and public indecency tending to corrupt the morals of the community. Again to protect the honor of chaste women, the evidence of four instead of the usual two witnesses is required to discourage people from false allegations. Rape on the other hand is a crime to be investigated as any other crime like murder, robbery etc.

God commands the believers that,

1. "If any of your women are guilty of lewdness,

Take the evidence of four (reliable) witnesses from among you against them; and if they testify, confine them to houses until death does claim them or Allah ordains for them some (other) way.

2. If two men among you are guilty of lewdness, punish them both.
If they repent and amend, leave them alone, for Allah is Oft-Returning, Most Merciful" (Qur'an 4:15-16).

5.2 ACCUSING CHASTE WOMEN IS A PUNISHABLE CRIME

The requirement of four witnesses is to discourage people from falsely accusing chaste women. It has nothing to do with rape which is an assault by a man on a woman. It should be proven in the same way as any other type of assault—like if someone stops a car, beats the driver, steals his money and takes away the car. Islam does not require the rape victim to produce four witnesses.

God commands the believers concerning false accusations that,

"Those who launch a charge against chaste women and produce not four witnesses (to support their allegations)—flog them with eighty stripes, and reject their evidence ever after, for such men are wicked transgressors—Unless they repent thereafter and mend (their conduct), for Allah is Oft-Forgiving, Most Merciful" (Qur'an 24:4-5).

5.3 ESTABLISHING A CHARGE WITHOUT FOUR WITNESSES

Four witnesses are not always required to prove adultery as is explained below in case of those who launch a charge against their spouses. This could also be used in investigating rape cases where four witnesses are not available.

God tells the believers that,

1. "And for those who launch a charge against their spouses and have (in support) no evidence but their own, their solitary evidence (can be received) if they bear witness four times (with an oath) by Allah that they are solemnly telling the truth, and the fifth (oath should be) that they solemnly invoke the curse of Allah on themselves if they tell a lie.
2. But it would avert the punishment from the wife, if she bears witness four times (with an oath) by Allah that (her husband) is telling a lie, and the fifth (oath) should be that she solemnly invokes the wrath of Allah on herself if (her accuser) is telling the truth" (Qur'an 24:6-9).

A seduction charge against Joseph was investigated without four witnesses by a circumstantial evidence as given below. This is an other example of —how to investigate a charge in the absences of witnesses.

"So they both raced each other to the door, and she tore his shirt from the back: they both found her lord near the door. She said: What is the (fitting) punishment for one who formed an evil design against your wife, but prison or a grievous chastisement? He said: It was she that sought to seduce me— from my (true) self.

3. And one of her household saw (this) and bore witness, (thus)— If it be that his shirt is rent from the front, then is her tale true, and he is a liar! But if it be that his shirt is torn from the back, then is she the liar, and he is telling the truth! So when he saw his shirt— that it was torn at the back—

(her husband) said: Behold! It is a snare of you women! Truly, mighty is your snare! O Joseph, pass this over! (O wife), ask forgiveness for your sin, for truly you have been at fault" (Qur'an 12:25-29).

5.4 GOSSIP NOT PROVEN BY WITNESSES IS CERTAINLY A LIE

Referring to the spreading of a scandal against Aisha, the Messenger's wife, without any evidence in which both men and women were involved, the believers have been told that gossip not proven by witnesses is certainly a lie. The obvious duty of people involved was to put the best, and not the worst construction on the acts of one of the 'mothers of the believers'. If any person took it seriously, it was their duty to search for and produce evidence, in the absence of which they themselves became guilty of slander—

God tells the believers that, "Those who brought forward the lie are a body among yourselves; think it not to be an evil to you. On the contrary, it is good for you. To every man among them (will come the punishment) of the sin that he earned, and to him who took on himself the lead among them will be a penalty grievous.

1. Why did not the believers, men and women, when you heard of the affair, put the best construction on it in their own minds and say, 'This (charge) is an obvious lie?'
2. Why did they not bring four witnesses to prove it? When they have not brought the witnesses, such men in the sight of Allah (stand forth) themselves as liars!" (Qur'an 24:11-13).

5.5 SLANDERING A CHASTE PERSON IS SERIOUS MISCONDUCT

Again, referring to the spreading of a scandal against Aisha without any evidence, the believers have been warned that slandering of any chaste person is a serious misconduct which is forbidden to the believers—

God asks the believers that,

1. "And why did you not, when you heard it, say, 'It is not right of us to speak of this. Glory to Allah! This is a most serious slander!'

Allah does admonish you that you may never repeat such (conduct) if you are (true) believers. And Allah makes the Signs plain to you: for Allah is full of knowledge and wisdom.

2. Those who love (to see) scandal published broadcast among the believers will have a grievous penalty in this life and in the Hereafter: Allah knows, and you know not" (Qur'an 24:16-19).

5.6 RESOLVE NOT AGAINST HELPING ONE'S KINSMEN IN NEED

One of the slanderers of Aisha was a cousin of her father Abu Bakr, whom he had been supporting financially. Naturally, he wished to stop that aid, but according to the highest standard of Islamic ethics, he was asked to forgive and forget, which he did, resulting in peace and unity of the Islamic community at that time and set an example to be followed by the believers under similar situations in the future.

God commands the believers that,

1. "Let not those among you who are endued with grace and amplitude of means resolve by oath against helping their kinsmen, those in want and those who have left their homes in Allah's Cause.
2. Let them forgive and overlook; do you not wish that Allah should forgive you?

For Allah is Oft-Forgiving, Most Merciful" (Qur'an 24:22).

5.7 THE SLANDERING OF CHASTE WOMEN IS CURSED BY GOD

Concluding the incident of the slandering of Aisha—

God warns the believers that, "Those who slander chaste women, indiscreet but believing, are cursed in this life and in the Hereafter. For them is a grievous penalty" (Qur'an 24:23).

5.8 BEING ENVIOUS IS ONE OF THE MOST HEINOUS CRIMES

People receive their provisions from God—some greater than others. The provisions seem unequal, but it is assured that Providence has allotted them by a scheme, 'by which people receive what they earn'. One must not be jealous if other people have more—in wealth, position, strength, honor, talent or happiness. Things are equalized in the aggregate or in the long run, or equated to needs and merits on the scale which one cannot understand. If people want more, instead of being jealous, they should pray to God and place before Him their needs. Though He knows all, our prayer may reveal to us our weaknesses and enable us to deserve more of God's bounty by making ourselves fit for it.

God commands the believers that,

1. "And in nowise covet those things in which Allah has bestowed His gifts more freely on some of you than on others.
2. To men is allotted what they earn, and to women what they earn, but ask Allah of His bounty. For Allah has full knowledge of all things" (Qur'an 4:32).

5.9 ENTER NOT OTHER PEOPLE'S HOMES WITHOUT APPROVAL

The conventions of propriety and privacy are essential to a refined life of goodness and purity. Therefore, entering other people's homes without their permission is forbidden to the believers.

God tells the believers that, "O you who believe!

1. Enter not houses other than your own until you have asked permission and saluted those in them. That is best for you, in order that you may heed (what is seemly).

If you find no one in the house, enter not until permission is given to you. If you are asked to go back, go back. That makes for greater purity for yourselves, and Allah knows well all that you do.

1. It is no fault on your part to enter houses not used for living in, which serve some (other) use for you; and Allah has knowledge of what you reveal and what you conceal" (Qur'an 24:27-29).

5.10 STARING AT OTHERS IS FORBIDDEN FOR MEN & WOMEN

The rule of modesty applies to men as well as to women. A brazen stare by a man at a women or even a man is a breach of good manners and should be avoided by the believers. It is one of the tricks of showy or unchaste women to tinkle their ankle ornaments to draw people's attention to themselves. That is why the believing women are forbidden to display their beauty and ornaments in any unusual ways.

The believing men and women are told to,

1. "Say to the believing men that they should lower their gaze and guard their modesty. That will make for greater purity for them, and Allah is well-acquainted with all that they do.

2. And say to the believing women that they should lower their gaze and guard their modesty; that they should not display their beauty and ornaments except what (must ordinarily) appear thereof …" (Qur'an 24:30-31).

5.11 FEMALE BELIEVERS ARE ASKED TO DRESS MODESTLY

All believing women are commanded to dress modestly and cover themselves with outer garments when in public. This is not to restrict their liberty but to protect them from harm and molestation. Elderly women on the other hand are exempt from wearing the outer garment if they like. However it is best for them to be modest.

The Messenger is told,

1. "O Prophet! Tell your wives and daughters, and the believing women, that they should cast their outer garments over their persons (when abroad).

That is most convenient that they should be known (as such) and not molested, and Allah is Oft-Forgiving, Most Merciful" (Qur'an 33:59).

2. "Such elderly women as are past the prospect of marriage—there is no blame on them if they lay aside their (outer) garments, provided they make not a wanton display of their beauty.

But it is best for them to be modest, and Allah is One Who sees and knows all things" (Qur'an 24:60).

5.12 FAMILY MEMBERS SHOULD NOT DIVULGE THEIR SECRETS
Citing an incident from the Messenger's household, the believers are advised to guard their family secrets, and not disclose them to anyone even to their closest friends: "When the Prophet disclosed a matter in confidence to one of his consorts, and she then divulged it (to another), and Allah made it known to him, he confronted her with part thereof and held back a part. Then when he told her thereof, she said, 'Who told you this?' He said, 'He told me Who knows and is well-acquainted (with all things)'" (Qur'an 66:3).

Chapter 13

Believers—Defend Themselves
(Believers Defend What They Believe In)

Jihad, the struggle to protect human society, can be a simple action, such as standing firm in defense of the Cause of Islam. This may require speaking out in public against ignoring Islamic principles, writing articles, or publishing books. It may also take the form of reminding people of their Islamic duties and of motivating them to conduct their lives according to Islam. It may also take the form of fighting the enemies of Islam in battle in order to foil their attempts to smother the call of Islam. Striving, making efforts, and trying to convince oneself or others about the truth of Islam are all different aspects of Jihad. It does not only mean fighting on a battlefield. But if a situation arises where the believers are attacked, then they have no choice but to defend themselves. The believers fight only with those unbelievers who attack them. The believers are forbidden to be the aggressors.

The 'Divine Law of War and Peace' is highlighted in *Surah Al-Baqarah* as, "Fight in the Cause of Allah (with) those who fight (with) you, but do not transgress limits, for Allah loves not transgressors. '... But if they cease, let there be no hostility except to those who practice oppression' " (Qur'an 2:190, 193). In *Surah Al-Anfal*, God commands the believers, "But if the enemy incline towards peace, you do (also) incline towards peace, and trust in Allah, for He is One that hears and knows (all things)" (Qur'an 8:61). Believers guard against injustice and oppression in their own society. They fight in the Way of Allah for the sake of helpless men, women, and children who, being weak, have been oppressed. They fight with the aggressors and hostile unbelievers. The believers' lives, abilities, and assets are a trust from God that they have to return when demanded. For the believers, not defending themselves is a heinous sin.

1
BELIEVERS— DEFEND THEMSELVES IF ATTACKED

During difficulties and hard times, God is sufficient for the believers. People who strive hard for a good cause are better than those who do not strive. Believers are partners of each other and strive together for a good cause. God has permitted people to fight to defend themselves when attacked.

1.1 DURING DIFFICULTIES, GOD IS SUFFICIENT FOR BELIEVERS

God is sufficient for the believers during their life on earth. Believers are told that it is Satan that suggests to them to fear him and his followers. Contrarily, the believers are commanded that they, 'should not be afraid of Satan and his associates but fear only God if they are the believers.'

A year after the battle of Uhud, "Men said to them (the believers): 'A great army is gathering against you,' and frightened them, but it (only) increased their faith. They said: 'For us Allah is sufficient, and He is the best disposer of affairs.' And they returned with grace and bounty from Allah. No harm ever touched them, for they followed the good pleasure of Allah, and Allah is the Lord of bounties unbounded. It is only Satan that suggests to you the fear of his votaries. Be not afraid of them, but fear Me if you have faith" (Qur'an 3:173-175).

1.2 BELIEVERS WHO STRIVE FOR A GOOD CAUSE ARE BETTER

The reward is always proportional to the efforts of believers for a good cause. Although all believers have been promised good in this life as well as in the life hereafter, the believers who strive for a good cause are better than those who do not strive in God's Way.

God tells the believers that, "Not equal are those believers who sit (at home) and receive no hurt and those who strive and fight in the Cause of Allah with their goods and their persons. Allah has granted a grade higher to those who strive and fight with their goods and persons than to those who sit (at home). Unto all (in faith) Allah has promised good but those who strive and fight has He distinguished above those who sit (at home) by a special reward—" (Qur'an 4:95).

1.3 PARTNERS ARE ALL WHO STRIVE UNITED FOR A GOOD CAUSE

God's Providence and Justice may not always appear plain to our eyes. During this worldly struggle, the believers are told that if they help and support a good cause, they share in all its credit and in the eventual victory. If it looks otherwise, one should not be deceived by its appearance. This is because God has power over all things. Contrarily, one cannot support a bad cause without sharing in its evil consequence.

Striving for a good cause is all that matters to the believers as God commands, "Then fight in Allah's Cause—you are held responsible only for yourself— and rouse the believers. It may be that Allah will restrain the fury of the unbelievers, for Allah is the strongest in might and in punishment. Whoever recommends and helps a good cause becomes a partner therein, and whoever recommends and helps an evil cause shares in its burden. And Allah has power over all things" (Qur'an 4:84-85).

1.4 GOD PERMITS PEOPLE TO FIGHT AND DEFEND THEMSELVES

Since free choice on the basis of informed conviction is an inalienable human right, Islam permits its members to defend themselves if they are persecuted because of their religion.

God commands the believers, "To those against whom war is made, permission is given (to fight) because they are wronged—and verily Allah is most powerful for their aid— (They are) those who have been expelled from their homes in defiance of right, (for no cause) except that they say, 'Our Lord is Allah.' Had not Allah checked one set of people by means of another, there would surely have been pulled down monasteries, churches, synagogues, and mosques in which the name of Allah is commemorated in abundant measure. Allah will certainly aid those who aid His (Cause)..." (Qur'an 22:39-40).

1.5 But kill none—intentional killing is not permitted

God has ordained human life to be equally sacred for all people at all times and places. Citing the story of two sons of Adam in which one of them regretfully killed the other, God ordained that, "... if any one slew a person— unless it be for murder or for spreading mischief in the land— it would be as if he slew the whole people: and if any one saved a life, it would be as if he saved the life of the whole people. ..." (Qur'an 5:32).

But sometimes mistakes do happen for example, in road accidents. If someone is killed without an intention to kill, it is not murder. In such cases the family of the deceased is entitled to compensation unless they freely remit it. No compensation or forgiveness is available for intentional killing without a just cause and the destiny of such murderers is Hell. God commands the believers that, "Never should a believer kill a believer, but (if it so happens) by mistake, (compensation is due).... If a man kills a believer intentionally, his recompense is Hell, to abide therein (forever), and the wrath and the curse of Allah are upon him, and a dreadful penalty is prepared for him" (Qur'an 4:92-93).

2

Believers— Fight and Spend in their Defense

The Messenger sought the welfare of people, and the believers follow his example in order to succeed in life. It is unfortunate that some people say things they do not do. This results in corruption if people do not resist it. Therefore, the believers fight and spend in God's Way to eradicate corruption from their communities. That is why the individual who dies striving in His Way lives on forever.

2.1 Messenger sought welfare— follow him to succeed

God tells people that He has sent a true teacher for their guidance, who is grieved if any of his students do not pay attention, and wastes his or her life. He is attentive to the needs of his followers, and whenever any of them shows signs of Faith, his kindness and mercy surrounds him— "Now has come unto you a Messenger from among yourselves. It grieves him that you should perish. Ardently anxious is he over you; to the believers is he most kind and merciful.

But if they turn away, say: 'Allah suffices (sufficient for) me; there is no god but He; on Him is my trust. He the Lord of the throne (of glory) supreme' " (Qur'an 9:128-129).

2.2 BELIEVERS PRACTICE FIRST WHAT THEY PREACH TO OTHERS
Referring to the breach of discipline by some fighters at the battle of Uhud, God tells the believers that when their deeds are not commensurate with their words, their behavior is questionable and under such circumstances, it is only His Mercy which can save them from disasters. Therefore, in any struggle, when a large number of people are involved, they should behave like— a solid wall of order, discipline, cohesion and courage.

God asks "O you who believe!

1. Why you say that which you do not (do)?
   Grievously odious is it in the sight of Allah that you say that which you do not.
2. Truly Allah loves those who fight in His Cause in battle array, as if they were a solid cemented structure" (Qur'an 61:2-4).

2.3 CORRUPTION SPREADS— IF GOOD PEOPLE DO NOT RESIST IT
Persistent corruption is like a cancer which spreads and destroys society if not resisted by its members. Since it is humanly impossible to have a corruption free society, efforts should always be made to minimize it. Communities are not destroyed for a single wrongdoing if its members are likely to repent and reform.

God asks people, "Why were there not, among the generations before you, persons possessed of balanced good sense, prohibiting (men) from mischief in the earth— except a few among them whom We saved (from harm)? But the wrongdoers pursued the enjoyment of the good things of life that were given them, and persisted in sin. Nor would your Lord be the One to destroy communities for a single wrongdoing if its members were likely to mend. If your Lord had so Willed, He could have made mankind one people; but they will not cease to dispute" (Qur'an 11:116-118).

2.4 BELIEVERS STRIVE HARD AND SPEND IN THE CAUSE OF GOD

Citing an unknown episode from history, the believers are told that if they are not prepared to fight for their faith, with their lives and resources, both their lives and resources will be wiped out by their enemies. God gives life which cannot be saved by cowardice. History confirms that people who readily agreed to leave their homes even more in number than their enemies, had the sentence of death pronounced on them because of their cowardice and they deserved this. God restores people to life if they strive to preserve it. This is a lesson to every generation.

God asks the believers, "Did you not turn your vision to those who abandoned their homes, though they were thousands (In number), for fear of death? Allah said to them: 'Die.' Then He restored them to life, for Allah is full of bounty to mankind, but most of them are ungrateful.

1. Then (O believers) fight in the Cause of Allah, and know that Allah hears and knows all things.
2. Who is he that will loan to Allah a beautiful loan which Allah will double unto his credit and multiply many times?

It is Allah that gives (you) want or plenty, and to Him shall be your return" (Qur'an 2:243-245).

2.5 A PERSON WHO DIES STRIVING IN GOD'S WAY— DIES NOT

People who die striving in God's Way are not dead—they rejoice at the bliss they have achieved. Besides, they have saved their dear ones from fear, sorrow, humiliation, and grief that results by not striving in this life, even before they come to share in the glories of the Hereafter. So the people left behind have no cause to grieve at the death of their Martyrs.

God commands the believers, "Think not of those who are slain in Allah's Way as dead. Nay, they live, finding their sustenance in the presence of their Lord. They rejoice in the bounty provided by Allah: And with regard to those left behind, who have not yet joined them (in their bliss), the (Martyrs) glory in the fact that on them is no fear, nor have they (cause to) grieve" (Qur'an 3:169-170).

3

Believers—Fight but Commit no Aggression

God commands the believers to fight with those who fight against them during a war, but He forbids transgression. Since the law of equality applies universally, it is also applicable to prohibitions. Therefore, fighting is permitted in the prohibited months only if the believers are attacked. The believers should take precautions while fighting to defend themselves and should not take unbelievers or hypocrites as allies or protectors. Being an unbelievers' ally is hypocritical and an open proof against such believers. The hypocrites will be in the lowest depths of the Fire. The believers are also forbidden to run away from the battlefield during a war.

3.1 Fight those who fight against you but exceed not

War is permissible in self-defense and under well-defined limits. When undertaken, it must be pursued with vigor, but only to restore peace and freedom of religion. In any case strict limits should not be transgressed: women, children, and elderly should not be molested, nor trees and crops cut down, or peace denied when the enemy is inclined towards peace.

The believers are commanded to, "Fight in the Cause of Allah those who fight you, but do not transgress limits; for Allah loves not transgressors.

1. And slay them wherever you catch them (in the battlefield), and turn them out from where they have turned you out; for tumult and oppression are worse than slaughter;

2. But fight them not at the Sacred Mosque, unless they (first) fight you there, but if they fight you, slay them. Such is the reward of those who suppress faith.

3. But if they cease, Allah is Oft-Forgiving, Most Merciful.

4. And fight them (the oppressors) on until there is no more tumult or oppression and there prevail (in your community) justice and faith in Allah. But if they cease, let there be no hostility except to those who practice oppression" (Qur'an 2:190-193).

3.2 The law of equality applies— to all prohibitions

Any convention or agreement is useless if one party does not respect it. There must be a law of equality: if one party breaks it and attacks the other party, the attacked party is free to defend themselves. At the same time the believers are commanded to exercise self-restraint as much as possible.

The believers are told that, "The prohibited month— for the prohibited month, and so for all things prohibited—

1. There is the law of equality. If then anyone transgresses the prohibition against you, transgress you likewise against him. But fear Allah, and know that Allah is with those who restrain themselves.
2. And spend of your substance in the Cause of Allah, and make not your own hands contribute to (your) destruction, But do good, for Allah loves those who do good" (Qur'an 2:194-195).

3.3 Fighting is permitted even in the prohibited months

To fight in the cause of Truth is one of the highest forms of charity. What one can offer which is more precious than one's own life? Intolerance and persecution in any society, like the persecution of early Muslims by the unbelievers in Makkah, cause untold hardships to people and therefore should be eliminated even by force. Tumult and oppression are worse than slaughter. Therefore, no one should be subjected to discrimination or exploitation in any society.

Therefore, God informs the believers that,

1. "Fighting is prescribed upon you, and you dislike it.

But it is possible that you dislike a thing that is good for you and that you love a thing that is bad for you. But Allah knows, and you know not.

2. They ask you concerning fighting in the prohibited month. Say: 'Fighting therein is a grave (offence), but graver is it in the sight of Allah to prevent access to the path of Allah, to deny Him, to prevent

access to the Sacred Mosque, and drive out its members.' Tumult and oppression are worse than slaughter.

Nor will they cease fighting you until they turn you back from your faith if they can. And if any of you turn back from their faith and die in unbelief, their works will bear no fruit in this life and in the Hereafter; they will be companions of the Fire and will abide therein" (Qur'an 2:216-217).

3.4 TAKE PRECAUTIONS WHILE FIGHTING IN THE WAY OF GOD

Fighting should not be undertaken without the required preparations and precautions. When all preparations have been completed, then the believers must go boldly forward either in small groups or all together to fight in God's Cause and for those who, being weak, are ill-treated and oppressed— men, women, and children— to rescue them from the oppressors. God also assures that the believers will be rewarded whether they are slain or achieve victory.

God tells the believers as,

1. "O you who believe! Take your precautions (when in danger), and either go forth in parties or go forth all together" (Qur'an 4:71).
2. "Let those fight in the Cause of Allah who sell the life of this world for the Hereafter. To him who fights in the Cause of Allah— whether he is slain or gets victory— soon shall We give him a reward of great (value).
3. And why should you not fight in the Cause of Allah and of those who, being weak, are ill-treated (and oppressed)?—men, women, and children whose cry is, 'Our Lord! Rescue us from this town whose people are oppressors; and raise for us from You one who will protect; and raise for us from You one who will help!'
4. Those who believe, fight in the Cause of Allah, and those who reject faith fight in the cause of evil. So you fight against the friends of Satan; feeble indeed is the cunning of Satan" (Qur'an 4:74-76).

3.5 TAKE NOT UNBELIEVERS OR HYPOCRITES—AS PROTECTORS

Hypocrites have no principles, they look for an opportunity to turn an event to their benefit. There is a continual fight between good and evil in this world. If the good seems to win, hypocrites align themselves on its side, taking a great part of the credit for themselves. Contrarily, when the balance tilts the other way, they make their peace with evil, providing an open proof for their punishment.

That is why the believers are forbidden to take unbelievers or hypocrites as their allies, "O you who believe! Take not for allies unbelievers rather than believers. Do you wish to offer Allah an open proof against yourselves? The hypocrites will be in the lowest depths of the Fire; no helper will you find for them—" (Qur'an 4:144-145).

4

BELIEVERS—FIGHT INJUSTICE AND AGGRESSION

The believers guard against injustice and oppression in society and fight to establish peace and justice. They are firm, remember God, remain united and patient during their struggle for justice, and if the unbelievers persist in fighting with them, the believers continue fighting till justice is restored. However, the believers have no reason to continue fighting if the enemy desires peace. Efforts to establish peace should be encouraged and reciprocated by the believers.

God commands the Messenger to motivate believers to defend themselves and He is with those who patiently persevere during such struggles. The believers are commanded to fight with all those aggressors who violate their oaths to maintain peace, and taunt believers due to their faith.

4.1 GUARD AGAINST INJUSTICE AND OPPRESSION AMONG YOU

'Fitnah' in Arabic has many meanings. It can be a trial or punishment, injustice or oppression in society, or discard and civil war. Normally this happens in the absence of the rule of law. Under such situations, both guilty and innocent people are affected alike. Therefore, believers should be sensitive and help to eliminate injustice and oppression from society.

This is why God warns the believers, "Fear tumult or oppression, which affects not in particular (only) those of you who do wrong, and know that Allah is strict in punishment" (Qur'an 8:25).

4.2 Be firm; remember God much— united and patient

How can one be successful in the trials of life? For success and prosperity people have to be confident in their efforts and keep striving. This can be achieved: 1) by always remembering God; 2) by following what He commands; 3) by keeping unity among one another; and 4) by patiently pursuing one's goals.

God commands the believers, "O you who believe!

1. When you meet a force, be firm, and call Allah in remembrance much (and often); that you may prosper.
2. And obey (the commands of) Allah and His Messenger,
3. And fall into no disputes, lest you lose heart and your power depart.
4. And be patient and persevering, for Allah is with those who patiently persevere.

And be not like those who started from their homes insolently and to be seen of men, and to hinder (men/women) from the path of Allah; for Allah compasses round about all that they do" (Qur'an 8:45-47).

4.3 If fighting persists— fight until peace is restored

The believers are commanded to keep defending themselves until the end of the hostilities. If the unbelievers cease fighting and cease the persecution of truth, then God will judge them by their actions and motives and He will not wish them further hostility. But if they refuse to cease their fight, then the righteous have nothing to fear: God will help and protect them.

God commands the believers to, "Say to the unbelievers, if (now) they desist (from fighting or persecution of the believers), their past will be forgiven them, but if they persist, the punishment of those before them is already (a matter of warning for them). And fight them on until there is no more tumult or oppression and there prevail justice and faith in Allah altogether and everywhere. But if they cease, verily Allah does see all that they do. If they refuse, be sure that Allah is your protector— the best to protect and the best to help" (Qur'an 8:38-40).

4.4 KEEP FIGHTING BUT RECIPROCATE IF ENEMY DESIRES PEACE

There is no benefit in fighting merely for the sake of fighting. It is a duty to establish peace, righteousness and justice. While believers must always be ready to fight, if it is forced on them, they should also be ready for peace even in the middle of fighting, if there is even a slight inclination towards peace on the other side.

God commands the believers:

1. "Against them make ready your strength to the utmost of your power,

    Including steeds of war to strike fear into (the hearts of) the enemies of Allah and your enemies and others besides whom you may not know, but whom Allah does know. Whatever you shall spend in the Cause of Allah shall be repaid unto you, and you shall not be treated unjustly.

2. But if the enemy inclines towards peace, you do (also) incline towards peace, and trust in Allah, for He is One that hears and knows (all things). ..." (Qur'an 8:60-61).

4.5 ROUSE BELIEVERS TO DEFEND AND PATIENTLY PERSEVERE

Mere vocal profession of belief, or even a belief that does not result in action is not enough to the believers. Sincere believers trust God and fearlessly strive in His service without any consideration for consequences on their life on earth. Fulfillment of what God commands is their goal. He assures them that their success will be proportional to the magnitude of their preparations, efforts, patience and perseverance.

That is why God commands the Messenger to rouse the believers to the fight, "O Prophet! Rouse the believers to the fight. If there are twenty amongst you, patient and persevering, they will vanquish two hundred. If a hundred, they will vanquish a thousand of the unbelievers, for these are a people without understanding. For the present, Allah has lightened your (task), for He knows that there is a weak spot in you. But (even so), if there are a hundred of you, patient and persevering, they will vanquish two hundred, and if a thousand, they will vanquish two thousand, with the leave of Allah, for Allah is with those who patiently persevere" (Qur'an 8:65-66).

4.6 Fight those who violate their oaths and taunt faith

Violation of oaths or treaties by unbelievers is a good enough reason to initiate a fight with those who break their treaties. Not fighting under such circumstances is like being afraid of fighting. Therefore, treaties must be maintained even if need be, by force.

God commands the believers to fight those who violate their treaties and taunt the believers about their Faith, "But if they violate their oaths after their covenant, and taunt you for your Faith— you fight (with) the chiefs of unfaith; for their oaths are nothing to them, that thus they may be restrained" (Qur'an 9:12).

4.7 Fight with aggressors— who violate their treaties

God asks the believers— do they fear the unbelievers? Then He tells them that they should fear Him instead— if they really believe. The believers are commanded to fight to defend themselves.

God asks the believers, "Will you not fight people who violated their oaths, plotted to expel the Messenger, and took the aggression by being the first (to assault) you? Do you fear them? Nay, it is Allah Whom you should more justly fear, if you believe! Fight them, and Allah will punish them by your hands, cover them with shame, help you (to victory) over them, heal the breasts of believers, and (will) still the indignation of their hearts. ..." (Qur'an 9:13-15).

5

Believers— Fight with Hostile Unbelievers

It is an obligation of the believers to defend themselves if attacked and to strive in God's Way. Striving for His Cause is so important that it is given priority even over members of one's own family who disbelieve. The struggle against violations of the divine law should continue until it is established in society. In addition, violations by hostile hypocrites should firmly be persecuted. The Messenger (or the ruler of an Islamic state) and the believers are to strive hard against hostile unbelievers and hypocrites in their communities, and be firm in persecuting them if they violate the state rules. God commands the Messenger, "O Prophet! Strive hard against the unbelievers and the hypocrites, and be firm against them. Their abode is Hell— an evil refuge (indeed)" (Qur'an 66:9).

5.1 THE BELIEVERS' DUTY IS TO DEFEND THEMSELVES IN WAR
Both the lives of this world and of the Hereafter are important to the believers— They live their life in this world as God commands to assure a better life in the Hereafter. The violators of divine law think that they are getting ahead of those who are careful to observe them. But lawless people lose both guidance and faith, and eventual success.

God asks the believers,

1. "O you who believe! What is the matter with you, that, when you are asked to go forth in the Cause of Allah, you cling heavily to the earth?

Do you prefer the life of this world to the Hereafter? But little is the comfort of this life, as compared with the Hereafter.

2. Unless you go forth, He will punish you with a grievous penalty, and put others in your place; but Him you would not harm in the least. For Allah has power over all things" (Qur'an 9:38-39).

5.2 A BELIEVER'S DUTY IS TO STRIVE HARD IN GOD'S CAUSE
The believers striving hard with their selves and their resources, fight to establish a just and humane society. They are firm in the establishment of the rule of the law in society and their governments are sincere in persecuting all mischief makers and the corrupt, who violate the law of the land.

The believers are commanded, if their communities are attacked to,

1. "You go forth, (whether equipped) lightly or heavily, and strive and struggle with your goods and your persons in the Cause of Allah. That is best for you, if you (but) knew.

2. O Prophet! Strive hard against the unbelievers and the hypocrites, and be firm against them. Their abode is Hell, an evil refuge indeed" (Qur'an 9:41,73).

5.3 FIGHT WITH VIOLATORS UNTIL DIVINE LAW IS RESTORED

It is an obligation for Muslims to establish the rule of law and justice in their communities and prosecute violators. Non believers can live in Islamic societies as law abiding citizens where their security and freedom of religion is fully assured as tax paying citizens.

Contrarily, God commands believers to, "Fight those who believe neither in Allah nor the Last Day, nor hold that forbidden which has been forbidden by Allah and His Messenger, nor acknowledge the religion of truth, (even if they are) of the People of the Book, until they pay the Jizya (a tax) with willing submission and feel themselves (law abiding citizens) subdued" (Qur'an 9:29).

5.4 STRIVING FOR GOD'S WAY HAS PRIORITY EVEN OVER A KIN

One's faith has a priority even over family ties. It is highly unlikely that unbelieving relatives will side with the believers in their struggle against unbelievers. That is why believers are forbidden to develop any type of alliance with unbelievers and hypocrites, even if they are their near relatives, in war situations. God commands the believers, "O you who believe! Take not for protectors your fathers and your brothers if they love infidelity above Faith. If any of you do so, they do wrong" (Qur'an 9:23).

On the other hand, God enjoins kindness to parents but forbids obeying them in unbelief and sin. He tells believers, "We have enjoined on man kindness to parents: but if they (either of them) strive (to force) you to join with Me (in worship) anything of which you have no knowledge, obey them not. You have (all) to return to me, and I will tell you (the truth) of all that you did" (Qur'an 29:8).

Contrarily, if believers fight with their resources and defend themselves, they will certainly succeed and prosper. God assures them good things and prosperity, "But the Messenger and those who believe with him strive and fight with their wealth and their persons. For them are (all) good things, and it is they who will prosper" (Qur'an 9:88).

5.5 ENFORCE THE LAW AND PERSECUTE HOSTILE HYPOCRITES

Hypocrites are those Muslims in an Islamic society who pay only lip service to their religion. Citing an example from history, the Messenger (or an Islamic state) is commanded to persecute the violations of the law by the hypocrites as well as other citizens of the state.

God tells the Messenger (or the government) that, "O Prophet! Strive hard against the unbelievers and the Hypocrites, and be firm against them. Their abode is Hell— an evil refuge indeed. They swear by Allah that they said nothing (evil), but indeed they uttered blasphemy, and they did it after accepting Islam; and they meditated a plot which they were unable to carry out: this revenge of theirs was (their) only return for the bounty with which Allah and His Messenger had enriched them! If they repent, it will be best for them; but if they turn back (to their evil ways), Allah will punish them with a grievous penalty in this life and in the Hereafter: They shall have none on earth to protect or help them" (Qur'an 9:73-74).

5.6 BE FIRM WITH HOSTILE UNBELIEVERS AND PERSECUTE THEM

Concluding the relationship with unbelievers, the believers are to live in this world with dignity and freedom. Believers cannot be the unbelievers' puppets under any circumstances. They are commanded to be firm and defend their beliefs. The believers enforce their law firmly, persecute and punish the violators in their society. Since believers live as God commands, most of the violators are either unbelievers or hypocrites, 'in whose heart is a disease, - which worsens by doubts after doubt and they die in a state of disbelief.

According to the Qur'an, hypocrites and unbelievers are, "Those in whose hearts is a disease— it will add doubt to their doubt, and they will die in a state of unbelief. See they not that they are tried every year once or twice? Yet they turn not in repentance, and they take no heed. Whenever there comes down a *Surah*, they look at each other, (saying), 'does anyone see you'? Then they turn aside: Allah has turned their hearts (from the light); for they are a people that understand not" (Qur'an 9:125-127).

When conflict becomes inevitable, the first thing necessary is to clear all evil from the surroundings, for it is evil that one can rightly fight. To evil, the believer must put up a stout and stiff resistance. Merely mouthed compromises are not right for soldiers of truth and righteousness. Such behavior is often a mixture of cowardice, weariness, greed and corruption and thus not suitable for a believer. Contrarily, God commands the believers, "O you who believe! Fight the unbelievers who gird you about, and let them find firmness in you, and know that Allah is with those who fear Him" (Qur'an 9:123).

6
BELIEVERS— NOT DEFENDING ISLAM IS A SIN

The lives, abilities, and assets of the believers are a Divine trust. Believers, therefore, seek no relief from striving in God's Way. God promises believers that they will fully be rewarded for their efforts in His Way. Studying the Qur'an to understand and follow what God commands is a duty of all Muslims. Therefore, a group of people among Muslims should prepare themselves as religious teachers to guide and teach people about Islam. Learning and teaching how to live and behave as Muslims, and fighting in the Way of God— both are integral parts of Jihad. Since security and peace will be lost if the community is not defended and secured, the believers are commanded to be forceful and concentrate to achieve their objective even before taking prisoners of war. The establishment of peace and security is of such an importance that for the believers not defending what they believe in— is a heinous sin. So, believers are forbidden to run away from the battlefield.

6.1 BELIEVERS' LIVES, ABILITIES AND ASSETS ARE GOD'S TRUST

Although, the believers' lives, abilities, and assets are God's given trust which must be returned on His demand, still, God has offered a bargain to people that if they live in this world as He commands, they will earn an everlasting salvation. The same promise was given to the followers of previous religions.

God tells about this bargain as, "Allah has purchased of the believers their persons and their goods; for theirs (in return) is the Garden (of Paradise). They fight in His Cause and slay and are slain—

A promise binding on Him in truth through the Law, the Gospel, and the Qur'an; and who is more faithful to his Covenant than Allah? Then rejoice in the bargain which you have concluded; that is the achievement supreme" (Qur'an 9:111).

6.2 SOME BELIEVERS— SHOULD DEVOTE TO RELIGIOUS STUDIES

It is the duty of all Muslims to study the Qur'an, to understand it themselves and follow what God commands. Therefore, a group of people among Muslims should prepare themselves as religious teachers to guide and teach people about Islam. Both the students and teachers are soldiers of Jihad in the spirit of their obedience and discipline. Learning and teaching how to live and behave as Muslims, and fighting in the Way of God— both are integral parts of Jihad.

God commands the believers:

1. "O you who believe! Fear Allah, and be with those who are true (in word and deed).
2. Nor should the believers all go forth together; if a contingent from every expedition remained behind, they could devote themselves to studies in religion and admonish the people when they return to them— that thus they (may learn) to guard themselves" (Qur'an 9:119, 122).

6.3 SECURITY WILL BE LOST— IF NOT DEFENDED AND SECURED

People can either lead a beastly life— trying to satisfying all their desires or live a life— based on truth and justice as God commands. God is the source of all energy and life, therefore, the corrupt will fail to achieve their goals and satisfactions they desire, because their desires will be endless. Since God protects those who believe, He will make it easier and easier for the righteous who fight in His Cause.

The believers are promised security and protection only if they defend themselves, "O you who believe! If you will aid (the Cause of) Allah, He will aid you and plant your feet firmly. That is because Allah is the Protector of those who believe, but those who reject Allah have no protector" (Qur'an 47:7, 11).

6.4 BE FORCEFUL IN WAR, TAKE NO PRISONERS BEFORE SUCCESS

Defending oneself is a serious business. It should be avoided as much as possible but when it is entered upon, it should be carried out with the utmost vigor following a well thought out strategy. One cannot win a war half heartedly. Taking prisoners, or releasing them comes only after the victory when the enemy is not likely to seek persecution of the Truth and of the believers again.

Fighting is a trial for the believers "Therefore, when you meet the unbelievers (in a battlefield), smite at their necks. At length, when you have thoroughly subdued them, bind a bond firmly (on them). Thereafter (is the time for) either generosity or ransom until the war lays down its burdens. Thus (are you commanded), but if it had been Allah's Will, He could certainly have exacted retribution from them (Himself); but (He lets you fight) in order to test you, some with others. But those who are slain in the way of Allah—He will never let their deeds be lost" (Qur'an 47:4).

6.5 LEAVING THE BATTLEFIELD DURING FIGHTING IS FORBIDDEN

Wars can only be won by strictly following military values and discipline. Believers should meet their enemy fairly and squarely, not rashly, but after due planning and preparation. When in combat, fighting should be carried through without any second thoughts until death or victory is achieved. Running away from the battlefield is forbidden except as a strategic move to mislead the enemy.

God warns the believers that, "O you who believe! When you meet the unbelievers in hostile array, never turn your backs to them. If any do turn his back to them on such a day, unless it be in a stratagem of war or to retreat to a troop (of his own), he draws on himself the wrath of Allah, and his abode is Hell, an evil refuge (indeed)!" (Qur'an 8:15-16).

Chapter 14

The Qur'an—Guidance for Humanity
(Humanity Needs Guidance for Progress)

God created people with a conscience and free will, and He gave them guidance. He offered each one of us, male or female, rich or poor, to be His *Khalifah* (trustee) on earth, to serve Him by implementing His commands in managing our affairs and in building a just human society in the world. God desires people to be His trustee on earth. Those who wish to be God's trustee believe and worship Him, learn to be human, reform themselves, and do good deeds. They take this assignment as a challenge and a trial from Him. It is up to us to accept or reject God's offer of trusteeship. Those who accept the assignment become the believers. As a token of acceptance to be God's trustee, the believers worship Him and remember Him during every moment of their lives, in order to develop a relationship and trust with Him.

The believers desire and intend to succeed as God's trustee on earth. Since it is through knowledge and understanding that people attain closeness to God, the believers strive to gain knowledge by reading and understanding the Qur'an and by following His Messenger as their role model. The importance of learning what God commands in the Qur'an is such that people should exert their best efforts to accomplish this task, and no one is exempt from this duty.

Why is it important to learn what God says in the Qur'an? God has shown us in numerous ways that He loves people. That is why He commands only those things that are good for us. Islam expects its followers to live their lives by following all moral and ethical principles. How we live in this world will very much determine our life in the Hereafter. People's welfare in this life, as well as in the Hereafter, depends on their efforts and good deeds. God tells us: "Every soul is (held) in pledge for its own deeds" (Qur'an 74:38). The believers are commanded to wish for others as they wish for themselves. This thought and feeling inspires numerous such activities that help establish all that is good and eliminates those things that are harmful to the welfare of people. Eventually, people's proper belief and cumulative righteous activities make the entire community an example for humanity.

Previous communities suffered because they ignored the importance of doing what is right and of forbidding what is wrong. Abdullah ibn Masud reported God's Messenger[PBUH] as saying: 'The first defect that permeated Banu Isra'il was that a man (of them) met another man and said: 'O so-and-so, fear Allah, and abandon what you are doing, for it is not lawful for you.' He then met him the next day, and that did not refrain him from eating with him, drinking with him, and sitting with him. When they did so, Allah mingled their hearts with one another.' He (the Prophet) then recited the verse: 'Curses were pronounced on those among the Children of Isra'il who rejected faith by the tongue of David and of Jesus, the son of Mary' because they disobeyed and persisted in Excesses' (Qur'an 5:78). The Messenger was saying this as he reclined, but at this point he sat up and said: 'By Him Who holds my soul in His hand, you must make them (the wrongdoers) turn back to what is right' (Abu Dawud: 37.4322).

When people's character and behavior keeps on deteriorating, and when corruption is on the rise, some corrective measures need to be taken to save the community from destruction. Amirah al-Kindi narrated that the Messenger[PBUH] said: 'When a sin is committed on earth, a person who witnesses it and denounces it is the same as one who has not seen it, but the one who has been absent and approves of it is considered like one who has taken part in it' (Abu Dawud 37:4331). It is, therefore, a matter of utmost importance that people repent, do good deeds, and avoid what is bad for the welfare of people in the society. The entire Islamic code is for the benefit of people; it either prevents harm or brings benefit. When God addresses the believers in the Qur'an, one will find either something good that people are encouraged to do or something evil that they are required to avoid or a combination of both. Compliance with God's commands is the only way to receive His Mercy and avoid His punishment.

Learning to develop a capability to earn an honest living is obligatory, and working hard in one's selected professional area for earning an honest living is an act of God's worship. Misappropriating property or using it to bribe judges is forbidden in Islam. God commands, "And do not eat up your property among yourselves for vanities, nor use it as bait for the judges, with intent that you may eat up wrongfully and knowingly a little of (other) people's property" (Qur'an 2:188).

God desires that a well balanced human personality be developed for the progress of humanity. Therefore, every aspect of human life needs to be addressed, in order to nurture an honest, hardworking, and competent individual. For this He has given people an ability to pursue every field of learning endeavor to acquire all kinds of knowledge: "And He taught Adam the names of all things…" (Qur'an 2:31).

Therefore, the schools that only stress either religious or secular aspects of life are not helping the society. People need an integrated educational system for the development of all human faculties. God's first command to both men and women is "Iqra" or "Proclaim! (Or read!) In the name of your Lord and Cherisher, Who created- Created man, out of a (mere) clot of congealed blood: Proclaim! And your Lord is Most Bountiful, - He Who taught (the use of) the pen, - Taught man (woman) that which he (she) knew not" (Qur'an 96:1-5). Hence, we cannot be a believer or even a civilized human being, unless we educate ourselves and arrange to educate our children both in religious as well as in other fields of learning.

Books Cited or Recommended

Akbar, Muhammad (trans. Tafhim-ul-Qur'an). *The Meaning of Holy Qur'an by Syed Abul Ala Maududi*. Lahore: Islamic Publications (Pvt) Limited, 2000.

'Ali, 'Abdullah Yusuf. *The Meaning of Holy Qur'an*. Beltsville, Maryland: Amana Publications, 11th ed., 2009, and www.usc.edu/schools/college/crcc/engagement/resources/texts/

At-Tarjumana, A'isha `Abdarahman and Johnson, Ya`qub, (trans.). *Malik's Muwatta* www.usc.edu/schools/college/crcc/engagement/resources/texts/

Hafeez, Muhammad A. *Human Character and Behavior. An Islamic Perspective.* Beltsville, MD, USA. Amana Publications, 2011.

Hafeez, Muhammad A. *The Mission and Destiny of Humankind: An Exercise in Understanding the Qur'an.* Beltsville, MD, USA. Amana Publications, 2012.

Hasan Prof. Ahmad, (trans.). *Sunan Abu-Dawud.*
www.usc.edu/schools/college/crcc/engagement/resources/texts/

Irving, Thomas Ballantine, Ahmed, Khurshid and Ahsan, Muhammad Manazir. *The Qur'an: Basic Teaching(s).* Leicester, England: The Islamic Foundation, 1994.

Karim, Maulana Fazlul. *Al-Hadith*, trans.*Mishkat-ul-Masabih*. New Delhi: Islamic Book Service, 2006.

Khan, Dr. Muhammad Muhsin and al-Hilali, Dr. Taqi-ud-Din. *The Noble Qur'an*. Riyadh, Saudi Arabia: Darussalam, 1996.

Khan, Dr. Muhammad Muhsin (trans.). *Sahih Bukhari*. www.usc.edu/schools/college/crcc/engagement/resources/texts/

Maududi, Syed Abul Ala, *Tafhim-ul-Qur'an*. Lahore, Pakistan: Idara Tarjuman -ul-Qur'an, 2003

Maududi, Syed Abul Ala, *Surah Introductions to the Qur'an*. www.usc.edu/schools/college/crcc/engagement/resources/texts/muslim/maududi/

Maududi, Syed Abul Ala, (trans. Ansari, Zafar Iqbal). *Towards Understanding the Qur'an*.
Leicester, England: The Islamic Foundation, 2006.

Salahi, Adil, (ed.). *Our Dialogue*. www.ourdialogue.com.

Siddique, Abdul Hamid, (trans.). *Sahih Muslim*. www.usc.edu/schools/college/crcc/engagement/resources/texts/

Tantavi, Sheikh Ali. *Introduction to Islam*. Lahore, Pakistan: the Qur'an Ahsan Tareek, 2004.

Author Biography

D r. Muhammad Abdul Hafeez, the author of *Human Character and Behavior* and *The Mission and Destiny of Humankind,* holds a master's degree in history, a master's degree in chemical technology from the University of Panjab, Lahore, Pakistan, and a Ph.D. in chemical engineering from the City University, London, England. He has extensively researched and studied the religion of Islam within its theological, historical, and cultural perspectives in the light of the Qur'an and the *Ahadith* of its Prophet. He has been trying to learn what God tells us in the Qur'an and how it was interpreted by His Messenger from translations of the Qur'an and *Sunnah.*

Originally from Pakistan, the author lived and worked in Saudi Arabia for over 20 years (1983 to 2004). His stay in Saudi Arabia tremendously helped him in his study and learning of the religion of Islam from various sources, specifically from study circles of the Qur'an. He has benefited from various religious scholars there who helped him in comprehending Islam as a *"Deen"* compatible with the modern age. He is indebted to all those teachers, commentators, friends, and scholars who have played a role in imparting knowledge of Islamic studies to him. He owes a special gratitude to all those scholars whose works in Urdu, as well as in English, have been of great help and guidance to him.

He migrated to the United States of America in 1973 and lives in Liverpool, New York.

Made in the USA
Middletown, DE
28 September 2022

11324688R00151